Inflation in a Monetary Union

Springer

Berlin
Heidelberg
New York
Barcelona
Hong Kong
London
Milan
Paris
Tokyo

Michael Carlberg

Inflation
in a
Monetary Union

With 2 Figures
and 26 Tables

 Springer

Professor Michael Carlberg
Federal University of Hamburg
Department of Economics
Holstenhofweg 85
22043 Hamburg
Germany

ISBN 3-540-43359-7 Springer-Verlag Berlin Heidelberg New York

Library of Congress Cataloging-in-Publication Data applied for
Die Deutsche Bibliothek – CIP-Einheitsaufnahme
Carlberg, Michael: Inflation in a Monetary Union: with 26 Tables / Michael Carlberg. –
Berlin; Heidelberg; New York; Barcelona; Hong Kong; London; Milan; Paris; Tokyo: Springer, 2002
    ISBN 3-540-43359-7

Springer-Verlag Berlin Heidelberg New York
a member of BertelsmannSpringer Science + Business Media GmbH

http://www.springer.de
© Springer-Verlag Berlin Heidelberg 2002
Printed in Germany

Cover design: Erich Kirchner, Heidelberg

SPIN 10873918   42/2202-5 4 3 2 1 0 – Printed on acid-free paper

Preface

This book studies the causes and cures of inflation in a monetary union. It carefully discusses the effects of money growth and output growth on inflation. The focus is on producer inflation, currency depreciation and consumer inflation. For instance, what determines the rate of consumer inflation in Europe, and what in America? Moreover, what determines the rate of consumer inflation in Germany, and what in France? Further topics are real depreciation, nominal and real interest rates, the growth of nominal wages, the growth of producer real wages, and the growth of consumer real wages. Here productivity growth and labour growth play significant roles. Another important issue is target inflation and required money growth. A special feature of this book is the numerical estimation of shock and policy multipliers.

The present book is part of a larger research project on monetary union, see Carlberg (1999, 2000, 2001). Over the years, in working on this project, I have benefited from comments by Iain Begg, Christopher Bliss, Volker Clausen, Peter Flaschel, Wilfried Fuhrmann, Michael Funke, Franz X. Hof, Jay H. Levin, Alfred Maußner, Hans G. Monissen, Manfred J. M. Neumann, Klaus Neusser, Franco Reither, Michael Schmid, Jürgen von Hagen, and Helmut Wagner. In addition, Michael Bräuninger and Alkis Otto carefully discussed with me all parts of the manuscript. Last but not least, Doris Ehrich did the secretarial work as excellently as ever. I would like to thank all of them.

February 2002   Michael Carlberg

Executive Summary

1) The world of two monetary regions, say Europe and America. First consider producer inflation. Producer inflation in Europe refers to the price of European goods. As a result, producer inflation in Europe is determined by money growth in Europe and by output growth in Europe. For instance, let output growth in Europe be 2 percent, let output growth in America be 3 percent, let money growth in Europe be 3 percent, and let money growth in America be 5 percent. Then producer inflation in Europe is 1 percent, and producer inflation in America is 2 percent.

Second consider nominal depreciation. As a result, the rate of depreciation is determined by money growth in Europe and by money growth in America. If money growth in Europe is high, the euro will depreciate. If money growth in Europe is low, the euro will appreciate. For instance, let money growth in Europe be 3 percent, and let money growth in America be 5 percent. Then the price of the euro grows at a constant rate of 2 percent. In other words, the price of the dollar declines at a constant rate of 2 percent. But be careful. The rate of depreciation does not depend on producer inflation in Europe or on producer inflation in America.

Third consider real depreciation. The real exchange rate is defined as the price of American goods, as measured in European goods. As a result, the growth of the relative price of American goods is determined by output growth in Europe and by output growth in America. If output growth in America is high, the relative price of American goods will decline. If output growth in America is low, the relative price of American goods will increase. For instance, let output growth in Europe be 2 percent, and let output growth in America be 3 percent. Then the relative price of American goods declines at a constant rate of 1 percent.

Fourth consider consumer inflation. European consumption includes both European goods and American goods. Therefore, the consumer price index of Europe includes the price of European goods, the price of American goods, and the price of the dollar. Accordingly, consumer inflation in Europe includes producer inflation in Europe, producer inflation in America, and the appreciation of the dollar. As a result, consumer inflation in Europe is determined by money growth in Europe, by output growth in Europe, and by output growth in America. For instance, let output growth in Europe be 2 percent, let output growth in America be 3 percent, let money growth in Europe be 3 percent, and let money growth in America be 5 percent. Further, let the share of American goods in European consumption be 0.1, and let the share of European goods in American consumption be equally 0.1. Then consumer inflation in Europe is 0.9 percent, and consumer inflation in America is 2.1 percent.

2) The monetary union of two countries, say Germany and France. First consider producer inflation. Producer inflation in Germany refers to the price of German goods. As a result, producer inflation in Germany is determined by money growth in Europe and by output growth in Germany. For instance, let output growth in Germany be 1 percent, let output growth in France be 3 percent, and let money growth in Europe be 3 percent. Then producer inflation in Germany is 2 percent, and producer inflation in France is 0 percent.

Second consider consumer inflation. Consumer inflation in Germany includes producer inflation in Germany, producer inflation in France, producer inflation in America, and the appreciation of the dollar. As a result, consumer inflation in Germany is determined by money growth in Europe, by output growth in Germany, by output growth in France, and by output growth in America. For instance, let output growth in Germany be 1 percent, let output growth in France be 3 percent, let output growth in America be 2 percent, and let money growth in Europe be 3 percent. Besides, let the share of French goods in German consumption be 0.2, and let the share of American goods in German consumption be 0.1. By symmetry, let the share of German goods in French consumption be 0.2, and let the share of American goods in French consumption be 0.1. Then consumer inflation in Germany is 1.5 percent, and consumer inflation in France is 0.5 percent.

Contents in Brief

Contents

Introduction

This book studies the causes and cures of inflation in a monetary union. It carefully discusses the effects of money growth and output growth on inflation. Further topics are the effects on currency depreciation, wage growth, and interest rate levels. This book takes new approaches that are firmly grounded on modern macroeconomics.

The framework of analysis is as follows. The monetary union is defined as a group of countries that share a common currency. The monetary union is an open economy with international trade and capital mobility. The exchange rate between the monetary union and the rest of the world is flexible. As a rule we assume that the union countries are the same size and have the same behavioural functions. This assumption proves to be particularly useful. As an exception we assume that the union countries differ in size and behavioural functions. A special feature of this book is the numerical estimation of shock and policy multipliers.

This book consists of five major parts:
> The Closed Economy
> The World of Two Monetary Regions
> The Monetary Union of Two Countries
> A One-Good Model of the World Economy
> Microfoundations for a Monetary Union.

Now the approach will be presented in greater detail.

Part One. The Closed Economy. First consider the model. Understanding the closed economy is helpful in understanding the world of two monetary regions as well as the monetary union of two countries. Here the focus is on steady-state inflation, given steady-state growth. Nominal wages and prices are flexible, so there is full employment. Aggregate demand equals aggregate supply, and money demand equals money supply. Output growth is determined by productivity growth and labour growth. Nominal wage growth is determined by productivity growth and inflation.

Second consider inflation and wage growth. To illustrate this, take a numerical example. Let productivity grow at a constant rate of 2 percent, let labour supply grow at a constant rate of 1 percent, and let money supply grow at a constant rate of 4 percent. Then, at what rate does output grow? At what rate does the price level grow? At what rate do nominal wages grow? And at what rate do real wages grow? Moreover, what is the nominal interest rate? And what is the real interest rate?

Third consider target inflation and required money growth. The objective of the central bank is to maintain price stability. Strictly speaking, the objective of the central bank is to keep inflation at target level. Let target inflation be 1 percent, let productivity growth be 2 percent, and let labour growth be 1 percent. Then, what rate of money growth is required? Besides, what is the rate of growth of nominal wages? What is the nominal interest rate? And what is the real interest rate?

Part Two. The World of Two Monetary Regions. First consider the model. The world consists of two monetary regions, say Europe and America. The exchange rate between Europe and America is flexible. Here the focus is on steady-state inflation in Europe and America, given steady-state growth. Nominal wages and prices are flexible, so there is full employment in Europe and America. European goods and American goods are imperfect substitutes for each other. The demand for European goods equals the supply of European goods. The demand for American goods equals the supply of American goods. European money demand equals European money supply. And American money demand equals American money supply. There is perfect capital mobility between Europe and America. The nominal interest rate in Europe equals the sum of the nominal interest rate in America and the rate of currency depreciation. The monetary regions are the same size and have the same behavioural functions.

Second consider inflation and currency depreciation. To illustrate this, have a look at a numerical example. Let European output grow at a constant rate of 2 percent, let American output grow at a constant rate of 3 percent, let European money supply grow at a constant rate of 3 percent, and let American money supply grow at a constant rate of 5 percent. This gives rise to a number of questions. At what rate does the price of European goods grow? At what rate does the price of American goods grow? At what rate does the price of the euro change? And at what rate does the price of the dollar change? The real exchange rate is defined as the price of American goods, as measured in European goods. Then at what rate does the relative price of American goods change?

European consumption includes both European goods and American goods. Accordingly, the consumer price index of Europe includes the price of European goods, the price of American goods, and the price of the dollar. Let the share of American goods in European consumption be 0.1. Then at what rate does the consumer price index of Europe grow? Similarly, American consumption includes both American goods and European goods. Hence the consumer price index of America includes the price of American goods, the price of European goods, and the price of the euro. Let the share of European goods in American consumption be equally 0.1. Then at what rate does the consumer price index of America grow? In addition, what is the nominal interest rate in Europe? What is the nominal interest rate in America? What is the real interest rate in Europe? And what is the real interest rate in America?

Third consider wage growth and productivity growth. Let European productivity grow at a constant rate of 2 percent, let American productivity grow at a constant rate of 3 percent, let European money supply grow at a constant rate of 3 percent, and let American money supply grow at a constant rate of 5 percent. Then at what rate do nominal wages grow in Europe? And at what rate do nominal wages grow in America? Producer real wages in Europe are defined as nominal wages in Europe divided by the price of European goods. Producer real wages in America are defined as nominal wages in America divided by the price of American goods. Then at what rate do producer real wages grow in Europe? And at what rate do producer real wages grow in America? Consumer real wages in Europe are defined as nominal wages in Europe divided by the consumer price index of Europe. Consumer real wages in America are defined as nominal wages in America divided by the consumer price index of America. Then at what rate do consumer real wages grow in Europe? And at what rate do consumer real wages grow in America?

Fourth consider wage growth and labour growth. Let labour growth in Europe be 0 percent, let labour growth in America be 1 percent, let money growth in Europe be 1 percent, and let money growth in America be 3 percent. Then, at what rate do nominal wages grow in Europe? At what rate do nominal wages grow in America? At what rate do producer real wages grow in Europe? At what rate do producer real wages grow in America? At what rate do consumer real wages grow in Europe? And at what rate do consumer real wages grow in America?

Fifth consider target inflation and required money growth. The objective of the European central bank is to maintain price stability in Europe. Strictly speaking, the objective of the European central bank is to keep consumer inflation in Europe at target level. The objective of the American central bank is to maintain price stability in America. Strictly speaking, the objective of the American central bank is to keep consumer inflation in America at target level. Let target inflation in Europe be 1 percent, let target inflation in America be 2 percent, let output growth in Europe be 2 percent, and let output growth in America be 3 percent. Then, what rate of money growth is required in Europe? And what rate of money growth is required in America? Further, what is the rate of currency depreciation? What is the nominal interest rate in Europe? And what is the nominal interest rate in America?

Part Three. The Monetary Union of Two Countries. First consider the model. The world consists of two monetary regions, say Europe and America. The exchange rate between Europe and America is flexible. Europe in turn consists of two countries, say Germany and France. Germany and France form a monetary union. Here the focus is on steady-state inflation in Germany, France and America, given steady-state growth. Nominal wages and prices are flexible, thus there is full employment in Germany, France and America.

German goods, French goods and American goods are imperfect substitutes for each other. The demand for German goods equals the supply of German goods. The demand for French goods equals the supply of French goods. And the demand for American goods equals the supply of American goods. The sum of German money demand and French money demand equals European money supply. And American money demand equals American money supply. There is perfect capital mobility between Germany, France and America. The nominal interest rate in Germany equals the nominal interest rate in France. The nominal interest rate in Europe equals the sum of the nominal interest rate in America and the rate of currency depreciation. The monetary regions are the same size and have the same behavioural functions. The union countries are the same size and have the same behavioural functions.

Second consider inflation and currency depreciation. To illustrate this, take a numerical example. Let German output grow at a constant rate of 1 percent, let French output grow at a constant rate of 3 percent, let American output grow at a constant rate of 2 percent, let European money supply grow at a constant rate of 3 percent, and let American money supply grow at a constant rate of 4 percent. This raises a number of questions. At what rate does the price of German goods grow? At what rate does the price of French goods grow? At what rate does the price of the euro change? And at what rate does the price of the dollar change? The real exchange rate can be defined as the price of French goods, as measured in German goods. Then at what rate does the relative price of French goods change?

German consumption includes German goods, French goods and American goods. Accordingly, the consumer price index of Germany includes the price of German goods, the price of French goods, the price of American goods, and the price of the dollar. Let the share of French goods in German consumption be 0.2, and let the share of American goods in German consumption be 0.1. Then at what rate does the consumer price index of Germany grow? Similarly, French consumption includes French goods, German goods and American goods. Hence the consumer price index of France includes the price of French goods, the price of German goods, the price of American goods, and the price of the dollar. Let the share of German goods in French consumption be 0.2, and let the share of American goods in French consumption be 0.1. Then at what rate does the consumer price index of France grow? Moreover, what is the nominal interest rate in Germany? What is the nominal interest rate in France? What is the real interest rate in Germany? And what is the real interest rate in France?

Third consider wage growth and productivity growth. Let German productivity grow at a constant rate of 1 percent, let French productivity grow at a constant rate of 3 percent, let American productivity grow at a constant rate of 2 percent, and let European money supply grow at a constant rate of 3 percent. Then, at what rate do nominal wages grow in Germany? And at what rate do nominal wages grow in France? Producer real wages in Germany are defined as nominal wages in Germany divided by the price of German goods. Producer real wages in France are defined as nominal wages in France divided by the price of French goods. Then, at what rate do producer real wages grow in Germany? And at what rate do producer real wages grow in France? Consumer real wages in Germany are defined as nominal wages in Germany divided by the consumer price index of Germany. Consumer real wages in France are defined as nominal wages in France divided by the consumer price index of France. Then, at what rate do consumer real wages grow in Germany? And at what rate do consumer real wages grow in France?

Fourth consider wage growth and labour growth. Let labour growth in Germany be −1 percent, let labour growth in France be 1 percent, let labour growth in America be 1 percent, and let money growth in Europe be 1 percent. Then, at what rate do nominal wages grow in Germany? At what rate do nominal wages grow in France? At what rate do producer real wages grow in Germany? At what rate do producer real wages grow in France? At what rate do consumer real wages grow in Germany? And at what rate do consumer real wages grow in France?

Fifth consider target inflation and required money growth. The objective of the European central bank is to maintain price stability in Europe. Strictly speaking, the objective of the European central bank is to keep consumer inflation in Europe at target level. European consumption includes German goods, French goods and American goods. Accordingly, the consumer price index of Europe includes the price of German goods, the price of French goods, the price of American goods, and the price of the dollar. That is, consumer inflation in Europe includes producer inflation in Germany, producer inflation in France, producer inflation in America, and the appreciation of the dollar. Let target inflation in Europe be 1 percent, let output growth in Germany be 1 percent, let output growth in France be 3 percent, and let output growth in America be 2 percent. Then, what rate of money growth is required in Europe? Further, what is consumer inflation in Germany? And what is consumer inflation in France?

Part Four. A One-Good Model of the World Economy. In Chapter 1, the world consists of two monetary regions, say Europe and America. The exchange rate between Europe and America is flexible. So far, in Parts Two and Three, we assumed that European goods and American goods were imperfect substitutes for each other. Now, in Part Four, we assume that there is a single good in the world economy. This good is produced in both Europe and America. Apart from this we take the same approach as before.

First consider given money growth. Let European output grow at a constant rate of 2 percent, let American output grow at a constant rate of 3 percent, let European money supply grow at a constant rate of 3 percent, and let American money supply grow at a constant rate of 5 percent. Then, at what rate does the price of European goods grow? At what rate does the price of American goods grow? At what rate does the price of the euro change? And at what rate does the price of the dollar change? In addition, what is the nominal interest rate in Europe? What is the nominal interest rate in America? What is the real interest rate in Europe? And what is the real interest rate in America?

Second consider target inflation and required money growth. Let target inflation in Europe be 1 percent, let target inflation in America be 2 percent, let output growth in Europe be 2 percent, and let output growth in America be 3 percent. Then, what rate of money growth is required in Europe? And what rate of money growth is required in America? Moreover, what is the rate of currency depreciation? What is the nominal interest rate in Europe? And what is the nominal interest rate in America?

In Chapter 2, Europe consists of two countries, say Germany and France. There is only one good in the world economy. This good is produced in Germany, France and America. First consider given money growth. Let output growth in Germany be 1 percent, let output growth in France be 3 percent, let the initial share of Germany in European output be 0.5, and let money growth in Europe be 3 percent. Then, what is the rate of inflation in Germany? And what is the rate of inflation in France? Second consider target inflation and required money growth. Let target inflation in Europe be 1 percent, let output growth in Germany be 1 percent, let output growth in France be 3 percent, and let the initial share of Germany in European output be 0.5. Then what rate of money growth is required in Europe?

Part Five. Microfoundations for a Monetary Union. First consider the world of two monetary regions, say Europe and America. The exchange rate between Europe and America is flexible. The monetary regions are completely specialized

8

in production. Europe produces European goods, while America produces American goods. European goods and American goods are imperfect substitutes in consumption.

European households consume both European goods and American goods. European households maximize utility subject to the budget constraint. The exogenous variables are European income, the price of European goods, the price of American goods, and the price of the dollar. The endogenous variables are the European consumption of European goods and the European consumption of American goods. Then what are the demand functions of European households?

American households consume both American goods and European goods. American households maximize utility subject to the budget constraint. The exogenous variables are American income, the price of American goods, the price of European goods, and the price of the euro. The endogenous variables are the American consumption of American goods and the American consumption of European goods. Then what are the demand functions of American households?

Next have a look at the market for European goods. European output is determined by the European consumption of European goods, by the American consumption of European goods, and by the autonomous demand for European goods. That is, European output is determined by the autonomous demand for European goods, by American income, by the price of European goods, by the price of American goods, and by the price of the euro.

Besides have a look at the market for American goods. American output is determined by the American consumption of American goods, by the European consumption of American goods, and by the autonomous demand for American goods. That is, American output is determined by the autonomous demand for American goods, by European income, by the price of American goods, by the price of European goods, and by the price of the dollar.

Further topics are:
- a first model of Europe and America
- the consumption, export and import functions of Europe
- the consumption, export and import functions of America
- a second model of Europe and America

- the monetary regions differ in size.

Second consider the large monetary union of two countries. The world still consists of two monetary regions, say Europe and America. The exchange rate between Europe and America is flexible. Europe in turn consists of two countries, say Germany and France. Germany and France form a monetary union. The three spatial units are completely specialized in production. Germany produces German goods, France produces French goods, and America produces American goods. These goods are imperfect substitutes in consumption.

German households consume German goods, French goods and American goods. German households maximize utility subject to the budget constraint. The exogenous variables are German income, the price of German goods, the price of French goods, the price of American goods, and the price of the dollar. The endogenous variables are the German consumption of German goods, the German consumption of French goods, and the German consumption of American goods. Then what are the demand functions of German households?

French households consume French goods, German goods and American goods. French households maximize utility subject to the budget constraint. The exogenous variables are French income, the price of French goods, the price of German goods, the price of American goods, and the price of the dollar. The endogenous variables are the French consumption of French goods, the French consumption of German goods, and the French consumption of American goods. Then what are the demand functions of French households?

American households consume American goods, German goods and French goods. American households maximize utility subject to the budget constraint. The exogenous variables are American income, the price of American goods, the price of German goods, the price of French goods, and the price of the euro. The endogenous variables are the American consumption of American goods, the American consumption of German goods, and the American consumption of French goods. Then what are the demand functions of American households?

The market for German goods. German output is determined by the German consumption of German goods, by the French consumption of German goods, by the American consumption of German goods, and by the autonomous demand for

German goods. That is, German output is determined by the autonomous demand for German goods, by French income, by American income, by the price of German goods, by the price of French goods, by the price of American goods, and by the price of the euro.

The market for French goods. French output is driven by the French consumption of French goods, by the German consumption of French goods, by the American consumption of French goods, and by the autonomous demand for French goods. That is, French output is driven by the autonomous demand for French goods, by German income, by American income, by the price of French goods, by the price of German goods, by the price of American goods, and by the price of the euro.

The market for American goods. American output is determined by the American consumption of American goods, by the German consumption of American goods, by the French consumption of American goods, and by the autonomous demand for American goods. That is, American output is determined by the autonomous demand for American goods, by German income, by French income, by the price of American goods, by the price of German goods, by the price of French goods, and by the price of the dollar.

Further topics are:
- a first model of Germany, France and America
- the consumption, export and import functions of Germany
- the consumption, export and import functions of France
- the consumption, export and import functions of America
- a second model of Germany, France and America.

Part One

The Closed Economy

1. The Static Model

1.1. Fixed Wages

Understanding the closed economy is helpful in understanding the world of two monetary regions as well as the monetary union of two countries. Consider for example an increase in money supply. Then what will be the effect on the interest rate, and what on output? Alternatively consider an increase in investment, in nominal wages or in productivity.

Let us begin with the goods market. The behavioural functions are as follows:

$$C = cY \tag{1}$$

$$I = br^{-\varepsilon} \tag{2}$$

Equation (1) is the consumption function. It states that consumption is an increasing function of income. Here C denotes real consumption, Y is real income, and c is the marginal consumption rate with $0 < c < 1$. Equation (2) is the investment function. It states that investment is a decreasing function of the interest rate. I symbolizes real investment, r is the interest rate, ε is the interest elasticity of investment with $\varepsilon > 0$, and b is a shift parameter with $b > 0$. The message of equation (2) is that a 1 percent increase in the interest rate causes an ε percent decrease in investment. Aggregate supply is determined by aggregate demand $Y = C + I$. Taking account of the behavioural functions, we arrive at the goods market equation:

$$Y = cY + br^{-\varepsilon} \tag{3}$$

Let us go on to the money market. The behavioural functions look like this:

$$L = kPYr^{-\eta} \tag{4}$$

$$M = \text{const} \tag{5}$$

Equation (4) is the money demand function. It states that money demand is an increasing function of income and a decreasing function of the interest rate. L stands for nominal money demand, Y is real income, P is the price level, PY is nominal income, r is the interest rate, η is the interest elasticity of money demand with $\eta > 0$, and k is a shift parameter with $k > 0$. Obviously, a 1 percent increase in real income causes a 1 percent increase in money demand. Similarly, a 1 percent increase in the price level causes a 1 percent increase in money demand. And a 1 percent increase in the interest rate causes an η percent decrease in money demand. Equation (5) is the money supply function. It states that the central bank fixes the nominal supply of money. Further, the nominal demand for money equals the nominal supply of money $L = M$. Taking account of the behavioural functions, we reach the money market equation:

$$kPYr^{-\eta} = M = const \tag{6}$$

The production function is characterized by fixed coefficients:

$$Y = aN \tag{7}$$

Here N designates labour input, a is labour productivity, and Y is output. Accordingly, labour demand is:

$$N = Y/a \tag{8}$$

That is to say, a 1 percent increase in output requires a 1 percent increase in labour demand. Conversely, a 1 percent increase in labour productivity allows a 1 percent decrease in labour demand. Firms set prices as a markup over unit labour cost:

$$P = gw/a \tag{9}$$

Here w is the nominal wage rate, w/a is unit labour cost, g is the markup factor, and P is the price level. A 1 percent increase in nominal wages causes a 1 percent increase in the price level. The other way round, a 1 percent increase in labour productivity causes a 1 percent decrease in the price level.

On this basis, the model can be represented by a system of four equations:

$$Y = cY + br^{-\varepsilon} \tag{10}$$

$$M = kPYr^{-\eta} \tag{11}$$

$$P = gw / a \tag{12}$$

$$N = Y / a \tag{13}$$

Equation (10) is the goods market equation, (11) is the money market equation, (12) is the price equation, and (13) is the labour demand equation. The exogenous variables are money supply M, the investment parameter b, nominal wages w, and labour productivity a. The endogenous variables are output Y, the interest rate r, the price level P, and labour demand N. Equation (12) gives the price level. Then equations (10) and (11) give output and the interest rate. Finally equation (13) gives labour demand.

Now have a brief look at some shocks. First consider an investment shock. An increase in autonomous investment raises the interest rate. This in turn lowers investment. The net effect is that output moves up. In a numerical example, we assume that the dampening effect of the money market on the investment multiplier is 0.5. Then, as a result, a 1 percent increase in autonomous investment (relative to output) causes a 1.79 percent increase in output. For the proof see Carlberg (2001). Second consider monetary policy. An increase in money supply lowers the interest rate. This in turn raises investment and output. In the numerical example, a 1 percent increase in money supply causes a 0.5 percent increase in output.

Third consider a wage shock. An increase in nominal wages causes an increase in the price level. This in turn lowers real balances, thereby raising the interest rate. As a consequence, investment and output move down. In the numerical example, a 1 percent increase in nominal wages causes a 1 percent increase in the price level and a 0.5 percent decrease in output. Fourth consider a productivity shock. An increase in labour productivity reduces the price level. This in turn drives up real balances, thus bringing down the interest rate. Therefore investment and output move up. In the numerical example, a 1 percent increase in labour productivity causes a 1 percent decrease in the price level and a 0.5 percent increase in output.

1.2. Flexible Wages

Take for example an increase in money supply. Then what will be the effect on nominal wages and the price level? Alternatively take an increase in investment, in labour supply or in labour productivity.

Under flexible wages, labour demand equals labour supply. As a consequence there is always full employment. Here N denotes labour supply. It is assumed that labour supply is given exogenously N = const. Then the model can be represented by a system of four equations:

$$Y = cY + br^{-\varepsilon} \tag{1}$$

$$M = kPYr^{-\eta} \tag{2}$$

$$Y = aN \tag{3}$$

$$w = aP / g \tag{4}$$

Equation (1) is the goods market equation, (2) is the money market equation, (3) is the production function, and (4) is the wage equation. The exogenous variables are money supply M, the investment parameter b, labour supply N, and productivity a. The endogenous variables are the price level P, nominal wages w, the interest rate r, and output Y. Equation (3) gives output. Then equations (1) and (2) give the price level and the interest rate. Finally equation (4) gives nominal wages.

Next have a look at some shocks. First take monetary policy. An increase in money supply pushes up nominal wages and the price level. In a numerical example, a 1 percent increase in money supply causes a 1 percent increase in nominal wages and a 1 percent increase in the price level. For the proof see Carlberg (2001). Second take an investment shock. An increase in autonomous investment drives up nominal wages and the price level. In the numerical example, a 1 percent increase in autonomous investment (relative to output) causes a 3.57 percent increase in nominal wages and a 3.57 percent increase in the price level.

Third take a labour supply shock. An increase in labour supply lowers nominal wages and the price level. In the numerical example, a 1 percent increase in labour supply causes a 2 percent decrease in nominal wages and a 2 percent decrease in the price level. Fourth take a productivity shock. An increase in labour productivity reduces nominal wages and the price level. In the numerical example, a 1 percent increase in labour productivity causes a 1 percent decrease in nominal wages and a 2 percent decrease in the price level.

2. Given Money Growth

2.1. The Dynamic Model

Here the focus is on steady-state inflation, given steady-state growth. We assume that nominal wages and prices are flexible, so there is always full employment. To illustrate the problem, consider a numerical example. Let productivity grow at a constant rate of 2 percent, let labour supply grow at a constant rate of 1 percent, and let money supply grow at a constant rate of 4 percent. Then, at what rate does output grow? At what rate does the price level grow? At what rate do nominal wages grow? And at what rate do real wages grow? Besides, what is the nominal interest rate? And what is the real interest rate?

For easy reference, the static model with flexible wages is reproduced here:

$$Y = cY + br^{-\varepsilon} \tag{1}$$

$$M = kPYr^{-\eta} \tag{2}$$

$$Y = aN \tag{3}$$

$$w = aP / g \tag{4}$$

Equation (1) is the goods market equation, (2) is the money market equation, (3) is the production function, and (4) is the wage equation.

Now the model is restated in terms of growth rates:

$$\hat{Y} = \hat{b} - \varepsilon\hat{r} \tag{5}$$

$$\hat{M} = \hat{P} + \hat{Y} - \eta\hat{i} \tag{6}$$

$$\hat{Y} = \hat{a} + \hat{N} \tag{7}$$

$$\hat{w} = \hat{a} + \hat{P} \tag{8}$$

Equation (5) is the goods market equation. $\hat{Y}$ denotes the rate of growth of output. It is defined as $\hat{Y} = \dot{Y}/Y$, where $\dot{Y}$ is the time derivative dY/dt. Correspondingly, $\hat{b}$ is the rate of growth of autonomous investment. r is the real interest rate, and $\hat{r}$ is the rate of growth of the real interest rate. Equation (6) is the money market equation. $\hat{M}$ symbolizes the rate of growth of money supply. $\hat{P}$ is the rate of growth of the price level. Put another way, $\hat{P}$ is the rate of inflation. i is the nominal interest rate, and $\hat{i}$ is the rate of growth of the nominal interest rate. Equation (7) is the production function. $\hat{a}$ stands for the rate of growth of productivity, and $\hat{N}$ is the rate of growth of labour supply. Equation (8) is the wage equation. $\hat{w}$ designates the rate of growth of nominal wages.

In the dynamic model, we make the following assumptions:

$$\hat{M} = \text{const} \tag{9}$$

$$\hat{N} = \text{const} \tag{10}$$

$$\hat{a} = \text{const} \tag{11}$$

$$\hat{b} = \hat{Y} \tag{12}$$

Equation (9) has it that money supply grows at the constant rate $\hat{M}$. Equation (10) has it that labour supply grows at the constant rate $\hat{N}$. Equation (11) has it that productivity grows at the constant rate $\hat{a}$. And equation (12) has it that, in the steady state, the growth of autonomous investment equals the growth of output. This is a natural assumption.

Equations (5) and (12) yield $\hat{r} = 0$. That means, in the steady state, the real interest rate is constant. Next have a look at the Fisher equation $i = r + \hat{P}$. It states that the nominal interest rate is determined by the real interest rate and by the (expected) rate of inflation. An increase in the (expected) rate of inflation raises the nominal interest rate. In the steady state, by definition, the rate of inflation is constant. This together with $\hat{r} = 0$ yields $\hat{i} = 0$. That is to say, in the steady state, the nominal interest rate is constant too. Moreover we assume that, in the steady state, the real interest rate is determined by productivity growth and labour growth $r = \hat{a} + \hat{N} + z$. Here z is a (positive) constant. From the point of view of growth theory, this is a natural assumption. An increase in productivity growth raises the real interest rate. And an increase in labour growth has the same effect.

On this foundation, the dynamic model can be characterized by a system of five equations:

$$\hat{M} = \hat{P} + \hat{Y} \tag{13}$$

$$\hat{Y} = \hat{a} + \hat{N} \tag{14}$$

$$\hat{w} = \hat{a} + \hat{P} \tag{15}$$

$$i = r + \hat{P} \tag{16}$$

$$r = \hat{a} + \hat{N} + z \tag{17}$$

Equation (13) is the money market equation, (14) is the production function, (15) is the wage equation, (16) is the Fisher equation, and (17) is the real interest equation. The exogenous variables are money growth $\hat{M}$, productivity growth $\hat{a}$, and labour growth $\hat{N}$. The endogenous variables are inflation $\hat{P}$, output growth $\hat{Y}$, nominal wage growth $\hat{w}$, the nominal interest rate i, and the real interest rate r.

2.2. Inflation and Wage Growth

The model can be condensed to a system of three equations:

$$\hat{M} = \hat{P} + \hat{Y} \tag{1}$$

$$\hat{Y} = \hat{a} + \hat{N} \tag{2}$$

$$\hat{w} = \hat{a} + \hat{P} \tag{3}$$

Equation (1) is the money market equation, (2) is the production function, and (3) is the wage equation. The exogenous variables are money growth $\hat{M}$, productivity growth $\hat{a}$, and labour growth $\hat{N}$. The endogenous variables are inflation $\hat{P}$, output growth $\hat{Y}$, and nominal wage growth $\hat{w}$.

The model can be solved as follows:

$$\hat{Y} = \hat{a} + \hat{N} \tag{4}$$

$$\hat{P} = \hat{M} - \hat{a} - \hat{N} \tag{5}$$

$$\hat{w} = \hat{M} - \hat{N} \tag{6}$$

$$\hat{w} - \hat{P} = \hat{a} \tag{7}$$

As a result, according to equation (4), output grows at a constant rate. Output growth is determined by productivity growth and labour growth. According to equation (5), the price level grows at a constant rate. The rate of inflation is determined by money growth, productivity growth, and labour growth. An increase in money growth raises inflation. On the other hand, an increase in productivity growth lowers inflation. And an increase in labour growth lowers inflation as well.

According to equation (6), nominal wages grow at a constant rate. Nominal wage growth depends on money growth and labour growth. However, it does not depend on productivity growth. An increase in money growth raises nominal wage growth. Conversely, an increase in labour growth lowers nominal wage growth. And an increase in productivity growth has no effect on nominal wage growth. How can this be explained? An increase in money growth raises inflation and, hence, nominal wage growth. An increase in labour growth raises output growth. This in turn lowers inflation and, hence, nominal wage growth. And an increase in productivity growth has two counteracting effects. The direct effect is to raise nominal wage growth. The indirect effect is to raise output growth. This in turn lowers inflation and, hence, nominal wage growth. The net effect is that nominal wage growth does not respond. According to equation (7), real wages grow at a constant rate. Real wage growth depends on productivity growth but not on labour growth.

To illustrate this, consider a numerical example. Let productivity grow at a constant rate of 2 percent, let labour supply grow at a constant rate of 1 percent, and let money supply grow at a constant rate of 4 percent. Then, as a result, output grows at a constant rate of 3 percent, the price level grows at a constant rate of 1 percent, nominal wages grow at a constant rate of 3 percent, and real wages grow at a constant rate of 2 percent. Table 1 presents a synopsis, containing some more examples.

Table 1
Inflation and Wage Growth
Given Productivity Growth, Labour Growth, and Money Growth

Productivity Growth	2	2	2
Labour Growth	0	1	1
Money Growth	3	4	5
Output Growth	2	3	3
Inflation	1	1	2
Nominal Wage Growth	3	3	4
Real Wage Growth	2	2	2

2.3. Nominal and Real Interest Rates

The model can be compressed to a system of three equations:

$$\hat{M} = \hat{P} + \hat{Y} \tag{1}$$

$$i = r + \hat{P} \tag{2}$$

$$r = \hat{Y} + z \tag{3}$$

Equation (1) is the money market equation, (2) is the Fisher equation, and (3) is the real interest equation. Here the exogenous variables are money growth $\hat{M}$ and output growth $\hat{Y}$. The endogenous variables are the nominal interest rate i, the real interest rate r, and the rate of inflation $\hat{P}$.

The model can be solved this way:

$$r = \hat{Y} + z \tag{4}$$

$$\hat{P} = \hat{M} - \hat{Y} \tag{5}$$

$$i = \hat{M} + z \tag{6}$$

As a result, according to equation (4), the real interest rate is determined by output growth. An increase in output growth raises the real interest rate. According to equation (5), the rate of inflation is determined by money growth and output growth. An increase in money growth raises the rate of inflation. Conversely, an increase in output growth lowers the rate of inflation. According to equation (6), the nominal interest rate is determined by money growth. An increase in money growth raises the nominal interest rate. An increase in output growth, however, has no effect on the nominal interest rate.

Have a look at a numerical example. Let output growth be 3 percent, let money growth be 4 percent, and let the constant z be 1 percent. Then the real interest rate is 4 percent, the rate of inflation is 1 percent, and the nominal interest rate is 5 percent. In other words, if the real interest rate exceeds output growth by 1 percentage point, then the nominal interest rate exceeds money growth by equally 1 percentage point. Table 2 gives an overview, containing some more examples.

Table 2
Nominal and Real Interest Rates
Given Output Growth and Money Growth

Output Growth	3	3	4
Money Growth	4	5	5
Real Interest Rate	4	4	5
Inflation	1	2	1
Nominal Interest Rate	5	6	6

3. Target Inflation and Required Money Growth

The objective of the central bank is to maintain price stability. Strictly speaking, the objective of the central bank is to keep inflation at target level. Then what monetary policy is needed? To illustrate this, take a numerical example. Let target inflation be 1 percent, let productivity growth be 2 percent, and let labour growth be 1 percent. Then, what rate of money growth is required? Besides, what is the ensuing growth of nominal wages? What is the nominal interest rate, and what is the real interest rate?

The model can be characterized by a system of three equations:

$$\hat{M} = \hat{P} + \hat{Y} \tag{1}$$

$$\hat{Y} = \hat{a} + \hat{N} \tag{2}$$

$$\hat{w} = \hat{a} + \hat{P} \tag{3}$$

Here $\hat{P}$ denotes the target rate of inflation. The exogenous variables are target inflation, productivity growth, and labour growth. The endogenous variables are required money growth, nominal wage growth, and output growth.

The solution to this problem is:

$$\hat{M} = \hat{P} + \hat{a} + \hat{N} \tag{4}$$

$$\hat{w} = \hat{P} + \hat{a} \tag{5}$$

Equation (4) shows the required rate of money growth. As a result, required money growth is determined by target inflation, productivity growth, and labour growth. An increase in target inflation calls for an increase in money growth. And the same holds for an increase in productivity growth or labour growth. Equation (5) shows the ensuing rate of nominal wage growth. As a result, nominal wage growth depends on target inflation and productivity growth. However, it does not depend on labour growth. An increase in target inflation raises nominal wage growth. The same applies to an increase in productivity growth. But an increase in labour growth has no effect on nominal wage growth.

Have a look at a numerical example. Let target inflation be 1 percent, let productivity growth be 2 percent, and let labour growth be 1 percent. Then required money growth is 4 percent. Besides, nominal wage growth is 3 percent. Table 3 presents a synopsis.

The next point refers to nominal and real interest rates. The model can be reduced to a system of two equations:

$$i = r + \hat{P} \tag{6}$$

$$r = \hat{Y} + z \tag{7}$$

Equation (6) is the Fisher equation, and equation (7) is the real interest equation. The exogenous variables are target inflation and output growth. The endogenous variables are the nominal interest rate and the real interest rate.

Obviously the solution is:

$$r = \hat{Y} + z \tag{8}$$

$$i = \hat{P} + \hat{Y} + z \tag{9}$$

As a result, according to equation (8), the real interest rate is determined by output growth. According to equation (9), the nominal interest rate is determined by target inflation and output growth. An increase in target inflation raises the nominal interest rate. And the same holds for an increase in output growth. For instance, let target inflation be 1 percent, let output growth be 3 percent, and let the constant z be 1 percent. Then the real interest rate is 4 percent, and the nominal interest rate is 5 percent.

Table 3
Required Money Growth
Given Target Inflation, Productivity Growth, and Labour Growth

Target Inflation	1	1	2
Productivity Growth	2	2	2
Labour Growth	0	1	1
Required Money Growth	3	4	5
Nominal Wage Growth	3	3	4

Part Two

The World of
Two Monetary Regions

Chapter 1
The Static Model

1. Fixed Wages

1) Introduction. In this chapter we consider a world of two monetary regions, let us say Europe and America. The exchange rate between Europe and America is flexible. Take for example an increase in European money supply. Then what will be the effect on European output, and what on American output? Alternatively take an increase in European investment, European nominal wages, or European productivity.

In doing the analysis, we make the following assumptions. European goods and American goods are imperfect substitutes for each other. European output is determined by the demand for European goods. American output is determined by the demand for American goods. European money demand equals European money supply. And American money demand equals American money supply. There is perfect capital mobility between Europe and America, so the European interest rate equals the American interest rate. The monetary regions are the same size and have the same behavioural functions.

2) The market for European goods. The behavioural functions underlying the analysis are as follows:

$$C_1 = cY_1 \tag{1}$$

$$I_1 = b_1 r^{-\varepsilon} \tag{2}$$

$$X_1 = qeP_2 Y_2 / P_1 \tag{3}$$

$$Q_1 = qY_1 \tag{4}$$

Equation (1) is the consumption function of Europe. It states that European consumption is an increasing function of European income. Here C_1 denotes European consumption, as measured in European goods. Y_1 is European income, as measured in European goods. And c is the marginal consumption rate of Europe, with $0 < c < 1$. Equation (2) is the investment function of Europe. It states that European investment is a decreasing function of the world interest rate. I_1 symbolizes European investment, as measured in European goods. r is the world interest rate. ε is the interest elasticity of European investment, with $\varepsilon > 0$. And b_1 is a shift parameter, with $b_1 > 0$. The message of equation (2) is that a 1 percent increase in the world interest rate causes an ε percent decrease in European investment.

Equation (3) is the export function of Europe. It states that European exports are an increasing function of American income. X_1 stands for European exports to America, as measured in European goods. P_1 is the price of European goods, as measured in euros. P_2 is the price of American goods, as measured in dollars. e is the exchange rate between the dollar and the euro. More exactly, e is the price of the dollar, as measured in euros. Then eP_2 is the price of American goods, as measured in euros. Y_2 is American income, as measured in American goods. P_2Y_2 is American income, as measured in dollars. eP_2Y_2 is American income, as measured in euros. eP_2Y_2 / P_1 is American income, as measured in European goods. And q is the marginal import rate of America, with $q > 0$. The message of equation (3) is that a 1 percent increase in American income causes a 1 percent increase in European exports. Further, a 1 percent depreciation of the euro causes a 1 percent increase in European exports. On the other hand, a 1 percent increase in the price of European goods causes a 1 percent decrease in European exports. And a 1 percent increase in the price of American goods causes a 1 percent increase in European exports.

Equation (4) is the import function of Europe. It states that European imports are an increasing function of European income. Q_1 designates European imports from America, as measured in European goods. Y_1 is European income, as measured in European goods. And q is the marginal import rate of Europe, with $q > 0$. European output is determined by the demand for European goods $Y_1 = C_1 + I_1 + X_1 - Q_1$. Taking account of the behavioural functions (1) until (4), we arrive at the goods market equation of Europe:

$$Y_1 = cY_1 + b_1 r^{-\varepsilon} + qeP_2Y_2 / P_1 - qY_1 \tag{5}$$

3) The market for American goods. The behavioural functions are as follows:

$$C_2 = cY_2 \tag{6}$$
$$I_2 = b_2 r^{-\varepsilon} \tag{7}$$
$$X_2 = qP_1Y_1 / eP_2 \tag{8}$$
$$Q_2 = qY_2 \tag{9}$$

Equation (6) is the consumption function of America. It states that American consumption is an increasing function of American income. Here C_2 denotes American consumption, as measured in American goods. Y_2 is American income, as measured in American goods. And c is the marginal consumption rate of America, with $0 < c < 1$. Equation (7) is the investment function of America. It states that American investment is a decreasing function of the world interest rate. I_2 symbolizes American investment, as measured in American goods. r is the world interest rate. ε is the interest elasticity of American investment, with $\varepsilon > 0$. And b_2 is a shift parameter, with $b_2 > 0$. The message of equation (7) is that a 1 percent increase in the world interest rate causes an ε percent decrease in American investment.

Equation (8) is the export function of America. It states that American exports are an increasing function of European income. X_2 stands for American exports to Europe, as measured in American goods. Y_1 is European income, as measured in European goods. P_1Y_1 is European income, as measured in euros. P_1Y_1 / e is European income, as measured in dollars. P_1Y_1 / eP_2 is European income, as measured in American goods. And q is the marginal import rate of Europe, with $q > 0$. The message of equation (8) is that a 1 percent increase in European income causes a 1 percent increase in American exports. Moreover, a 1 percent depreciation of the dollar causes a 1 percent increase in American exports. The other way round, a 1 percent increase in the price of American goods causes a 1 percent decrease in American exports. And a 1 percent increase in the price of European goods causes a 1 percent increase in American exports. Of course, American exports to Europe are identical with European imports from America, as long as both are measured in American goods.

Equation (9) is the import function of America. It states that American imports are an increasing function of American income. Q_2 designates American imports from Europe, as measured in American goods. Y_2 is American income, as measured in American goods. And q is the marginal import rate of America, with $q > 0$. American output is determined by the demand for American goods $Y_2 = C_2 + I_2 + X_2 - Q_2$. Upon substituting the behavioural functions (6) until (9), we reach the goods market equation of America:

$$Y_2 = cY_2 + b_2 r^{-\varepsilon} + qP_1 Y_1 / eP_2 - qY_2 \qquad (10)$$

4) The European money market. The behavioural functions are as follows.

$$L_1 = kP_1 Y_1 r^{-\eta} \qquad (11)$$

$$M_1 = const \qquad (12)$$

Equation (11) is the money demand function of Europe. It states that European money demand is an increasing function of European income and a decreasing function of the world interest rate. Here L_1 denotes European money demand, as measured in euros. Y_1 is European income, as measured in European goods. P_1 is the price of European goods, as measured in euros. $P_1 Y_1$ is European income, as measured in euros. r is the world interest rate. η is the interest elasticity of European money demand, with $\eta > 0$. And k is a shift parameter, with $k > 0$. The message of equation (11) is that a 1 percent increase in European income causes a 1 percent increase in European money demand. Similarly, a 1 percent increase in the price of European goods causes a 1 percent increase in European money demand. And a 1 percent increase in the world interest rate causes an η percent decrease in European money demand.

Equation (12) is the money supply function of Europe. It states that the European central bank fixes the money supply of Europe. M_1 is European money supply, as measured in euros. European money demand equals European money supply $L_1 = M_1$. Taking account of the behavioural functions (11) and (12), we arrive at the money market equation of Europe:

$$kP_1 Y_1 r^{-\eta} = M_1 = const \qquad (13)$$

5) The American money market. The behavioural functions are as follows:

$$L_2 = kP_2Y_2r^{-\eta} \tag{14}$$

$$M_2 = \text{const} \tag{15}$$

Equation (14) is the money demand function of America. It states that American money demand is an increasing function of American income and a decreasing function of the world interest rate. L_2 symbolizes American money demand, as measured in dollars. Y_2 is American income, as measured in American goods. P_2 is the price of American goods, as measured in dollars. P_2Y_2 is American income, as measured in dollars. r is the world interest rate. η is the interest elasticity of American money demand, with $\eta > 0$. And k is a shift parameter, with $k > 0$. The message of equation (14) is that a 1 percent increase in American income causes a 1 percent increase in American money demand. Likewise, a 1 percent increase in the price of American goods causes a 1 percent increase in American money demand. And a 1 percent increase in the world interest rate causes an η percent decrease in American money demand.

Equation (15) is the money supply function of America. It states that the American central bank fixes the money supply of America. M_2 is American money supply, as measured in dollars. American money demand equals American money supply $L_2 = M_2$. Upon substituting the behavioural functions (14) and (15), we reach the money market equation of America:

$$kP_2Y_2r^{-\eta} = M_2 = \text{const} \tag{16}$$

6) Technology and price setting. The production function of Europe is characterized by fixed coefficients:

$$Y_1 = a_1N_1 \tag{17}$$

Here N_1 stands for European labour input. a_1 is European labour productivity, as measured in European goods. And Y_1 is European output, as measured in European goods. Accordingly, European labour demand is:

$$N_1 = Y_1 / a_1 \tag{18}$$

That means, a 1 percent increase in European output requires a 1 percent increase in European labour demand. On the other hand, a 1 percent increase in European productivity allows a 1 percent decrease in European labour demand.

European firms set the price of European goods as a markup over unit labour cost in Europe:

$$P_1 = gw_1 / a_1 \tag{19}$$

Here w_1 is the nominal wage rate in Europe, as measured in euros. w_1 / a_1 is unit labour cost in Europe, as measured in euros. g is the markup factor in Europe. And P_1 is the price of European goods, as measured in euros. The message of equation (19) is that a 1 percent increase in European nominal wages causes a 1 percent increase in the price of European goods. Conversely, a 1 percent increase in European productivity causes a 1 percent decrease in the price of European goods.

The production function of America is characterized by fixed coefficients:

$$Y_2 = a_2 N_2 \tag{20}$$

Here N_2 designates American labour input. a_2 is American labour productivity, as measured in American goods. And Y_2 is American output, as measured in American goods. Accordingly, American labour demand is:

$$N_2 = Y_2 / a_2 \tag{21}$$

That is to say, a 1 percent increase in American output requires a 1 percent increase in American labour demand. The other way round, a 1 percent increase in American productivity allows a 1 percent decrease in American labour demand.

American firms set the price of American goods as a markup over unit labour cost in America:

$$P_2 = gw_2 / a_2 \tag{22}$$

Here w_2 is the nominal wage rate in America, as measured in dollars. w_2 / a_2 is unit labour cost in America, as measured in dollars. g is the markup factor in America. And P_2 is the price of American goods, as measured in dollars. The message of equation (22) is that a 1 percent increase in American nominal wages causes a 1 percent increase in the price of American goods. Conversely, a 1 percent increase in American productivity causes a 1 percent decrease in the price of American goods.

7) The model. On this foundation, the full model can be represented by a system of eight equations:

$$Y_1 = cY_1 + b_1 r^{-\varepsilon} + qeP_2 Y_2 / P_1 - qY_1 \tag{23}$$

$$Y_2 = cY_2 + b_2 r^{-\varepsilon} + qP_1 Y_1 / eP_2 - qY_2 \tag{24}$$

$$M_1 = kP_1 Y_1 r^{-\eta} \tag{25}$$

$$M_2 = kP_2 Y_2 r^{-\eta} \tag{26}$$

$$P_1 = gw_1 / a_1 \tag{27}$$

$$P_2 = gw_2 / a_2 \tag{28}$$

$$N_1 = Y_1 / a_1 \tag{29}$$

$$N_2 = Y_2 / a_2 \tag{30}$$

Equation (23) is the goods market equation of Europe, as measured in European goods. (24) is the goods market equation of America, as measured in American goods. (25) is the money market equation of Europe, as measured in euros. (26) is the money market equation of America, as measured in dollars. (27) is the price equation of Europe, as measured in euros. (28) is the price equation of America, as measured in dollars. (29) is the labour demand equation of Europe, and (30) is the labour demand equation of America.

The exogenous variables are European money supply M_1, American money supply M_2, the European investment parameter b_1, the American investment parameter b_2, European nominal wages w_1, American nominal wages w_2,

European productivity a_1, and American productivity a_2. The endogenous variables are European output Y_1, American output Y_2, the exchange rate e, the world interest rate r, the price of European goods P_1, the price of American goods P_2, European labour demand N_1, and American labour demand N_2. Equation (27) gives the price of European goods, and equation (28) gives the price of American goods. Then equations (23) until (26) give European output, American output, the exchange rate, and the world interest rate. Finally equation (29) gives European labour demand, and equation (30) gives American labour demand.

Now it proves very useful to rewrite the goods market equations as follows:

$$P_1Y_1 = cP_1Y_1 + P_1b_1r^{-\epsilon} + qeP_2Y_2 - qP_1Y_1 \tag{31}$$

$$P_2Y_2 = cP_2Y_2 + P_2b_2r^{-\epsilon} + qP_1Y_1 / e - qP_2Y_2 \tag{32}$$

Equation (31) is the goods market equation of Europe, as measured in euros. P_1Y_1 is European income, as measured in euros. cP_1Y_1 is European consumption, as measured in euros. $P_1b_1r^{-\epsilon}$ is European investment, as measured in euros. qeP_2Y_2 is American imports from Europe, as measured in euros. Put another way, qeP_2Y_2 is European exports to America, as measured in euros. And qP_1Y_1 is European imports from America, as measured in euros. Equation (32) is the goods market equation of America, as measured in dollars. P_2Y_2 is American income, as measured in dollars. cP_2Y_2 is American consumption, as measured in dollars. $P_2b_2r^{-\epsilon}$ is American investment, as measured in dollars. qP_1Y_1 / e is European imports from America, as measured in dollars. Put differently, qP_1Y_1 / e is American exports to Europe, as measured in dollars. And qP_2Y_2 is American imports from Europe, as measured in dollars. It is worth pointing out here that the goods market equations (31) and (32) are well consistent with microfoundations, see Part Five below. European income P_1Y_1 is spent on European goods $(c-q)P_1Y_1$ and American goods qP_1Y_1. American income is spent on American goods $(c-q)P_2Y_2$ and on European goods qP_2Y_2.

8) Some shocks. First consider monetary policy. An increase in European money supply causes a depreciation of the euro, an appreciation of the dollar, and a decrease in the world interest rate. The depreciation of the euro, in turn, raises European exports. The appreciation of the dollar, however, lowers American

exports. And the decrease in the world interest rate raises both European investment and American investment. The net effect is that European output moves up. On the other hand, American output moves down. In a numerical example, a 1 percent increase in European money supply causes a 2.75 percent depreciation of the euro, a 2.75 percent appreciation of the dollar, a 0.75 percent increase in European output, and a 0.25 percent decrease in American output. For the proof see Carlberg (2001).

Second consider fiscal policy. An increase in European government purchases causes an appreciation of the euro, a depreciation of the dollar, and an increase in the world interest rate. The appreciation of the euro, in turn, lowers European exports. The depreciation of the dollar raises American exports. And the increase in the world interest rate lowers both European investment and American investment. The net effect is that European output and American output move up, at the same rate respectively. In the numerical example, a 1 percent increase in European government purchases (relative to European output) causes a 6.25 percent appreciation of the euro, a 6.25 percent depreciation of the dollar, a 0.89 percent increase in European output, and a 0.89 percent increase in American output.

Third consider a wage shock. An increase in European nominal wages pushes up the price of European goods. This in turn causes an appreciation of the euro, a depreciation of the dollar, and an increase in the world interest rate. The net effect is that European output moves down. On the other hand, American output moves up. In the numerical example, a 1 percent increase in European nominal wages causes a 1 percent increase in the price of European goods, a 1.75 percent appreciation of the euro, a 1.75 percent depreciation of the dollar, a 0.75 percent decrease in European output, and a 0.25 percent increase in American output.

Fourth consider a productivity shock. An increase in European productivity reduces the price of European goods. This in turn causes a depreciation of the euro, an appreciation of the dollar, and a decrease in the world interest rate. The net effect is that European output moves up. On the other hand, American output moves down. On balance, both European labour demand and American labour demand decline. In the numerical example, a 1 percent increase in European productivity causes a 1 percent decrease in the price of European goods, a 1.75

percent depreciation of the euro, a 1.75 percent appreciation of the dollar, a 0.75 percent increase in European output, and a 0.25 percent decrease in American output. Besides, it causes a 0.25 percent decrease in European labour demand and a 0.25 percent decrease in American labour demand.

2. Flexible Wages

Take for example an increase in European money supply. Then what will be the effect on the price of European goods, and what on the price of American goods? Alternatively take an increase in European investment, in European labour supply, or in European productivity.

Under flexible wages, European labour demand equals European labour supply. On the same grounds, American labour demand equals American labour supply. As a consequence there is always full employment in Europe and America. Here N_1 denotes European labour supply, and N_2 is American labour supply. It is assumed that European and American labour supply are given exogenously ($N_1 = \text{const}$, $N_2 = \text{const}$). Then the full model can be characterized by a system of eight equations:

$$Y_1 = cY_1 + b_1 r^{-\varepsilon} + qeP_2 Y_2 / P_1 - qY_1 \tag{1}$$

$$Y_2 = cY_2 + b_2 r^{-\varepsilon} + qP_1 Y_1 / eP_2 - qY_2 \tag{2}$$

$$M_1 = kP_1 Y_1 r^{-\eta} \tag{3}$$

$$M_2 = kP_2 Y_2 r^{-\eta} \tag{4}$$

$$Y_1 = a_1 N_1 \tag{5}$$

$$Y_2 = a_2 N_2 \tag{6}$$

$$w_1 = a_1 P_1 / g \tag{7}$$

$$w_2 = a_2 P_2 / g \tag{8}$$

Equation (1) is the goods market equation of Europe, (2) is the goods market equation of America, (3) is the money market equation of Europe, (4) is the money market equation of America, (5) is the production function of Europe, (6) is the production function of America, (7) is the wage equation of Europe, and (8) is the wage equation of America. The exogenous variables are European money supply M_1, American money supply M_2, the European investment parameter b_1, the American investment parameter b_2, European labour supply N_1, American labour supply N_2, European productivity a_1, and American productivity a_2. The endogenous variables are the price of European goods P_1, the price of American goods P_2, European nominal wages w_1, American nominal wages w_2, the exchange rate e, the world interest rate r, European output Y_1, and American output Y_2. Equation (5) gives European output, and equation (6) gives American output. Then equations (1) until (4) give the price of European goods, the price of American goods, the exchange rate, and the world interest rate. Finally equation (7) gives European nominal wages, and equation (8) gives American nominal wages.

Next have a look at some shocks. First take monetary policy. An increase in European money supply causes a depreciation of the euro. This in turn raises European nominal wages and the price of European goods. On the other hand, American nominal wages and the price of American goods do not change. In a numerical example, a 1 percent increase in European money supply causes a 1 percent depreciation of the euro, a 1 percent increase in European nominal wages, and a 1 percent increase in the price of European goods. For the proof see Carlberg (2001).

Second take fiscal policy. An increase in European government purchases causes an appreciation of the euro, a depreciation of the dollar, and an increase in the world interest rate. The net effect is that both European and American nominal wages move up. As a consequence, the prices of European and American goods move up too. In the numerical example, a 1 percent increase in European government purchases (relative to European output) causes a 6.25 percent appreciation of the euro, a 6.25 percent depreciation of the dollar, a 1.79 percent increase in European nominal wages, a 1.79 percent increase in American nominal wages, a 1.79 percent increase in the price of European goods, and a 1.79 percent increase in the price of American goods.

Third take a labour supply shock. An increase in European labour supply lowers European nominal wages and the price of European goods. This in turn raises European output. As a secondary effect, American nominal wages and the price of American goods come down too. In the numerical example, a 1 percent increase in European labour supply causes a 1.5 percent decrease in European nominal wages, a 1.5 percent decrease in the price of European goods, and a 1 percent increase in European output. Moreover, it causes a 0.5 percent decrease in American nominal wages and a 0.5 percent decrease in the price of American goods.

Fourth take a productivity shock. An increase in European productivity lowers European nominal wages and the price of European goods. This in turn raises European output. As a secondary effect, American nominal wages and the price of American goods come down too. In the numerical example, a 1 percent increase in European productivity causes a 0.5 percent decrease in European nominal wages, a 1.5 percent decrease in the price of European goods, and a 1 percent increase in European output. Further, it causes a 0.5 percent decrease in American nominal wages and a 0.5 percent decrease in the price of American goods.

Chapter 2
Given Money Growth

1. The Dynamic Model

Here the focus is on steady-state inflation in Europe and America, given steady-state growth. We assume that nominal wages and prices are flexible, so there is always full employment in Europe and America. To illustrate the problem, consider a numerical example. Let European output grow at a constant rate of 2 percent, let American output grow at a constant rate of 3 percent, let European money supply grow at a constant rate of 3 percent, and let American money supply grow at a constant rate of 5 percent. This gives rise to a number of questions.

At what rate does the price of European goods grow? At what rate does the price of American goods grow? At what rate does the price of the euro change? At what rate does the price of the dollar change? And at what rate does the real exchange rate move? The consumer price index of Europe includes the price of European goods, the price of American goods, and the price of the dollar. Then at what rate does the consumer price index of Europe grow? Similarly, the consumer price index of America includes the price of American goods, the price of European goods, and the price of the euro. Then at what rate does the consumer price index of America grow?

For easy reference, the static model with flexible wages is reproduced here:

$$Y_1 = cY_1 + b_1 r^{-\varepsilon} + qeP_2 Y_2 / P_1 - qY_1 \tag{1}$$

$$Y_2 = cY_2 + b_2 r^{-\varepsilon} + qP_1 Y_1 / eP_2 - qY_2 \tag{2}$$

$$M_1 = kP_1 Y_1 r^{-\eta} \tag{3}$$

$$M_2 = kP_2 Y_2 r^{-\eta} \tag{4}$$

$$Y_1 = a_1 N_1 \tag{5}$$

$$Y_2 = a_2 N_2 \tag{6}$$

$$w_1 = a_1 P_1 / g \tag{7}$$

$$w_2 = a_2 P_2 / g \tag{8}$$

Equation (1) is the goods market equation of Europe, (2) is the goods market equation of America, (3) is the money market equation of Europe, (4) is the money market equation of America, (5) is the production function of Europe, (6) is the production function of America, (7) is the wage equation of Europe, and (8) is the wage equation of America.

In the dynamic model, we make the following assumptions:

$$\hat{M}_1 = \text{const} \tag{9}$$

$$\hat{M}_2 = \text{const} \tag{10}$$

$$\hat{N}_1 = \text{const} \tag{11}$$

$$\hat{N}_2 = \text{const} \tag{12}$$

$$\hat{a}_1 = \text{const} \tag{13}$$

$$\hat{a}_2 = \text{const} \tag{14}$$

$$\hat{b}_1 = \hat{Y}_1 \tag{15}$$

$$\hat{b}_2 = \hat{Y}_2 \tag{16}$$

$$r = \text{const} \tag{17}$$

$\hat{M}_1$ denotes the rate of growth of European money supply. It is defined as $\hat{M}_1 = \dot{M}_1 / M_1$, where $\dot{M}_1$ is the time derivative dM_1 / dt. Correspondingly, $\hat{N}_1$ is the rate of growth of European labour supply. Equation (9) has it that European money supply grows at the constant rate $\hat{M}_1$. Equation (10) has it that American money supply grows at the constant rate $\hat{M}_2$. Equation (11) has it that European labour supply grows at the constant rate $\hat{N}_1$. Equation (12) has it that American labour supply grows at the constant rate $\hat{N}_2$. Equation (13) has it that European productivity grows at the constant rate $\hat{a}_1$. Equation (14) has it that American productivity grows at the constant rate $\hat{a}_2$.

In equation (15), $\hat{b}_1$ symbolizes the rate of growth of autonomous investment in Europe, and $\hat{Y}_1$ is the rate of growth of European output. Equation (15) has it that, in the steady state, the growth of autonomous investment in Europe equals output growth in Europe. This is a natural assumption. In equation (16), $\hat{b}_2$ stands for the rate of growth of autonomous investment in America, and $\hat{Y}_2$ is the rate of growth of American output. Equation (16) has it that, in the steady state, the growth of autonomous investment in America equals output growth in America. And equation (17) has it that, in the steady state, the world interest rate is constant. This is a natural assumption as well.

Now the static model will be restated in terms of growth rates. In equation (1), all terms except qeP_2Y_2 / P_1 grow at the rate $\hat{Y}_1$. As a consequence, qeP_2Y_2 / P_1 grows at the rate $\hat{Y}_1$ too. This implies:

$$\hat{P}_1 + \hat{Y}_1 = \hat{e} + \hat{P}_2 + \hat{Y}_2 \tag{18}$$

In equation (2), all terms except qP_1Y_1 / eP_2 grow at the rate $\hat{Y}_2$. As a consequence, qP_1Y_1 / eP_2 grows at the rate $\hat{Y}_2$ too. This implies:

$$\hat{P}_1 + \hat{Y}_1 = \hat{e} + \hat{P}_2 + \hat{Y}_2 \tag{19}$$

Of course, equations (18) and (19) are identical.

On this foundation, the dynamic model can be characterized by a system of seven equations:

$$\hat{P}_1 + \hat{Y}_1 = \hat{e} + \hat{P}_2 + \hat{Y}_2 \tag{20}$$
$$\hat{M}_1 = \hat{P}_1 + \hat{Y}_1 \tag{21}$$
$$\hat{M}_2 = \hat{P}_2 + \hat{Y}_2 \tag{22}$$
$$\hat{Y}_1 = \hat{a}_1 + \hat{N}_1 \tag{23}$$
$$\hat{Y}_2 = \hat{a}_2 + \hat{N}_2 \tag{24}$$
$$\hat{w}_1 = \hat{a}_1 + \hat{P}_1 \tag{25}$$
$$\hat{w}_2 = \hat{a}_2 + \hat{P}_2 \tag{26}$$

Equation (20) is called the goods market equation, (21) is the money market equation of Europe, (22) is the money market equation of America, (23) is the production function of Europe, (24) is the production function of America, (25) is the wage equation of Europe, and (26) is the wage equation of America.

In equation (20), $\hat{P}_1$ is the rate of growth of the price of European goods. Put another way, $\hat{P}_1$ is the rate of producer inflation in Europe. By analogy, $\hat{P}_2$ is the rate of growth of the price of American goods. Put differently, $\hat{P}_2$ is the rate of producer inflation in America. $\hat{e}$ is the rate of growth of the nominal exchange rate. In other words, $\hat{e}$ is the rate of depreciation. According to equation (20), European income as measured in euros $P_1 Y_1$ and American income as measured in euros $e P_2 Y_2$ grow at the same rate. According to equation (20), the rate of depreciation $\hat{e}$ depends on nominal income growth in Europe $\hat{P}_1 + \hat{Y}_1$ and on nominal income growth in America $\hat{P}_2 + \hat{Y}_2$.

According to equation (21), European money supply (as measured in euros) and European income (as measured in euros) grow at the same rate. That is to say, nominal income growth in Europe is determined by money growth in Europe. According to equation (22), American money supply (as measured in dollars) and American income (as measured in dollars) grow at the same rate. That is to say, nominal income growth in America is determined by money growth in America. According to equation (23), output growth in Europe is determined by productivity growth in Europe and by labour growth in Europe. According to Equation (24), output growth in America is determined by productivity growth in America and by labour growth in America.

In equation (25), $\hat{w}_1$ is the rate of growth of European nominal wages. According to equation (25), nominal wage growth in Europe depends on productivity growth in Europe and on producer inflation in Europe. In equation (26), $\hat{w}_2$ is the rate of growth of American nominal wages. According to equation (26), nominal wage growth in America depends on productivity growth in America and on producer inflation in America.

The exogenous variables are money growth in Europe $\hat{M}_1$, money growth in America $\hat{M}_2$, productivity growth in Europe $\hat{a}_1$, productivity growth in America $\hat{a}_2$, labour growth in Europe $\hat{N}_1$, and labour growth in America $\hat{N}_2$. The endogenous variables are producer inflation in Europe $\hat{P}_1$, producer inflation in

America $\hat{P}_2$, nominal depreciation $\hat{e}$, output growth in Europe $\hat{Y}_1$, output growth in America $\hat{Y}_2$, nominal wage growth in Europe $\hat{w}_1$, and nominal wage growth in America $\hat{w}_2$. Equation (23) gives output growth in Europe, and equation (24) gives output growth in America. Then equation (21) gives producer inflation in Europe, and equation (22) gives producer inflation in America. Then equation (20) gives nominal depreciation. Finally equation (25) gives nominal wage growth in Europe, and equation (26) gives nominal wage growth in America.

2. Inflation and Depreciation

2.1. Producer Inflation

Producer inflation in Europe refers to the price of European goods, as measured in euros. Producer inflation in America refers to the price of American goods, as measured in dollars. The model can be reduced to a system of two equations:

$$\hat{M}_1 = \hat{P}_1 + \hat{Y}_1 \tag{1}$$
$$\hat{M}_2 = \hat{P}_2 + \hat{Y}_2 \tag{2}$$

Equation (1) is the money market equation of Europe, and equation (2) is the money market equation of America. Here the exogenous variables are money growth in Europe, money growth in America, output growth in Europe, and output growth in America. The endogenous variables are producer inflation in Europe and producer inflation in America.

Obviously the solution is:

$$\hat{P}_1 = \hat{M}_1 - \hat{Y}_1 \tag{3}$$
$$\hat{P}_2 = \hat{M}_2 - \hat{Y}_2 \tag{4}$$

As a result, according to equation (3), the price of European goods grows at a constant rate. Producer inflation in Europe depends on money growth in Europe and on output growth in Europe. However, it does not depend on money growth in America or on output growth in America. An increase in European money growth raises producer inflation in Europe. On the other hand, an increase in European output growth lowers producer inflation in Europe. To illustrate this, consider a numerical example. Let European output grow at a constant rate of 2 percent, and let European money supply grow at a constant rate of 3 percent. Then, as a result, the price of European goods grows at a constant rate of 1 percent.

According to equation (4), the price of American goods also grows at a constant rate. Producer inflation in America is determined by money growth in America and by output growth in America. An increase in American money growth drives up producer inflation in America. Conversely, an increase in American output growth cuts down producer inflation in America. For instance, let output growth in America be 3 percent, and let money growth in America be 5 percent. Then producer inflation in America is 2 percent. In the region where money growth is high, other things being equal, producer inflation will be high. And in the region where money growth is low, producer inflation will be low. In the region where output growth is high, other things being equal, producer inflation will be low. And in the region where output growth is low, producer inflation will be high.

2.2. Nominal Depreciation

The model can be condensed to a system of three equations:

$$\hat{P}_1 + \hat{Y}_1 = \hat{e} + \hat{P}_2 + \hat{Y}_2 \tag{1}$$
$$\hat{M}_1 = \hat{P}_1 + \hat{Y}_1 \tag{2}$$

$$\hat{M}_2 = \hat{P}_2 + \hat{Y}_2 \tag{3}$$

Equation (1) is the goods market equation, (2) is the money market equation of Europe, and (3) is the money market equation of America. The exogenous variables are money growth in Europe, money growth in America, output growth in Europe, and output growth in America. The endogenous variables are nominal depreciation, producer inflation in Europe, and producer inflation in America.

Equations (1), (2) and (3) yield:

$$\hat{e} = \hat{M}_1 - \hat{M}_2 \tag{4}$$

As a result, the nominal exchange rate grows (or declines) at a constant rate. The rate of depreciation depends on money growth in Europe and on money growth in America. But it does not depend on output growth in Europe or on output growth in America. In the region where money growth is high, the currency will depreciate. And in the region where money growth is low, the currency will appreciate. To be more specific, if money growth in Europe is high, the euro will depreciate. And if money growth in Europe is low, the euro will appreciate. Correspondingly, if money growth in America is high, the dollar will depreciate. And if money growth in America is low, the dollar will appreciate.

To illustrate this, consider some numerical examples. Let us begin with numerical example number one. Let European money supply grow at a constant rate of 3 percent, and let American money supply grow at a constant rate of 5 percent. Then, as a result, the price of the dollar declines at a constant rate of 2 percent. And the price of the euro grows at a constant rate of 2 percent.

We proceed now to numerical example number two. Let output growth in Europe be 2 percent, let output growth in America be 3 percent, let money growth in Europe be 3 percent, and let money growth in America be 4 percent. Then producer inflation in Europe is 1 percent, producer inflation in America is 1 percent, the appreciation of the euro is 1 percent, and the depreciation of the dollar is 1 percent. Here we have an appreciation of the euro, in spite of the fact that producer inflation in Europe is equal to producer inflation in America. The general point is that the rate of depreciation does not depend on producer inflation in Europe or on producer inflation in America. This is in sharp contrast to a widely held view.

To sum up, the rate of depreciation is determined by money growth in Europe and by money growth in America. In short, the rate of depreciation is driven by the money growth differential.

2.3. Real Depreciation

The real exchange rate is defined as the price of American goods, as measured in European goods:

$$R = eP_2 / P_1 \tag{1}$$

An increase in the relative price of American goods raises the competitiveness of European goods. Equation (1) can be expressed in terms of growth rates as $\hat{R} = \hat{e} + \hat{P}_2 - \hat{P}_1$. Here $\hat{R}$ designates the rate of growth of the real exchange rate. Put another way, $\hat{R}$ is the rate of real depreciation. The model can be compressed to a system of two equations:

$$\hat{P}_1 + \hat{Y}_1 = \hat{e} + \hat{P}_2 + \hat{Y}_2 \tag{2}$$
$$\hat{R} = \hat{e} + \hat{P}_2 - \hat{P}_1 \tag{3}$$

Equation (2) is the goods market equation, and equation (3) defines the real exchange rate. The exogenous variables are output growth in Europe and output growth in America. The endogenous variable is real depreciation.

The model can be solved as follows:

$$\hat{R} = \hat{Y}_1 - \hat{Y}_2 \tag{4}$$

As a result, the real exchange rate grows at a constant rate. Put differently, the price of American goods, as measured in European goods, grows at a constant rate. That means, the competitiveness of European goods grows at a constant rate. According to equation (4), the growth of the relative price of American goods depends on output growth in Europe and on output growth in America. However, it does not depend on money growth in Europe or on money growth in America.

If output growth in America is high, the relative price of American goods will decline. And if output growth in America is low, the relative price of American goods will increase. If output growth in Europe is high, the relative price of American goods will increase. And if output growth in Europe is low, the relative price of American goods will decline. To see this more clearly, have a look at a numerical example. Let European output grow at a constant rate of 2 percent, and let American output grow at a constant rate of 3 percent. Then the relative price of American goods declines at a constant rate of 1 percent. That is to say, the relative price of European goods grows at a constant rate of 1 percent.

As regards competitiveness, the general findings can be restated as follows. If output growth in Europe is high, the competitiveness of European goods will increase. And if output growth in Europe is low, the competitiveness of European goods will decline.

We turn now to purchasing power. An increase in the relative price of American goods (as measured in European goods) reduces the purchasing power of European goods (as measured in American goods). As regards purchasing power, the general findings can be expressed as follows. If output growth in Europe is high, the purchasing power of European goods will decline. And if output growth in Europe is low, the purchasing power of European goods will increase. This is closely related to purchasing power parity. By definition, it means that purchasing power is constant. If European output and American output grow at the same rate, then the purchasing power of European goods will be constant. In other words, purchasing power parity will hold. If European output and American output grow at different rates, then the purchasing power of European goods will not be constant. Put another way, purchasing power parity will not hold.

Finally compare nominal depreciation and real depreciation. Nominal depreciation is determined by money growth in Europe and by money growth in America. Real depreciation, on the other hand, is determined by output growth in Europe and by output growth in America. In short, nominal depreciation is driven by the money growth differential. And real depreciation is driven by the output growth differential.

2.4. Consumer Inflation

1) The consumer price index of Europe. European consumption includes both European goods and American goods. Therefore, the consumer price index of Europe includes the price of European goods, the price of American goods, and the price of the dollar. The consumer price index of Europe is defined as follows:

$$J_1 = P_1^{\alpha}(eP_2)^{\beta} \tag{1}$$

Here P_1 denotes the price of European goods, as measured in euros. P_2 is the price of American goods, as measured in dollars. e is the price of the dollar, as measured in euros. Hence eP_2 is the price of American goods, as measured in euros. α is the share of European goods in European consumption, and β is the share of American goods in European consumption, with $\alpha + \beta = 1$. Then J_1 is the consumer price index of Europe, as measured in euros.

Equation (1) can be expressed in terms of growth rates:

$$\hat{J}_1 = \alpha\hat{P}_1 + \beta\hat{P}_2 + \beta\hat{e} \tag{2}$$

$\hat{J}_1$ symbolizes the rate of growth of the consumer price index in Europe. Put differently, $\hat{J}_1$ is the rate of consumer inflation in Europe. According to equation (2), consumer inflation in Europe includes producer inflation in Europe, producer inflation in America, and the appreciation of the dollar.

2) The consumer price index of America. American consumption includes both American goods and European goods. Therefore, the consumer price index of America includes the price of American goods, the price of European goods, and the price of the euro. The consumer price index of America is defined as:

$$J_2 = P_2^\alpha (P_1 / e)^\beta \tag{3}$$

Here P_2 stands for the price of American goods, as measured in dollars. P_1/e is the price of European goods, as measured in dollars. α is the share of American goods in American consumption, and β is the share of European goods in American consumption. Then J_2 is the consumer price index of America, as measured in dollars.

Equation (3) can be reformulated in terms of growth rates:

$$\hat{J}_2 = \alpha \hat{P}_2 + \beta \hat{P}_1 - \beta \hat{e} \tag{4}$$

$\hat{J}_2$ designates the rate of growth of the consumer price index in America. In other words, $\hat{J}_2$ is the rate of consumer inflation in America. According to equation (4), consumer inflation in America includes producer inflation in America, producer inflation in Europe, and the appreciation of the euro.

3) The model. On this basis, the model can be captured by a system of five equations:

$$\hat{P}_1 + \hat{Y}_1 = \hat{e} + \hat{P}_2 + \hat{Y}_2 \tag{5}$$

$$\hat{M}_1 = \hat{P}_1 + \hat{Y}_1 \tag{6}$$

$$\hat{M}_2 = \hat{P}_2 + \hat{Y}_2 \tag{7}$$

$$\hat{J}_1 = \alpha \hat{P}_1 + \beta \hat{P}_2 + \beta \hat{e} \tag{8}$$

$$\hat{J}_2 = \alpha \hat{P}_2 + \beta \hat{P}_1 - \beta \hat{e} \tag{9}$$

Equation (5) is the goods market equation, (6) is the money market equation of Europe, (7) is the money market equation of America, (8) is the consumer price index of Europe, and (9) is the consumer price index of America. The exogenous variables are money growth in Europe, money growth in America, output growth in Europe, and output growth in America. The endogenous variables are producer inflation in Europe, producer inflation in America, nominal depreciation, consumer inflation in Europe, and consumer inflation in America.

4) Consumer inflation in Europe. Equations (5), (6) and (7) yield:

$$\hat{P}_1 = \hat{M}_1 - \hat{Y}_1 \tag{10}$$

$$\hat{P}_2 = \hat{M}_2 - \hat{Y}_2 \tag{11}$$

$$\hat{e} = \hat{M}_1 - \hat{M}_2 \tag{12}$$

Next substitute these equations into equation (8) to arrive at:

$$\hat{J}_1 = \hat{M}_1 - \alpha\hat{Y}_1 - \beta\hat{Y}_2 \tag{13}$$

As a result, according to equation (13), the consumer price index of Europe grows at a constant rate. Consumer inflation in Europe depends on money growth in Europe, on output growth in Europe, and on output growth in America. However, it does not depend on money growth in America. An increase in European money growth raises consumer inflation in Europe. An increase in European output growth lowers consumer inflation in Europe. And what is more, an increase in American output growth lowers consumer inflation in Europe too.

What is the chain of cause and effect? An increase in European money growth raises both producer inflation in Europe and the appreciation of the dollar. This in turn raises consumer inflation in Europe. An increase in European output growth lowers producer inflation in Europe and, hence, consumer inflation in Europe. An increase in American output growth lowers producer inflation in America and, hence, consumer inflation in Europe.

5) Consumer inflation in America. Insert equations (10), (11) and (12) into equation (9) to conclude:

$$\hat{J}_2 = \hat{M}_2 - \alpha\hat{Y}_2 - \beta\hat{Y}_1 \tag{14}$$

That means, the consumer price index of America grows at a constant rate. Consumer inflation in America depends on money growth in America, on output growth in America, and on output growth in Europe. But it does not depend on money growth in Europe. An increase in American money growth drives up consumer inflation in America. An increase in American output growth cuts down consumer inflation in America. And an increase in European output growth has the same effect.

In the region where money growth is high, consumer inflation will be high. And in the region where money growth is low, consumer inflation will be low. In the region where output growth is high, consumer inflation will be low. And in the region where output growth is low, consumer inflation will be high. Moreover, if $\hat{Y}_1 > \hat{Y}_2$, then $\hat{J}_1 > \hat{P}_1$. Conversely, if $\hat{Y}_1 < \hat{Y}_2$, then $\hat{J}_1 < \hat{P}_1$. That is to say, in the region where output growth is high, consumer inflation will exceed producer inflation. And in the region where output growth is low, consumer inflation will fall short of producer inflation.

6) Numerical examples. Let us begin with numerical example number one. Let output growth in Europe be 2 percent, let output growth in America be equally 2 percent, let money growth in Europe be 3 percent, and let money growth in America be 4 percent. Further, let the share of European goods in European consumption be 0.9, and let the share of American goods in European consumption be 0.1. By symmetry, let the share of American goods in American consumption be 0.9, and let the share of European goods in American consumption be 0.1. Then, as a result, consumer inflation in Europe is 1 percent, and consumer inflation in America is 2 percent. Compare this with producer inflation. Producer inflation in Europe is 1 percent, and producer inflation in America is 2 percent. Thus, in this case, consumer inflation is identical to producer inflation.

We come now to numerical example number two. Let output growth in Europe be 2 percent, let output growth in America be 3 percent, let money growth in Europe be 3 percent, and let money growth in America be 4 percent. Then consumer inflation in Europe is 0.9 percent, and consumer inflation in America is 1.1 percent. Compare this with producer inflation. Producer inflation in Europe is 1 percent, and producer inflation in America is 1 percent as well.

Thus, in this case, consumer inflation is different from producer inflation. Table 4 gives an overview of the conclusions drawn in Section 2.

Table 4

Inflation and Depreciation

Given Output Growth and Money Growth

Output Growth in Europe	2	2
Output Growth in America	2	3
Money Growth in Europe	3	3
Money Growth in America	4	4
Producer Inflation in Europe	1	1
Producer Inflation in America	2	1
Appreciation of the Euro	1	1
Depreciation of the Dollar	1	1
Decline of European Competitiveness	0	1
Growth of American Competitiveness	0	1
Consumer Inflation in Europe	1	0.9
Consumer Inflation in America	2	1.1

3. Wage Growth

3.1. Productivity Growth

1) The model. This section deals with the growth of nominal wages, producer real wages and consumer real wages, given productivity growth. The relevant model can be encapsulated in a system of seven equations:

$$\hat{P}_1 + \hat{Y}_1 = \hat{e} + \hat{P}_2 + \hat{Y}_2 \tag{1}$$

$$\hat{M}_1 = \hat{P}_1 + \hat{Y}_1 \tag{2}$$

$$\hat{M}_2 = \hat{P}_2 + \hat{Y}_2 \tag{3}$$

$$\hat{Y}_1 = \hat{a}_1 \tag{4}$$

$$\hat{Y}_2 = \hat{a}_2 \tag{5}$$

$$\hat{w}_1 = \hat{a}_1 + \hat{P}_1 \tag{6}$$

$$\hat{w}_2 = \hat{a}_2 + \hat{P}_2 \tag{7}$$

Equation (1) is the goods market equation, (2) is the money market equation of Europe, (3) is the money market equation of America, (4) is the production function of Europe, (5) is the production function of America, (6) is the wage equation of Europe, and (7) is the wage equation of America. The exogenous variables are money growth in Europe $\hat{M}_1$, money growth in America $\hat{M}_2$, productivity growth in Europe $\hat{a}_1$, and productivity growth in America $\hat{a}_2$. The endogenous variables are producer inflation in Europe $\hat{P}_1$, producer inflation in America $\hat{P}_2$, nominal depreciation $\hat{e}$, output growth in Europe $\hat{Y}_1$, output growth in America $\hat{Y}_2$, nominal wage growth in Europe $\hat{w}_1$, and nominal wage growth in America $\hat{w}_2$.

2) The growth of nominal wages. Equations (2) and (4) imply $\hat{P}_1 = \hat{M}_1 - \hat{a}_1$. This together with equation (6) yields:

$$\hat{w}_1 = \hat{M}_1 \tag{8}$$

As a result, according to equation (8), nominal wages in Europe grow at a constant rate. Nominal wage growth in Europe depends on money growth in Europe. However, it does not depend on productivity growth in Europe. By analogy we have:

$$\hat{w}_2 = \hat{M}_2 \tag{9}$$

That means, nominal wage growth in America is determined by money growth in America. In the region where money growth is high, nominal wage growth will be high. And in the region where money growth is low, nominal wage growth will be low. For instance, let money growth in Europe be 3 percent, and let money growth in America be 5 percent. Then nominal wage growth in Europe is 3 percent, and nominal wage growth in America is 5 percent.

3) The growth of producer real wages. Producer real wages in Europe are defined as nominal wages in Europe divided by the price of European goods w_1 / P_1. Correspondingly, producer real wages in America are defined as nominal wages in America divided by the price of American goods w_2 / P_2. Producer real wages in Europe measure the real cost of labour in Europe. And producer real wages in America measure the real cost of labour in America. Producer real wages can be expressed in terms of growth rates. $\hat{w}_1 - \hat{P}_1$ is the rate of growth of producer real wages in Europe. And $\hat{w}_2 - \hat{P}_2$ is the rate of growth of producer real wages in America. Now equations (6) and (7) provide:

$$\hat{w}_1 - \hat{P}_1 = \hat{a}_1 \tag{10}$$
$$\hat{w}_2 - \hat{P}_2 = \hat{a}_2 \tag{11}$$

As a result, according to equation (10), producer real wages in Europe grow at a constant rate. The growth of producer real wages in Europe is determined by productivity growth in Europe. And according to equation (11), the growth of producer real wages in America is driven by productivity growth in America. In the region where productivity growth is high, the growth of producer real wages will be high. And in the region where productivity growth is low, the growth of producer real wages will be low. For instance, let productivity growth in Europe be 2 percent, and let productivity growth in America be 3 percent. Then the growth of producer real wages in Europe is 2 percent, and the growth of producer real wages in America is 3 percent.

4) The growth of consumer real wages. Consumer real wages in Europe are defined as nominal wages in Europe divided by the consumer price index of Europe w_1 / J_1. Similarly, consumer real wages in America are defined as nominal wages in America divided by the consumer price index of America w_2 / J_2. European nominal wages are spent on European goods and on American goods. So consumer real wages in Europe measure the purchasing power of European nominal wages. American nominal wages are spent on American goods and on European goods. So consumer real wages in America measure the purchasing power of American nominal wages. Consumer real wages can be expressed in terms of growth rates. $\hat{w}_1 - \hat{J}_1$ is the rate of growth of consumer real wages in Europe. And $\hat{w}_2 - \hat{J}_2$ is the rate of growth of consumer real wages in America.

Consumer inflation in Europe is given by:

$$\hat{J}_1 = \hat{M}_1 - \alpha\hat{Y}_1 - \beta\hat{Y}_2 \tag{12}$$

For the proof see Section 2.4. above. Next substitute equations (4) and (5) into equation (12) to get $\hat{J}_1 = \hat{M}_1 - \alpha\hat{a}_1 - \beta\hat{a}_2$. Then take account of equation (8) and rearrange:

$$\hat{w}_1 - \hat{J}_1 = \alpha\hat{a}_1 + \beta\hat{a}_2 \tag{13}$$

As a result, according to equation (13), consumer real wages in Europe grow at a constant rate. The growth of consumer real wages in Europe depends on productivity growth in Europe and on productivity growth in America. But it does not depend on money growth in Europe or on money growth in America. An increase in European productivity growth raises the growth of consumer real wages in Europe. And what is more, an increase in American productivity growth also raises the growth of consumer real wages in Europe.

Along the same lines it can be shown that:

$$\hat{w}_2 - \hat{J}_2 = \alpha\hat{a}_2 + \beta\hat{a}_1 \tag{14}$$

That is to say, the growth of consumer real wages in America is determined by productivity growth in America and by productivity growth in Europe. In the region where productivity growth is high, the growth of consumer real wages will be high. And in the region where productivity growth is low, the growth of consumer real wages will be low.

To see this more clearly, have a look at some numerical examples. Let us begin with numerical example number one. Let productivity growth in Europe be 2 percent, and let productivity growth in America be 3 percent. In addition, let the share of American goods in European consumption be 0.1. Symmetrically, let the share of European goods in American consumption be equally 0.1. Then, as a result, the growth of consumer real wages in Europe is 2.1 percent, and the growth of consumer real wages in America is 2.9 percent. Compare this with the growth of producer real wages. The growth of producer real wages in Europe is 2 percent, and the growth of producer real wages in America is 3 percent. Hence, in this case, the growth of consumer real wages is different from the growth of producer real wages.

Let us proceed to numerical example number two. Let productivity growth in Europe be 2 percent, and let productivity growth in America be equally 2 percent. Then the growth of consumer real wages in Europe is 2 percent, and the growth of consumer real wages in America is equally 2 percent. In this case, the growth of consumer real wages is identical to the growth of producer real wages. Table 5 presents a synopsis.

Table 5
Wage Growth
Given Productivity Growth and Money Growth

Productivity Growth in Europe	2	2
Productivity Growth in America	3	2
Money Growth in Europe	3	3
Money Growth in America	4	4
Growth of Nominal Wages in Europe	3	3
Growth of Nominal Wages in America	4	4
Growth of Producer Real Wages in Europe	2	2
Growth of Producer Real Wages in America	3	2
Growth of Consumer Real Wages in Europe	2.1	2
Growth of Consumer Real Wages in America	2.9	2

3.2. Labour Growth

1) The model. This section is devoted to the growth of nominal wages, producer real wages and consumer real wages, given labour growth. The model can be enshrined in a system of seven equations:

$$\hat{P}_1 + \hat{Y}_1 = \hat{e} + \hat{P}_2 + \hat{Y}_2 \tag{1}$$

$$\hat{M}_1 = \hat{P}_1 + \hat{Y}_1 \tag{2}$$

$$\hat{M}_2 = \hat{P}_2 + \hat{Y}_2 \tag{3}$$

$$\hat{Y}_1 = \hat{N}_1 \tag{4}$$

$$\hat{Y}_2 = \hat{N}_2 \tag{5}$$

$$\hat{w}_1 = \hat{P}_1 \tag{6}$$

$$\hat{w}_2 = \hat{P}_2 \tag{7}$$

Equation (1) is the goods market equation, (2) is the money market equation of Europe, (3) is the money market equation of America, (4) is the production function of Europe, (5) is the production function of America, (6) is the wage equation of Europe, and (7) is the wage equation of America. The exogenous variables are money growth in Europe $\hat{M}_1$, money growth in America $\hat{M}_2$, labour growth in Europe $\hat{N}_1$, and labour growth in America $\hat{N}_2$. The endogenous variables are producer inflation in Europe $\hat{P}_1$, producer inflation in America $\hat{P}_2$, nominal depreciation $\hat{e}$, output growth in Europe $\hat{Y}_1$, output growth in America $\hat{Y}_2$, nominal wage growth in Europe $\hat{w}_1$, and nominal wage growth in America $\hat{w}_2$.

2) The growth of nominal wages. Equations (2) and (4) provide $\hat{P}_1 = \hat{M}_1 - \hat{N}_1$. This together with equation (6) yields:

$$\hat{w}_1 = \hat{M}_1 - \hat{N}_1 \tag{8}$$

As a result, according to equation (8), nominal wages in Europe grow at a constant rate. Nominal wage growth in Europe is determined by money growth in

Europe and by labour growth in Europe. An increase in European money growth raises nominal wage growth in Europe. On the other hand, an increase in European labour growth lowers nominal wage growth in Europe.

By analogy we have:

$$\hat{w}_2 = \hat{M}_2 - \hat{N}_2 \tag{9}$$

That means, nominal wage growth in America is determined by money growth in America and by labour growth in America. In the region where money growth is high, nominal wage growth will be high. And in the region where money growth is low, nominal wage growth will be low. In the region where labour growth is high, nominal wage growth will be low. And in the region where labour growth is low, nominal wage growth will be high.

To illustrate this, consider a series of numerical examples. Let us start with numerical example number one. Let labour growth in Europe be 1 percent, let labour growth in America be equally 1 percent, let money growth in Europe be 2 percent, and let money growth in America be 3 percent. Then nominal wage growth in Europe is 1 percent, and nominal wage growth in America is 2 percent. We proceed now to numerical example number two. Let labour growth in Europe be 0 percent, let labour growth in America be 1 percent, let money growth in Europe be 2 percent, and let money growth in America be equally 2 percent. Then nominal wage growth in Europe is 2 percent, and nominal wage growth in America is 1 percent.

Numerical example number three: Let labour growth in Europe be 0 percent, let labour growth in America be 1 percent, let money growth in Europe be 1 percent, and let money growth in America be 2 percent. Then nominal wage growth in Europe is 1 percent, and nominal wage growth in America is equally 1 percent. Numerical example number four: Let labour growth in Europe be 0 percent, let labour growth in America be 1 percent, let money growth in Europe be 1 percent, and let money growth in America be 3 percent. Then nominal wage growth in Europe is 1 percent, and nominal wage growth in America is 2 percent. Numerical example number five: Let labour growth in Europe be −1 percent, let labour growth in America be 1 percent, let money growth in Europe be 0 percent, and let money growth in America be 3 percent. Then nominal wage growth in Europe is 1 percent, and nominal wage growth in America is 2 percent.

3) The growth of producer real wages. From equations (6) and (7) it follows immediately that:

$$\hat{w}_1 - \hat{P}_1 = 0 \tag{10}$$

$$\hat{w}_2 - \hat{P}_2 = 0 \tag{11}$$

According to equation (10), producer real wages in Europe are constant. And according to equation (11), producer real wages in America are constant too. This holds although there is labour growth. And this holds although the regions differ in labour growth.

4) The growth of consumer real wages. Consumer inflation in Europe is given by:

$$\hat{J}_1 = \hat{M}_1 - \alpha\hat{Y}_1 - \beta\hat{Y}_2 \tag{12}$$

For the proof see Section 2.4. above. Next insert equations (4) and (5) into equation (12) to get $\hat{J}_1 = \hat{M}_1 - \alpha\hat{N}_1 - \beta\hat{N}_2$. Then take account of equation (8) and solve for:

$$\hat{w}_1 - \hat{J}_1 = \beta\hat{N}_2 - \beta\hat{N}_1 \tag{13}$$

As a result, according to equation (13), consumer real wages in Europe grow at a constant rate. The growth of consumer real wages in Europe depends on labour growth in Europe and on labour growth in America. However, it does not depend on money growth in Europe or on money growth in America. An increase in European labour growth cuts down the growth of consumer real wages in Europe. Conversely, an increase in American labour growth drives up the growth of consumer real wages in Europe.

What is the relationship between cause and effect? First consider an increase in European labour growth. Initially let European labour growth be equal to American labour growth. Therefore European output growth is equal to

American output growth. The relative price of American goods is constant. So consumer real wages in Europe are constant too. In this situation, European labour growth speeds up. Therefore European output growth speeds up. The relative price of American goods starts to grow. So consumer real wages in Europe start to decline.

Second consider an increase in American labour growth. Initially let American labour growth be equal to European labour growth. Therefore American output growth is equal to European output growth. The relative price of American goods is constant. So consumer real wages in Europe are constant as well. In this condition, American labour growth speeds up. Therefore American output growth speeds up. The relative price of American goods starts to decline. So consumer real wages in Europe start to grow.

In the same way it can be derived that:

$$\hat{w}_2 - \hat{J}_2 = \beta\hat{N}_1 - \beta\hat{N}_2 \tag{14}$$

That is to say, the growth of consumer real wages in America is determined by labour growth in America and by labour growth in Europe. In the region where labour growth is high, consumer real wages will decline. And in the region where labour growth is low, consumer real wages will increase.

To see this more clearly, have a look at some numerical examples. Let us begin with numerical example number one. Let labour growth in Europe be 0 percent, and let labour growth in America be 1 percent. Further, let the share of American goods in European consumption be 0.1. And let the share of European goods in American consumption be equally 0.1. Then, as a result, the growth of consumer real wages in Europe is 0.1 percent, and the growth of consumer real wages in America is − 0.1 percent. Compare this with the growth of producer real wages. The growth of producer real wages in Europe is zero, as is the growth of producer real wages in America. So, in this case, the growth of consumer real wages is different from the growth of producer real wages.

We turn now to numerical example number two. Let labour growth in Europe be 1 percent, and let labour growth in America be equally 1 percent. Then consumer real wages in Europe are constant, as are consumer real wages in

America. How does this compare with producer real wages? Producer real wages in Europe are constant, as are producer real wages in America. Hence, in this case, the growth of consumer real wages is identical to the growth of producer real wages. Tables 6 and 7 give an overview.

Table 6
Wage Growth
Given Labour Growth and Money Growth

Labour Growth in Europe	0	1
Labour Growth in America	1	1
Money Growth in Europe	2	2
Money Growth in America	2	3
Growth of Nominal Wages in Europe	2	1
Growth of Nominal Wages in America	1	2
Growth of Producer Real Wages in Europe	0	0
Growth of Producer Real Wages in America	0	0
Growth of Consumer Real Wages in Europe	0.1	0
Growth of Consumer Real Wages in America	− 0.1	0

Table 7
Comparing Productivity Growth and Labour Growth
Given Money Growth

Productivity Growth in Europe	2	0
Productivity Growth in America	3	0
Labour Growth in Europe	0	0
Labour Growth in America	0	1
Money Growth in Europe	3	1
Money Growth in America	4	2
Growth of Nominal Wages in Europe	3	1
Growth of Nominal Wages in America	4	1
Growth of Producer Real Wages in Europe	2	0
Growth of Producer Real Wages in America	3	0
Growth of Consumer Real Wages in Europe	2.1	0.1
Growth of Consumer Real Wages in America	2.9	− 0.1

4. Nominal and Real Interest Rates

1) The model. In this context, the real interest rate can be defined in two ways. Let us begin with definition number one: The real interest rate is the nominal interest rate as adjusted for producer inflation. This is the real interest rate from the point of view of producers. It measures the real cost of bonds. We come now to definition number two: The real interest rate is the nominal interest as adjusted for consumer inflation. This is the real interest rate from the point of view of consumers. It measures the real return on bonds. Here definition number one is adopted. The model can be captured by a system of six equations:

$$\hat{P}_1 + \hat{Y}_1 = \hat{e} + \hat{P}_2 + \hat{Y}_2 \tag{1}$$

$$\hat{M}_1 = \hat{P}_1 + \hat{Y}_1 \tag{2}$$

$$\hat{M}_2 = \hat{P}_2 + \hat{Y}_2 \tag{3}$$

$$i_1 = i_2 + \hat{e} \tag{4}$$

$$r_1 = i_1 - \hat{P}_1 \tag{5}$$

$$r_2 = i_2 - \hat{P}_2 \tag{6}$$

Equation (1) is the goods market equation, equation (2) is the money market equation of Europe, and equation (3) is the money market equation of America. Equation (4) is the open interest parity. i_1 denotes the nominal interest rate in Europe, i_2 is the nominal interest rate in America, and $\hat{e}$ is the rate of depreciation. The open interest parity is the result of interest arbitrage. Equation (5) is the Fisher equation of Europe. r_1 symbolizes the real interest rate in Europe. The real interest rate in Europe is defined as the nominal interest rate in Europe minus producer inflation in Europe. Correspondingly, equation (6) is the Fisher equation of America. r_2 stands for the real interest rate in America. The real interest rate in America is defined as the nominal interest rate in America minus producer inflation in America.

The exogenous variables are money growth in Europe, money growth in America, output growth in Europe, and output growth in America. The endogenous variables are the nominal interest rate in Europe, the nominal interest rate in America, the real interest rate in Europe, the real interest rate in America, producer inflation in Europe, producer inflation in America, and nominal depreciation.

2) Nominal interest rates. Equations (1), (2) and (3) give $\hat{e} = \hat{M}_1 - \hat{M}_2$. This together with equation (4) yields:

$$i_1 - i_2 = \hat{M}_1 - \hat{M}_2 \tag{7}$$

As a result, the nominal interest differential is determined by the money growth differential. In the region where money growth is high, the nominal interest rate will be high. And in the region where money growth is low, the nominal interest rate will be low. To illustrate this, consider some numerical examples. Let us start with numerical example number one. Let money growth in Europe be 3 percent, and let money growth in America be 5 percent. Then, as result, the nominal interest rate in America exceeds the nominal interest rate in Europe by 2 percentage points.

We proceed now to numerical example number two. Let output growth in Europe be 2 percent, let output growth in America be 3 percent, let money growth in Europe be 3 percent, and let money growth in America be 5 percent. Then the nominal interest rate in America exceeds the nominal interest rate in Europe by 2 percentage points. Compare this with producer inflation. Producer inflation in Europe is 1 percent, and producer inflation in America is 2 percent. So producer inflation in America exceeds producer inflation in Europe by 1 percentage point. By comparison, the nominal interest differential is greater than the inflation differential. The general point is that the nominal interest differential is not determined by the inflation differential. This is in remarkable contrast to a popular view.

3) Real interest rates. From equations (2), (3), (5) and (6) it can be derived that:

$$r_1 = i_1 - \hat{M}_1 + \hat{Y}_1 \tag{8}$$
$$r_2 = i_2 - \hat{M}_2 + \hat{Y}_2 \tag{9}$$

Next subtract equation (9) from equation (8), noting equation (7):

$$r_1 - r_2 = \hat{Y}_1 - \hat{Y}_2 \tag{10}$$

As a consequence, the real interest differential is determined by the output growth differential. In the region where output growth is high, the real interest rate will be high. And in the region where output growth is low, the real interest rate will be low. It is worth pointing out here that the real interest differential cannot be exploited by producers. For instance, let output growth in Europe be 2 percent, and let output growth in America be 3 percent. Then the real interest rate in America exceeds the real interest rate in Europe by 1 percentage point.

Finally compare the nominal interest differential and the real interest differential. The nominal interest differential is determined by the money growth differential. And the real interest differential is determined by the output growth differential.

4) An important special case. Assume for the moment that the real interest rate in Europe equals output growth in Europe $r_1 = \hat{Y}_1$. And assume for the moment that the real interest rate in America equals output growth in America $r_2 = \hat{Y}_2$. Then, as a result, the nominal interest rate in Europe equals money growth in Europe:

$$i_1 = \hat{M}_1 \tag{11}$$

And the nominal interest rate in America equals money growth in America:

$$i_2 = \hat{M}_2 \tag{12}$$

To see this more clearly, have a look at a numerical example. Let output growth in Europe be 2 percent, let output growth in America be 3 percent, let money growth in Europe be 3 percent, and let money growth in America be 5 percent. Accordingly, let the real interest rate in Europe be 2 percent, and let the real interest rate in America be 3 percent. Then producer inflation in Europe is 1 percent, and producer inflation in America is 2 percent. So the nominal interest rate in Europe is $2+1=3$ percent, and the nominal interest rate in America is $3+2=5$ percent.

Now assume instead that the real interest rate in Europe exceeds output growth in Europe by 1 percentage point. And assume instead that the real interest rate in America exceeds output growth in America by equally 1 percentage point. Then, as a result, the nominal interest rate in Europe exceeds money growth in Europe by 1 percentage point. And the nominal interest in America exceeds money growth in America by equally 1 percentage point.

For instance, let output growth in Europe be 2 percent, let output growth in America be 3 percent, let money growth in Europe be 3 percent, and let money growth in America be 5 percent. Accordingly, let the real interest rate in Europe be $2+1=3$ percent, and let the real interest rate in America be $3+1=4$ percent. Then producer inflation in Europe is 1 percent, and producer inflation in America is 2 percent. Thus the nominal interest rate in Europe is $3+1=4$ percent, and the nominal interest rate in America is $4+2=6$ percent. Table 8 presents a synopsis.

Table 8
Nominal and Real Interest Rates
Given Output Growth and Money Growth

Output Growth in Europe	2	2
Output Growth in America	3	3
Money Growth in Europe	3	3
Money Growth in America	5	5
Real Interest Rate in Europe	2	3
Real Interest Rate in America	3	4
Producer Inflation in Europe	1	1
Producer Inflation in America	2	2
Nominal Interest Rate in Europe	3	4
Nominal Interest Rate in America	5	6

Chapter 3
Target Inflation and Required Money Growth

1. Required Money Growth

1.1. The Dynamic Model

The objective of the European central bank is to maintain price stability in Europe. Strictly speaking, the objective of the European central bank is to keep consumer inflation in Europe at target level. Let $\hat{J}_1$ designate the target rate of consumer inflation in Europe. The objective of the American central bank is to maintain price stability in America. Strictly speaking, the objective of the American central bank is to keep consumer inflation in America at target level. Let $\hat{J}_2$ designate the target rate of consumer inflation in America.

To illustrate the problem, consider a numerical example. Let target inflation in Europe be 1 percent, let target inflation in America be 2 percent, let output growth in Europe be 2 percent, and let output growth in America be 3 percent. Then, what rate of money growth is required in Europe? And what rate of money growth is required in America? Further, what is the rate of depreciation?

The model can be characterized by a system of five equations:

$$\hat{P}_1 + \hat{Y}_1 = \hat{e} + \hat{P}_2 + \hat{Y}_2 \tag{1}$$

$$\hat{M}_1 = \hat{P}_1 + \hat{Y}_1 \tag{2}$$

$$\hat{M}_2 = \hat{P}_2 + \hat{Y}_2 \tag{3}$$

$$\hat{J}_1 = \alpha\hat{P}_1 + \beta\hat{P}_2 + \beta\hat{e} \tag{4}$$

$$\hat{J}_2 = \alpha\hat{P}_2 + \beta\hat{P}_1 - \beta\hat{e} \tag{5}$$

Equation (1) is the goods market equation, (2) is the money market equation of Europe, and (3) is the money market equation of America. Equation (4) defines consumer inflation in Europe, and (5) defines consumer inflation in America.

The exogenous variables are target inflation in Europe $\hat{J}_1$, target inflation in America $\hat{J}_2$, output growth in Europe $\hat{Y}_1$, and output growth in America $\hat{Y}_2$. The endogenous variables are money growth in Europe $\hat{M}_1$, money growth America $\hat{M}_2$, nominal depreciation $\hat{e}$, producer inflation in Europe $\hat{P}_1$, and producer inflation in America $\hat{P}_2$.

1.2. Required Money Growth

Eliminate $\hat{e} + \hat{P}_2$ in equation (4) of the model by means of equation (1) and solve for:

$$\hat{P}_1 = \hat{J}_1 - \beta\hat{Y}_1 + \beta\hat{Y}_2 \tag{6}$$

Then substitute this into equation (2) to arrive at:

$$\hat{M}_1 = \hat{J}_1 + \alpha\hat{Y}_1 + \beta\hat{Y}_2 \tag{7}$$

As a result, this is the required rate of money growth in Europe. Obviously, required money growth in Europe depends on target inflation in Europe, on output growth in Europe, and on output growth in America. However, it does not depend on target inflation in America. An increase in European target inflation calls for an increase in European money growth. An increase in European output growth calls for an increase in European money growth too. And what is more, an increase in American output growth calls for an increase in European money growth as well.

What is the chain of cause and effect? An increase in European money growth raises consumer inflation in Europe, as was demonstrated above. An increase in European output growth lowers consumer inflation in Europe. In order to prevent this, the European central bank has to raise its money growth.

An increase in American output growth lowers consumer inflation in Europe. To counteract this, the European central bank has to raise its money growth.

By analogy, required money growth in America is:

$$\hat{M}_2 = \hat{J}_2 + \alpha \hat{Y}_2 + \beta \hat{Y}_1 \tag{8}$$

It is determined by target inflation in America, by output growth in America, and by output growth in Europe. In the region where target inflation is high, money growth has to be high. And in the region where target inflation is low, money growth has to be low. In the region where output growth is high, money growth has to be high. And in the region where output growth is low, money growth has to be low.

To see this more clearly, have a look at a numerical example. Let the share of American goods in European consumption be 0.1, and let the share of European goods in American consumption be equally 0.1. First consider the case that output growth in Europe equals output growth in America. Let target inflation in Europe be 1 percent, let target inflation in America be 2 percent, let output growth in Europe be 2 percent, and let output growth in America be equally 2 percent. Then, as a result, required money growth in Europe is 3 percent. And required money growth in America is 4 percent.

Second consider the case that target inflation in Europe equals target inflation in America. Let output growth in Europe be 2 percent, let output growth in America be 3 percent, let target inflation in Europe be 1 percent, and let target inflation in America be equally 1 percent. Then, as a result, required money growth in Europe is 3.1 percent, and required money growth in America is 3.9 percent.

1.3. Nominal Depreciation

Equations (1), (2) and (3) give $\hat{e} = \hat{M}_1 - \hat{M}_2$. Next get rid of $\hat{M}_1$ and $\hat{M}_2$ by making use of equations (7) and (8):

$$\hat{e} = \hat{J}_1 - \hat{J}_2 + (\alpha - \beta)(\hat{Y}_1 - \hat{Y}_2) \tag{9}$$

As a result, this is the rate of depreciation. According to equation (9), nominal depreciation is determined by target inflation in Europe, by target inflation in America, by output growth in Europe, and by output growth in America.

First consider the case that output growth in Europe equals output growth in America. In this case we have:

$$\hat{e} = \hat{J}_1 - \hat{J}_2 \tag{10}$$

That means, the rate of depreciation is determined by the target inflation differential. In the region where target inflation is high, the currency will depreciate. And in the region where target inflation is low, the currency will appreciate. To be more specific, if target inflation in Europe is high, the euro will depreciate. And if target inflation in Europe is low, the euro will appreciate. Correspondingly, if target inflation in America is high, the dollar will depreciate. And if target inflation in America is low, the dollar will appreciate. For instance, let target inflation in Europe be 1 percent, and let target inflation in America be 2 percent. Then the appreciation of the euro is 1 percent. In other words, the depreciation of the dollar is 1 percent. How can this be explained? In the region where target inflation is high, money growth has to be high. And in the region where target inflation is low, money growth has to be low.

Second consider the case that target inflation in Europe equals target inflation in America. In this case we have:

$$\hat{e} = (\alpha - \beta)(\hat{Y}_1 - \hat{Y}_2) \tag{11}$$

That is to say, the rate of depreciation is determined by the output growth differential. Further, note that $\alpha > \beta$. In the region where output growth is high, the currency will depreciate. And in the region where output growth is low, the currency will appreciate. To be more explicit, if output growth in Europe is high, the euro will depreciate. And if output growth in Europe is low, the euro will appreciate. Correspondingly, if output growth in America is high, the dollar will depreciate. And if output growth in America is low, the dollar will appreciate. For instance, let output growth in Europe be 2 percent, and let output growth in America be 3 percent. Then the appreciation of the euro is 0.8 percent. Put differently, the depreciation of the dollar is 0.8 percent. What is the intuition about this result? In the region where output growth is high, money growth has to be high. And in the region where output growth is low, money growth has to be low.

To sum up, nominal depreciation is determined by the target inflation differential and by the output growth differential. This is in sharp contrast to the conclusions drawn under given money growth. There, nominal depreciation was determined by the money growth differential.

1.4. Nominal Interest Rates

Combine the open interest parity $i_1 = i_2 + \hat{e}$ with equation (9) to find out:

$$i_1 - i_2 = \hat{J}_1 - \hat{J}_2 + (\alpha - \beta)(\hat{Y}_1 - \hat{Y}_2) \tag{12}$$

As a result, the difference between the nominal interest rate in Europe and the nominal interest rate in America is determined by target inflation in Europe, by target inflation in America, by output growth in Europe, and by output growth in America.

First have a look at the case that output growth in Europe equals output growth in America. In this case we have:

$$i_1 - i_2 = \hat{J}_1 - \hat{J}_2 \tag{13}$$

That means, the nominal interest differential is determined by the target inflation differential. In the region where target inflation is high, the nominal interest rate will be high. And in the region where target inflation is low, the nominal interest rate will be low. For instance, let target inflation in Europe be 1 percent, and let target inflation in America be 2 percent. Then the nominal interest rate in America exceeds the nominal interest rate in Europe by 1 percentage point.

Second have a look at the case that target inflation in Europe equals target inflation in America. In this case we have:

$$i_1 - i_2 = (\alpha - \beta)(\hat{Y}_1 - \hat{Y}_2) \tag{14}$$

That is to say, the nominal interest differential is determined by the output growth differential. Besides, note that $\alpha > \beta$. In the region where output growth is high, the nominal interest rate will be high. And in the region where output growth is low, the nominal interest rate will be low. For instance, let output growth in Europe be 2 percent, and let output growth in America be 3 percent. Then the nominal interest rate in America exceeds the nominal interest rate in Europe by 0.8 percentage points. At first glance, this comes as a surprise.

To sum up, the nominal interest differential is determined by the target inflation differential and by the output growth differential. This is in remarkable contrast to the conclusions reached under given money growth. There, the nominal interest differential was determined by the money growth differential.

1.5. Producer Inflation

According to equation (6), producer inflation in Europe is given by:

$$\hat{P}_1 = \hat{J}_1 - \beta \hat{Y}_1 + \beta \hat{Y}_2 \tag{15}$$

As a result, producer inflation in Europe depends on target inflation in Europe, on output growth in Europe, and on output growth in America. However, it does not depend on target inflation in America. Producer inflation in America can be derived in the same way:

$$\hat{P}_2 = \hat{J}_2 - \beta \hat{Y}_2 + \beta \hat{Y}_1 \tag{16}$$

Obviously, producer inflation in America is determined by target inflation in America, by output growth in America, and by output growth in Europe.

First consider the case that output growth in Europe equals output growth in America. In this case we have:

$$\hat{P}_1 = \hat{J}_1 \tag{17}$$
$$\hat{P}_2 = \hat{J}_2 \tag{18}$$

That means, producer inflation in Europe equals target inflation in Europe. And producer inflation in America equals target inflation in America. Second consider the case that target inflation in Europe equals target inflation in America. In this case we have:

$$\hat{P}_1 - \hat{P}_2 = 2\beta(\hat{Y}_2 - \hat{Y}_1) \tag{19}$$

That is to say, in the region where output growth is high, producer inflation will be low. And in the region where output growth is low, producer inflation will be high.

To illustrate this, have a look at a numerical example. Let output growth in Europe be 2 percent, let output growth in America be 3 percent, let target inflation in Europe be 1 percent, and let target inflation in America be equally 1 percent. Then producer inflation in Europe is 1.1 percent, while producer inflation in America is 0.9 percent. Table 9 gives an overview.

Table 9
Required Money Growth
Given Target Inflation and Output Growth

Target Inflation in Europe	1	1
Target Inflation in America	2	1
Output Growth in Europe	2	2
Output Growth in America	2	3
Required Money Growth in Europe	3	3.1
Required Money Growth in America	4	3.9
Appreciation of the Euro	1	0.8
Depreciation of the Dollar	1	0.8
Nominal Interest Differential	− 1	− 0.8
Real Interest Differential	0	− 1
Producer Inflation in Europe	1	1.1
Producer Inflation in America	2	0.9

2. Wage Growth

2.1. The Dynamic Model

This section deals with the growth of nominal wages, given productivity growth and labour growth. For the growth of producer real wages or consumer real wages see Chapter 2 above. The model can be represented by a system of nine equations:

$$\hat{P}_1 + \hat{Y}_1 = \hat{e} + \hat{P}_2 + \hat{Y}_2 \tag{1}$$

$$\hat{M}_1 = \hat{P}_1 + \hat{Y}_1 \tag{2}$$

$$\hat{M}_2 = \hat{P}_2 + \hat{Y}_2 \tag{3}$$

$$\hat{Y}_1 = \hat{a}_1 + \hat{N}_1 \tag{4}$$

$$\hat{Y}_2 = \hat{a}_2 + \hat{N}_2 \tag{5}$$

$$\hat{w}_1 = \hat{a}_1 + \hat{P}_1 \tag{6}$$

$$\hat{w}_2 = \hat{a}_2 + \hat{P}_2 \tag{7}$$

$$\hat{J}_1 = \alpha\hat{P}_1 + \beta\hat{P}_2 + \beta\hat{e} \tag{8}$$

$$\hat{J}_2 = \alpha\hat{P}_2 + \beta\hat{P}_1 - \beta\hat{e} \tag{9}$$

Equation (1) is the goods market equation, (2) is the money market equation of Europe, (3) is the money market equation of America, (4) is the production function of Europe, (5) is the production function of America, (6) is the wage equation of Europe, (7) is the wage equation of America, (8) is consumer inflation in Europe, and (9) is consumer inflation in America. The exogenous variables are target inflation in Europe $\hat{J}_1$, target inflation in America $\hat{J}_2$, productivity growth in Europe $\hat{a}_1$, productivity growth in America $\hat{a}_2$, labour growth in Europe $\hat{N}_1$, and labour growth in America $\hat{N}_2$. The endogenous variables are nominal wage growth in Europe $\hat{w}_1$, nominal wage growth in America $\hat{w}_2$, money growth in Europe $\hat{M}_1$, money growth in America $\hat{M}_2$, nominal depreciation $\hat{e}$, producer inflation in Europe $\hat{P}_1$, producer inflation in America $\hat{P}_2$, output growth in Europe $\hat{Y}_1$, and output growth in America $\hat{Y}_2$.

2.2. Productivity Growth

For the time being, assume that there is no labour growth $\hat{N}_1 = \hat{N}_2 = 0$. Now eliminate $\hat{e} + \hat{P}_2$ in equation (8) with the help of equation (1) and solve for:

$$\hat{P}_1 = \hat{J}_1 - \beta\hat{Y}_1 + \beta\hat{Y}_2 \tag{10}$$

Then substitute equations (4) and (5), which gives $\hat{P}_1 = \hat{J}_1 - \beta\hat{a}_1 + \beta\hat{a}_2$. Finally put this into equation (6) to reach:

$$\hat{w}_1 = \hat{J}_1 + \alpha\hat{a}_1 + \beta\hat{a}_2 \tag{11}$$

As a result, nominal wage growth in Europe depends on target inflation in Europe, on productivity growth in Europe, and on productivity growth in America. However, it does not depend on target inflation in America. An increase in European target inflation raises nominal wage growth in Europe. An increase in European productivity growth raises nominal wage growth in Europe. And an increase in American productivity growth raises nominal wage growth in Europe too.

Nominal wage growth in America can be deduced along the same lines:

$$\hat{w}_2 = \hat{J}_2 + \alpha\hat{a}_2 + \beta\hat{a}_1 \tag{12}$$

Evidently, nominal wage growth in America is determined by target inflation in America, by productivity growth in America, and by productivity growth in Europe.

It proves useful to consider two distinct cases. Let us begin with the case that productivity growth in Europe equals productivity growth in America $\hat{a} = \hat{a}_1 = \hat{a}_2$. In this case we have:

$$\hat{w}_1 = \hat{J}_1 + \hat{a} \tag{13}$$

$$\hat{w}_2 = \hat{J}_2 + \hat{a} \tag{14}$$

That means, nominal wage growth in Europe equals target inflation in Europe plus productivity growth. Correspondingly, nominal wage growth in America equals target inflation in America plus productivity growth. In the region where target inflation is high, nominal wage growth will be high. And in the region where target inflation is low, nominal wage growth will be low. To illustrate this, consider a numerical example. Let target inflation in Europe be 1 percent, let target inflation in America be 2 percent, let productivity growth in Europe be 2 percent, and let productivity growth in America be equally 2 percent. Then nominal wage growth in Europe is 3 percent, and nominal wage growth in America is 4 percent.

We come now to the case that target inflation in Europe equals target inflation in America. In this case we have:

$$\hat{w}_1 - \hat{w}_2 = (\alpha - \beta)(\hat{a}_1 - \hat{a}_2) \tag{15}$$

Note that $\alpha > \beta$. In the region where productivity growth is high, nominal wage growth will be high. And in the region where productivity growth is low, nominal wage growth will be low. To see this more clearly, have a look at a numerical example. Let productivity growth in Europe be 2 percent, let productivity growth in America be 3 percent, let target inflation in Europe be 1 percent, and let target inflation in America be equally 1 percent. Moreover, let the share of American goods in European consumption be 0.1, and let the share of European goods in American consumption be equally 0.1. Then, as a result, nominal wage growth in Europe is 3.1 percent, and nominal wage growth in America is 3.9 percent. Table 10 presents a synopsis.

To sum up, nominal wage growth in Europe is determined by target inflation in Europe, by productivity growth in Europe, and by productivity growth in America. This differs widely from the conclusions drawn under given money growth. There nominal wage growth in Europe was determined by money growth in Europe.

Table 10
Wage Growth
Given Target Inflation and Productivity Growth

Target Inflation in Europe	1	1
Target Inflation in America	2	1
Productivity Growth in Europe	2	2
Productivity Growth in America	2	3
Growth of Nominal Wages in Europe	3	3.1
Growth of Nominal Wages in America	4	3.9
Growth of Producer Real Wages in Europe	2	2
Growth of Producer Real Wages in America	2	3
Growth of Consumer Real Wages in Europe	2	2.1
Growth of Consumer Real Wages in America	2	2.9

2.3. Labour Growth

For the time being, assume that there is no productivity growth $\hat{a}_1 = \hat{a}_2 = 0$. Insert equations (4) and (5) into equation (10), which gives $\hat{P}_1 = \hat{J}_1 - \beta\hat{N}_1 + \beta\hat{N}_2$. Next put this into equation (6) to get:

$$\hat{w}_1 = \hat{J}_1 - \beta\hat{N}_1 + \beta\hat{N}_2 \tag{16}$$

As an outcome, nominal wage growth in Europe depends on target inflation in Europe, on labour growth in Europe, and on labour growth in America. But it does not depend on target inflation in America. An increase in European target inflation drives up nominal wage growth in Europe. An increase in European labour growth cuts down nominal wage growth in Europe. And an increase in American labour growth drives up nominal wage growth in Europe.

Nominal wage growth in America can be derived in the same way:

$$\hat{w}_2 = \hat{J}_2 - \beta\hat{N}_2 + \beta\hat{N}_1 \tag{17}$$

Obviously, nominal wage growth in America is determined by target inflation in America, by labour growth in America, and by labour growth in Europe.

First consider the case that labour growth in Europe equals labour growth in America. In this case we have:

$$\hat{w}_1 = \hat{J}_1 \tag{18}$$
$$\hat{w}_2 = \hat{J}_2 \tag{19}$$

That is to say, nominal wage growth in Europe equals target inflation in Europe. Similarly, nominal wage growth in America equals target inflation in America. For instance, let target inflation in Europe be 1 percent, and let target inflation in America be 2 percent. Then nominal wage growth in Europe is 1 percent, and nominal wage growth in America is 2 percent.

Second consider the case that target inflation in Europe equals target inflation in America. In this case we have:

$$\hat{w}_1 - \hat{w}_2 = 2\beta(\hat{N}_2 - \hat{N}_1) \tag{20}$$

In the region where labour growth is high, nominal wage growth will be low. And in the region where labour growth is low, nominal wage growth will be high. For instance, let labour growth in Europe be 0 percent, let labour growth in America be 1 percent, let target inflation in Europe be 1 percent, and let target inflation in America be equally 1 percent. Then nominal wage growth in Europe is 1.1 percent, and nominal wage growth in America is 0.9 percent. Table 11 gives an overview.

To sum up, nominal wage growth in Europe is determined by target inflation in Europe, by labour growth in Europe, and by labour growth in America. This differs remarkably from the conclusions reached under given money growth. There nominal wage growth in Europe was determined by money growth in Europe and by labour growth in Europe.

Table 11
Wage Growth
Given Target Inflation and Labour Growth

Target Inflation in Europe	1	1
Target Inflation in America	2	1
Labour Growth in Europe	1	0
Labour Growth in America	1	1
Growth of Nominal Wages in Europe	1	1.1
Growth of Nominal Wages in America	2	0.9
Growth of Producer Real Wages in Europe	0	0
Growth of Producer Real Wages in America	0	0
Growth of Consumer Real Wages in Europe	0	0.1
Growth of Consumer Real Wages in America	0	− 0.1

Chapter 4
The Monetary Regions Differ in Size

1) The static model. According to the microfoundations given in Part Five below, the goods market equations are as follows:

$$Y_1 = A_1 + cY_1 + q_2 eP_2 Y_2 / P_1 - q_1 Y_1 \tag{1}$$

$$Y_2 = A_2 + cY_2 + q_1 P_1 Y_1 / eP_2 - q_2 Y_2 \tag{2}$$

Equation (1) is the goods market equation of Europe, as measured in European goods. And equation (2) is the goods market equation of America, as measured in American goods. A_1 denotes the autonomous demand for European goods, and A_2 is the autonomous demand for American goods. In addition, q_1 is the marginal import rate of Europe, and q_2 is the marginal import rate of America. Now assume that Europe is small and America is large. In terms of the model this means that the marginal import rate of Europe is large, and the marginal import rate of America is small $q_1 > q_2$.

Next the goods market equations are rewritten as follows:

$$P_1 Y_1 = P_1 A_1 + cP_1 Y_1 + q_2 eP_2 Y_2 - q_1 P_1 Y_1 \tag{3}$$

$$P_2 Y_2 = P_2 A_2 + cP_2 Y_2 + q_1 P_1 Y_1 / e - q_2 P_2 Y_2 \tag{4}$$

Here equation (3) is the goods market equation of Europe, as measured in euros. And equation (4) is the goods market equation of America, as measured in dollars. In equation (3), $P_1 Y_1$ is European income as measured in euros, $eP_2 Y_2$ is American income as measured in euros, $q_1 P_1 Y_1$ is European imports as measured in euros, and $q_2 eP_2 Y_2$ is European exports as measured in euros.

Further, assume for the moment that the current account of Europe is balanced $q_2 eP_2 Y_2 = q_1 P_1 Y_1$. This yields immediately:

$$\frac{P_1 Y_1}{e P_2 Y_2} = \frac{q_2}{q_1} \tag{5}$$

To illustrate this, consider a numerical example. Let the marginal import rate of Europe be $q_1 = 0.2$, and let the marginal import rate of America be $q_2 = 0.1$. In this case we have $e P_2 Y_2 = 2 P_1 Y_1$. That is to say, American income is twice as much as European income.

2) The dynamic model. Here the focus is on steady-state inflation in Europe and America, given steady-state growth. We assume that nominal wages and prices are flexible, hence there is always full employment in Europe and America. In equation (3), all terms except $q_2 e P_2 Y_2$ grow at the rate $\hat{P}_1 + \hat{Y}_1$. As a consequence, $q_2 e P_2 Y_2$ grows at the rate $\hat{P}_1 + \hat{Y}_1$, too. This implies $\hat{P}_1 + \hat{Y}_1 = \hat{e} + \hat{P}_2 + \hat{Y}_2$. So, along the same lines as in Chapter 2, the model can be characterized by a system of three equations:

$$\hat{P}_1 + \hat{Y}_1 = \hat{e} + \hat{P}_2 + \hat{Y}_2 \tag{6}$$

$$\hat{M}_1 = \hat{P}_1 + \hat{Y}_1 \tag{7}$$

$$\hat{M}_2 = \hat{P}_2 + \hat{Y}_2 \tag{8}$$

Equation (6) is the goods market equation, (7) is the money market equation of Europe, and (8) is the money market equation of America. The exogenous variables are money growth in Europe $\hat{M}_1$, money growth in America $\hat{M}_2$, output growth in Europe $\hat{Y}_1$, and output growth in America $\hat{Y}_2$. The endogenous variables are producer inflation in Europe $\hat{P}_1$, producer inflation in America $\hat{P}_2$, and nominal depreciation $\hat{e}$.

3) Producer inflation and nominal depreciation. The solution to this problem is as follows:

$$\hat{P}_1 = \hat{M}_1 - \hat{Y}_1 \tag{9}$$

$$\hat{P}_2 = \hat{M}_2 - \hat{Y}_2 \tag{10}$$

$$\hat{e} = \hat{M}_1 - \hat{M}_2 \tag{11}$$

According to equation (9), producer inflation in Europe is determined by money growth in Europe and by output growth in Europe. According to equation (11), the rate of depreciation is driven by money growth in Europe and by money growth in America. For instance, let output growth in Europe be 2 percent, let output growth in America be 3 percent, let money growth in Europe be 3 percent, and let money growth in America be 5 percent. Then producer inflation in Europe is 1 percent, producer inflation in America is 2 percent, the appreciation of the euro is 2 percent, and the depreciation of the dollar is 2 percent. All of this confirms the conclusions drawn in Chapter 2 above. Put another way, the relative size of regions does not matter here.

4) Consumer inflation. Consumer inflation in Europe is defined as:

$$\hat{J}_1 = \alpha_1 \hat{P}_1 + \beta_1 \hat{P}_2 + \beta_1 \hat{e} \tag{12}$$

α_1 is the share of European goods in European consumption, and β_1 is the share of American goods in European consumption, with $\alpha_1 + \beta_1 = 1$. Consumer inflation in America is defined as:

$$\hat{J}_2 = \alpha_2 \hat{P}_2 + \beta_2 \hat{P}_1 - \beta_2 \hat{e} \tag{13}$$

α_2 is the share of American goods in American consumption, and β_2 is the share of European goods in American consumption, with $\alpha_2 + \beta_2 = 1$. We still assume that Europe is small and America is large. In terms of the model this means that the share of American goods in European consumption is greater than the share of European goods in American consumption $\beta_1 > \beta_2$.

Now substitute equations (9), (10) and (11) into equation (12) to check:

$$\hat{J}_1 = \hat{M}_1 - \alpha_1 \hat{Y}_1 - \beta_1 \hat{Y}_2 \tag{14}$$

Obviously, consumer inflation in Europe is determined by money growth in Europe, by output growth in Europe, and by output growth in America. By analogy, consumer inflation in America is:

$$\hat{J}_2 = \hat{M}_2 - \alpha_2 \hat{Y}_2 - \beta_2 \hat{Y}_1 \tag{15}$$

To see this more clearly, have a look at a numerical example. Let output growth in Europe be 2 percent, let output growth in America be 3 percent, let money growth in Europe be 3 percent, and let money growth in America be 4 percent. Besides, let the share of European goods in European consumption be 0.8, and let the share of American goods in European consumption be 0.2. Asymmetrically, let the share of American goods in American consumption be 0.9, and let the share of European goods in American consumption be 0.1. Then, as a result, consumer inflation in Europe is 0.8 percent, and consumer inflation in America is 1.1 percent. This differs from the conclusions reached in Chapter 2 above. In other words, the relative size of regions does matter here.

5) Target inflation and required money growth. It proves useful to solve equations (14) and (15) for $\hat{M}_1$ and $\hat{M}_2$, respectively:

$$\hat{M}_1 = \hat{J}_1 + \alpha_1 \hat{Y}_1 + \beta_1 \hat{Y}_2 \tag{16}$$
$$\hat{M}_2 = \hat{J}_2 + \alpha_2 \hat{Y}_2 + \beta_2 \hat{Y}_1 \tag{17}$$

Here the exogenous variables are target inflation in Europe $\hat{J}_1$, target inflation in America $\hat{J}_2$, output growth in Europe $\hat{Y}_1$, and output growth in America $\hat{Y}_2$. The endogenous variables are money growth in Europe $\hat{M}_1$ and money growth in America $\hat{M}_2$. According to equation (16), required money growth in Europe is determined by target inflation in Europe, by output growth in Europe, and by output growth in America.

To illustrate this, consider a numerical example. Let output growth in Europe be 2 percent, let output growth in America be 3 percent, let target inflation in Europe be 1 percent, and let target inflation in America be equally 1 percent. Moreover, let the share of American goods in European consumption be 0.2, and let the share of European goods in American consumption be 0.1. Then, as a result, required money growth in Europe is 3.2 percent, and required money growth in America is 3.9 percent. This differs from the conclusions drawn in Chapter 3 above. That means, the relative size of regions does matter here.

Part Three

The Monetary Union
of Two Countries

Chapter 1
The Static Model

1. Fixed Wages

1) Introduction. The world consists of two monetary regions, let us say Europe and America. The exchange rate between Europe and America is flexible. Europe in turn consists of two countries, let us say Germany and France. Germany and France form a monetary union. Take for example an increase in European money supply. Then what will be the effect on German output, on French output, and on American output? Alternatively take an increase in German investment, German nominal wages, or German productivity.

In doing the analysis, we make the following assumptions. German goods, French goods and American goods are imperfect substitutes for each other. German output is determined by the demand for German goods. French output is determined by the demand for French goods. And American output is determined by the demand for American goods. The sum of German money demand and French money demand equals European money supply. And American money demand equals American money supply. There is perfect capital mobility between Germany, France and America. As a consequence, the German interest rate, the French interest rate, and the American interest rate are equalized. The monetary regions are the same size and have the same behavioural functions. Correspondingly, the union countries are the same size and have the same behavioural functions.

2) The market for German goods. The behavioural functions underlying the analysis are as follows:

$$C_1 = cY_1 \tag{1}$$

$$I_1 = b_1 r^{-\varepsilon} \tag{2}$$

$$X_{12} = mP_2 Y_2 / P_1 \tag{3}$$

$$X_{13} = 0.5qeP_3Y_3 / P_1 \tag{4}$$

$$Q_1 = (m+q)Y_1 \tag{5}$$

Equation (1) is the consumption function of Germany. It states that German consumption is an increasing function of German income. Here C_1 denotes German consumption, as measured in German goods. Y_1 is German income, as measured in German goods. And c is the marginal consumption rate of Germany, with $0 < c < 1$. Equation (2) is the investment function of Germany. It states that German investment is a decreasing function of the world interest rate. I_1 symbolizes German investment, as measured in German goods. r is the world interest rate. ε is the interest elasticity of German investment, with $\varepsilon > 0$. And b_1 is a shift parameter, with $b_1 > 0$. The message of equation (2) is that a 1 percent increase in the world interest rate causes an ε percent decline in German investment.

Equations (3) and (4) are the export functions of Germany. Equation (3) states that German exports to France are an increasing function of French income. X_{12} stands for German exports to France, as measured in German goods. P_1 is the price of German goods, as measured in euros. P_2 is the price of French goods, as measured in euros. Y_2 is French income, as measured in French goods. P_2Y_2 is French income, as measured in euros. P_2Y_2 / P_1 is French income, as measured in German goods. And m is the marginal import rate of France relative to Germany, with $m > 0$. The message of equation (3) is that a 1 percent increase in French income causes a 1 percent increase in German exports to France. On the other hand, a 1 percent increase in the price of German goods causes a 1 percent decline in German exports to France. Further, a 1 percent increase in the price of French goods causes a 1 percent increase in German exports to France.

Equation (4) states that German exports to America are an increasing function of American income. X_{13} designates German exports to America, as measured in German goods. P_3 is the price of American goods, as measured in dollars. e is the exchange rate between the dollar and the euro. More exactly, e is the price of the dollar, as measured in euros. eP_3 is the price of American goods, as measured in euros. Y_3 is American income, as measured in American goods. P_3Y_3 is American income, as measured in dollars. eP_3Y_3 is American income, as measured in euros. eP_3Y_3 / P_1 is American income, as measured in German goods. q is the marginal import rate of America relative to Europe, with $q > 0$. And $0.5q$ is the marginal import rate of America relative to Germany.

The message of equation (4) is that a 1 percent increase in American income causes a 1 percent increase in German exports to America. Conversely, a 1 percent increase in the price of the euro causes a 1 percent decline in German exports to America. Similarly, a 1 percent increase in the price of German goods causes a 1 percent decline in German exports to America. And a 1 percent increase in the price of American goods causes a 1 percent increase in German exports to America.

Equation (5) is the import function of Germany. It states that German imports are an increasing function of German income. Q_1 is German imports from France and from America, as measured in German goods. Y_1 is German income, as measured in German goods. m is the marginal import rate of Germany relative to France. q is the marginal import rate of Germany relative to America. And $m + q$ is the (overall) marginal import rate of Germany.

German output is determined by the demand for German goods $Y_1 = C_1 + I_1 + X_{12} + X_{13} - Q_1$. Taking account of the behavioural functions (1) until (5), we arrive at the goods market equation of Germany:

$$Y_1 = cY_1 + b_1 r^{-\varepsilon} + mP_2 Y_2 / P_1 + 0.5qeP_3 Y_3 / P_1 - (m + q)Y_1 \qquad (6)$$

3) The market for French goods. The behavioural functions are as follows:

$$C_2 = cY_2 \qquad (7)$$

$$I_2 = b_2 r^{-\varepsilon} \qquad (8)$$

$$X_{21} = mP_1 Y_1 / P_2 \qquad (9)$$

$$X_{23} = 0.5qeP_3 Y_3 / P_2 \qquad (10)$$

$$Q_2 = (m + q)Y_2 \qquad (11)$$

Equation (7) is the consumption function of France. It states that French consumption is an increasing function of French income. Here C_2 denotes French consumption, as measured in French goods. Y_2 is French income, as measured in French goods. And c is the marginal consumption rate of France. Equation (8) is the investment function of France. It states that French investment is a decreasing function of the world interest rate. I_2 symbolizes French investment, as measured in French goods. ε is the interest elasticity of French investment. And b_2 is a shift parameter, with $b_2 > 0$. The message of equation (8) is that a 1 percent increase in the world interest rate causes an ε percent decline in French investment.

Equations (9) and (10) are the export functions of France. Equation (9) states that French exports to Germany are an increasing function of German income. X_{21} stands for French exports to Germany, as measured in French goods. $P_1 Y_1$ is German income, as measured in euros. $P_1 Y_1 / P_2$ is German income, as measured in French goods. And m is the marginal import rate of Germany relative to France. The message of equation (9) is that a 1 percent increase in German income causes a 1 percent increase in French exports to Germany. The other way round, a 1 percent increase in the price of French goods causes a 1 percent decline in French exports to Germany. Moreover, a 1 percent increase in the price of German goods causes a 1 percent increase in French exports to Germany.

Equation (10) states that French exports to America are an increasing function of American income. X_{23} designates French exports to America, as measured in French goods. $P_3 Y_3$ is American income, as measured in dollars. $e P_3 Y_3$ is American income, as measured in euros. $e P_3 Y_3 / P_2$ is American income, as measured in French goods. q is the marginal import rate of America relative to Europe. And 0.5q is the marginal import rate of America relative to France. The message of equation (10) is that a 1 percent increase in American income causes a 1 percent increase in French exports to America. A 1 percent increase in the price of the euro causes a 1 percent decline in French exports to America. A 1 percent increase in the price of French goods causes a 1 percent decline in French exports to America. And a 1 percent increase in the price of American goods causes a 1 percent increase in French exports to America.

Equation (11) is the import function of France. It states that French imports are an increasing function of French income. Q_2 is French imports from Germany and from America, as measured in French goods. Y_2 is French income, as measured in French goods. m is the marginal import rate of France relative to

Germany. q is the marginal import rate of France relative to America. And $m+q$ is the (overall) marginal import rate of France.

French output is determined by the demand for French goods $Y_2 = C_2 + I_2 + X_{21} + X_{23} - Q_2$. Upon substituting the behavioural functions (7) until (11), we reach the goods market equation of France:

$$Y_2 = cY_2 + b_2 r^{-\varepsilon} + mP_1 Y_1 / P_2 + 0.5qeP_3 Y_3 / P_2 - (m+q)Y_2 \tag{12}$$

4) The market for American goods. The behavioural functions are as follows:

$$C_3 = cY_3 \tag{13}$$

$$I_3 = b_3 r^{-\varepsilon} \tag{14}$$

$$X_{31} = qP_1 Y_1 / eP_3 \tag{15}$$

$$X_{32} = qP_2 Y_2 / eP_3 \tag{16}$$

$$Q_3 = qY_3 \tag{17}$$

Equation (13) is the consumption function of America. It states that American consumption is an increasing function of American income. Here C_3 denotes American consumption, as measured in American goods. Y_3 is American income, as measured in American goods. And c is the marginal consumption rate of America. Equation (14) is the investment function of America. It states that American investment is a decreasing function of the world interest rate. I_3 symbolizes American investment, as measured in American goods. ε is the interest elasticity of American investment. And b_3 is a shift parameter, with $b_3 > 0$. The message of equation (14) is that a 1 percent increase in the world interest rate causes an ε percent decline in American investment.

Equations (15) and (16) are the export functions of America. Equation (15) states that American exports to Germany are an increasing function of German income. X_{31} stands for American exports to Germany, as measured in American goods. $P_1 Y_1$ is German income, as measured in euros. $P_1 Y_1 / e$ is German income, as measured in dollars. $P_1 Y_1 / eP_3$ is German income, as measured in American goods. And q is the marginal import rate of Germany relative to America. The message of equation (15) is that a 1 percent increase in German income causes a

1 percent increase in American exports to Germany. Conversely, a 1 percent increase in the price of the dollar causes a 1 percent decline in American exports to Germany. Similarly, a 1 percent increase in the price of American goods causes a 1 percent decline in American exports to Germany. And a 1 percent increase in the price of German goods causes a 1 percent increase in American exports to Germany.

Equation (16) states that American exports to France are an increasing function of French income. X_{32} designates American exports to France, as measured in American goods. $P_2 Y_2$ is French income, as measured in euros. $P_2 Y_2 / e$ is French income, as measured in dollars. $P_2 Y_2 / eP_3$ is French income, as measured in American goods. And q is the marginal import rate of France relative to America. The message of equation (16) is that a 1 percent increase in French income causes a 1 percent increase in American exports to France. A 1 percent increase in the price of the dollar causes a 1 percent decline in American exports to France. A 1 percent increase in the price of American goods causes a 1 percent decline in American exports to France. And a 1 percent increase in the price of French goods causes a 1 percent increase in American exports to France.

Equation (17) is the import function of America. It states that American imports are an increasing function of American income. Q_3 is American imports from Germany and from France, as measured in American goods. Y_3 is American income, as measured in American goods. And q is the marginal import rate of America.

American output is determined by the demand for American goods $Y_3 = C_3 + I_3 + X_{31} + X_{32} - Q_3$. Upon inserting the behavioural functions (13) until (17), we get to the goods market equation of America:

$$Y_3 = cY_3 + b_3 r^{-\varepsilon} + qP_1 Y_1 / eP_3 + qP_2 Y_2 / eP_3 - qY_3 \tag{18}$$

5) The European money market. The behavioural functions are as follows:

$$L_1 = kP_1 Y_1 r^{-\eta} \tag{19}$$

$$L_2 = kP_2 Y_2 r^{-\eta} \tag{20}$$

$$M_{12} = \text{const} \tag{21}$$

Equation (19) is the money demand function of Germany. It states that German money demand is an increasing function of German income and a decreasing function of the world interest rate. Here L_1 denotes German money demand, as measured in euros. Y_1 is German income, as measured in German goods. P_1 is the price of German goods, as measured in euros. $P_1 Y_1$ is German income, as measured in euros. r is the world interest rate. η is the interest elasticity of German money demand, with $\eta > 0$. And k is a shift parameter, with $k > 0$. The message of equation (19) is that a 1 percent increase in German income causes a 1 percent increase in German money demand. Further, a 1 percent increase in the price of German goods causes a 1 percent increase in German money demand. And a 1 percent increase in the world interest rate causes an η percent decline in German money demand.

Equation (20) is the money demand function of France. It states that French money demand is an increasing function of French income and a decreasing function of the world interest rate. L_2 symbolizes French money demand, as measured in euros. Y_2 is French income, as measured in French goods. P_2 is the price of French goods, as measured in euros. $P_2 Y_2$ is French income, as measured in euros. η is the interest elasticity of French money demand. And k is a shift parameter. The message of equation (20) is that a 1 percent increase in French income causes a 1 percent increase in French money demand. A 1 percent increase in the price of French goods causes a 1 percent increase in French money demand. And a 1 percent increase in the world interest rate causes an η percent decline in French money demand.

Equation (21) is the money supply function of Europe. It states that the European central bank fixes the money supply in Europe. M_{12} stands for European money supply, as measured in euros. European money demand equals European money supply $L_1 + L_2 = M_{12}$. Taking account of the behavioural functions (19) until (21), we arrive at the money market equation of Europe:

$$kP_1 Y_1 r^{-\eta} + kP_2 Y_2 r^{-\eta} = M_{12} = const \qquad (22)$$

6) The American money market. The behavioural functions are as follows:

$$L_3 = kP_3Y_3r^{-\eta} \tag{23}$$

$$M_3 = \text{const} \tag{24}$$

Equation (23) is the money demand function of America. It states that American money demand is an increasing function of American income and a decreasing function of the world interest rate. L_3 designates American money demand, as measured in dollars. Y_3 is American income, as measured in American goods. P_3 is the price of American goods, as measured in dollars. P_3Y_3 is American income, as measured in dollars. η is the interest elasticity of American money demand. And k is a shift parameter. The message of equation (23) is that a 1 percent increase in American income causes a 1 percent increase in American money demand. A 1 percent increase in the price of American goods causes a 1 percent increase in American money demand. And a 1 percent increase in the world interest rate causes an η percent decline in American money demand.

Equation (24) is the money supply function of America. It states that the American central bank fixes the money supply in America. M_3 is American money supply, as measured in dollars. American money demand equals American money supply $L_3 = M_3$. Upon substituting the behavioural functions (23) and (24), we reach the money market equation of America:

$$kP_3Y_3r^{-\eta} = M_3 = \text{const} \tag{25}$$

7) Technology and price setting. The production function of Germany is characterized by fixed coefficients:

$$Y_1 = a_1N_1 \tag{26}$$

Here N_1 denotes German labour input. a_1 is German labour productivity, as measured in German goods. And Y_1 is German output, as measured in German goods. Accordingly, German labour demand is:

$$N_1 = Y_1 / a_1 \tag{27}$$

That means, a 1 percent increase in German output requires a 1 percent increase in German labour demand. On the other hand, a 1 percent increase in German productivity allows a 1 percent reduction in German labour demand.

German firms set the price of German goods as a markup over unit labour cost in Germany:

$$P_1 = gw_1 / a_1 \tag{28}$$

Here w_1 is the nominal wage rate in Germany, as measured in euros. w_1 / a_1 is unit labour cost in Germany, as measured in euros. g is the markup factor in Germany. And P_1 is the price of German goods, as measured in euros. The message of equation (28) is that a 1 percent increase in German nominal wages causes a 1 percent increase in the price of German goods. Conversely, a 1 percent increase in German productivity causes a 1 percent reduction in the price of German goods.

The production function of France is characterized by fixed coefficients:

$$Y_2 = a_2 N_2 \tag{29}$$

Here N_2 symbolizes French labour input. a_2 is French labour productivity, as measured in French goods. And Y_2 is French output, as measured in French goods. Accordingly, French labour demand is:

$$N_2 = Y_2 / a_2 \tag{30}$$

That is to say, a 1 percent increase in French output requires a 1 percent increase in French labour demand. The other way round, a 1 percent increase in French productivity allows a 1 percent reduction in French labour demand.

French firms set the price of French goods as a markup over unit labour cost in France:

$$P_2 = gw_2 / a_2 \tag{31}$$

Here w_2 is the nominal wage rate of France, as measured in euros. w_2 / a_2 is unit labour cost in France, as measured in euros. g is the markup factor in France. And P_2 is the price of French goods, as measured in euros. The message of equation (31) is that a 1 percent increase in French nominal wages causes a 1 percent increase in the price of French goods. Conversely, a 1 percent increase in French productivity causes a 1 percent reduction in the price of French goods.

The production function of America is characterized by fixed coefficients:

$$Y_3 = a_3 N_3 \tag{32}$$

Here N_3 stands for American labour input. a_3 is American labour productivity, as measured in American goods. And Y_3 is American output, as measured in American goods. Accordingly, American labour demand is:

$$N_3 = Y_3 / a_3 \tag{33}$$

That means, a 1 percent increase in American output requires a 1 percent increase in American labour demand. On the other hand, a 1 percent increase in American productivity allows a 1 percent reduction in American labour demand.

American firms set the price of American goods as a markup over unit labour cost in America:

$$P_3 = gw_3 / a_3 \tag{34}$$

Here w_3 is the nominal wage rate in America, as measured in dollars. w_3 / a_3 is unit labour cost in America, as measured in dollars. g is the markup factor in America. And P_3 is the price of American goods, as measured in dollars. The message of equation (34) is that a 1 percent increase in American nominal wages causes a 1 percent increase in the price of American goods. Conversely, a 1 percent increase in American productivity causes a 1 percent reduction in the price of American goods.

8) The model. On this foundation, the full model can be represented by a system of eleven equations:

$$Y_1 = cY_1 + b_1 r^{-\varepsilon} + mP_2 Y_2 / P_1 + 0.5qeP_3 Y_3 / P_1 - (m+q)Y_1 \tag{35}$$

$$Y_2 = cY_2 + b_2 r^{-\varepsilon} + mP_1 Y_1 / P_2 + 0.5qeP_3 Y_3 / P_2 - (m+q)Y_2 \tag{36}$$

$$Y_3 = cY_3 + b_3 r^{-\varepsilon} + qP_1 Y_1 / eP_3 + qP_2 Y_2 / eP_3 - qY_3 \tag{37}$$

$$M_{12} = kP_1 Y_1 r^{-\eta} + kP_2 Y_2 r^{-\eta} \tag{38}$$

$$M_3 = kP_3 Y_3 r^{-\eta} \tag{39}$$

$$P_1 = gw_1 / a_1 \tag{40}$$

$$P_2 = gw_2 / a_2 \tag{41}$$

$$P_3 = gw_3 / a_3 \tag{42}$$

$$N_1 = Y_1 / a_1 \tag{43}$$

$$N_2 = Y_2 / a_2 \tag{44}$$

$$N_3 = Y_3 / a_3 \tag{45}$$

Equation (35) is the goods market equation of Germany, as measured in German goods. (36) is the goods market equation of France, as measured in French goods. (37) is the goods market equation of America, as measured in American goods. (38) is the money market equation of Europe, as measured in euros. (39) is the money market equation of America, as measured in dollars. (40) is the price equation of Germany, as measured in euros. (41) is the price equation of France, as measured in euros. (42) is the price equation of America, as measured in dollars. (43) is the labour demand equation of Germany. (44) is the labour demand equation of France. And (45) is the labour demand equation of America.

The exogenous variables are European money supply M_{12}, American money supply M_3, the German investment parameter b_1, the French investment parameter b_2, the American investment parameter b_3, German nominal wages w_1, French nominal wages w_2, American nominal wages w_3, German productivity a_1, French productivity a_2, and American productivity a_3. The endogenous variables are German output Y_1, French output Y_2, American output Y_3, the exchange rate e, the world interest rate r, the price of German goods P_1, the price of French goods P_2, the price of American goods P_3, German labour demand N_1, French labour demand N_2, and American labour demand N_3. Equation (40) gives the price of German goods, (41) gives the price of French goods, and (42) gives the price of American goods. Then equations (35) until (39) give German output, French output, American output, the exchange rate, and the world interest rate. Finally equation (43) gives German labour demand, (44) gives French labour demand, and (45) gives American labour demand.

Now it proves very useful to rewrite the goods market equations as follows:

$$P_1Y_1 = cP_1Y_1 + P_1b_1r^{-\varepsilon} + mP_2Y_2 + 0.5qeP_3Y_3 - (m+q)P_1Y_1 \tag{46}$$

$$P_2Y_2 = cP_2Y_2 + P_2b_2r^{-\varepsilon} + mP_1Y_1 + 0.5qeP_3Y_3 - (m+q)P_2Y_2 \tag{47}$$

$$P_3Y_3 = cP_3Y_3 + P_3b_3r^{-\varepsilon} + qP_1Y_1/e + qP_2Y_2/e - qP_3Y_3 \tag{48}$$

Equation (46) is the goods market equation of Germany, as measured in euros. P_1Y_1 is German income, as measured in euros. cP_1Y_1 is German consumption, as measured in euros. $P_1b_1r^{-\varepsilon}$ is German investment, as measured in euros. mP_2Y_2 is French imports from Germany, as measured in euros. Put another way, mP_2Y_2 is German exports to France, as measured in euros. $0.5qeP_3Y_3$ is American imports from Germany, as measured in euros. Put differently, $0.5qeP_3Y_3$ is German exports to America, as measured in euros. $(m+q)P_1Y_1$ is German imports from France and from America, as measured in euros.

Equation (47) is the goods market equation of France, as measured in euros. P_2Y_2 is French income, as measured in euros. cP_2Y_2 is French consumption, as measured in euros. $P_2b_2r^{-\varepsilon}$ is French investment, as measured in euros. mP_1Y_1 is German imports from France, as measured in euros. Put another way, mP_1Y_1 is French exports to Germany, as measured in euros. $0.5qeP_3Y_3$ is American imports from France, as measured in euros. Put differently, $0.5qeP_3Y_3$ is French exports to America, as measured in euros. $(m+q)P_2Y_2$ is French imports from Germany and from America, as measured in euros.

Equation (48) is the goods market equation of America, as measured in dollars. P_3Y_3 is American income, as measured in dollars. cP_3Y_3 is American consumption, as measured in dollars. $P_3b_3r^{-\varepsilon}$ is American investment, as measured in dollars. qP_1Y_1/e is German imports from America, as measured in dollars. Put another way, qP_1Y_1/e is American exports to Germany, as measured in dollars. qP_2Y_2/e is French imports from America, as measured in dollars. Put differently, qP_2Y_2/e is American exports to France, as measured in dollars. qP_3Y_3 is American imports from Germany and from France, as measured in dollars.

It is worth pointing out here that the goods market equations (46) until (48) are well consistent with microfoundations, see Part Five below. German income P_1Y_1 is spent on German goods $(c-m-q)P_1Y_1$, on French goods mP_1Y_1, and on American goods qP_1Y_1. French income P_2Y_2 is spent on French goods $(c-m-q)P_2Y_2$, on German goods mP_2Y_2, and on American goods qP_2Y_2. American income P_3Y_3 is spent on American goods $(c-q)P_3Y_3$, on German goods $0.5qP_3Y_3$, and on French goods $0.5qeP_3Y_3$.

9) Monetary policy in Europe. An increase in European money supply causes a depreciation of the euro, an appreciation of the dollar, and a decline in the world interest rate. The depreciation of the euro, in turn, raises both German exports and French exports. The appreciation of the dollar, however, lowers American exports. And the decline in the world interest rate raises German investment, French investment as well as American investment. The net effect is that German output and French output move up. On the other hand, American output moves down. In a numerical example, a 1 percent increase in European money supply causes a 2.75 percent depreciation of the euro, a 2.75 percent appreciation of the dollar, a 0.75 percent increase in German output, an 0.75 percent increase in French output, and a 0.25 percent decline in American output. For the proof see Carlberg (2001).

2. Flexible Wages

Take for example an increase in European money supply. Then what will be the effect on the price of German goods, on the price of French goods, and on the price of American goods? Alternatively take an increase in German investment, in German labour supply, or in German productivity.

Under flexible wages, German labour demand equals German labour supply. On the same grounds, French labour demand equals French labour supply. And American labour demand equals American labour supply. As a consequence there is always full employment in Germany, France and America. Here N_1 denotes German labour supply, N_2 is French labour supply, and N_3 is American labour supply. It is assumed that German labour supply, French labour supply, and American labour supply are given exogenously ($N_1 = $ const, $N_2 = $ const, $N_3 = $ const). Now the full model can be characterized by a system of eleven equations:

$$Y_1 = cY_1 + b_1 r^{-\varepsilon} + mP_2 Y_2 / P_1 + 0.5qeP_3 Y_3 / P_1 - (m+q)Y_1 \tag{1}$$

$$Y_2 = cY_2 + b_2 r^{-\varepsilon} + mP_1 Y_1 / P_2 + 0.5qeP_3 Y_3 / P_2 - (m+q)Y_2 \tag{2}$$

$$Y_3 = cY_3 + b_3 r^{-\varepsilon} + qP_1 Y_1 / eP_3 + qP_2 Y_2 / eP_3 - qY_3 \tag{3}$$

$$M_{12} = kP_1 Y_1 r^{-\eta} + kP_2 Y_2 r^{-\eta} \tag{4}$$

$$M_3 = kP_3 Y_3 r^{-\eta} \tag{5}$$

$$Y_1 = a_1 N_1 \tag{6}$$

$$Y_2 = a_2 N_2 \tag{7}$$

$$Y_3 = a_3 N_3 \tag{8}$$

$$w_1 = a_1 P_1 / g \tag{9}$$

$$w_2 = a_2 P_2 / g \tag{10}$$

$$w_3 = a_3 P_3 / g \tag{11}$$

Equation (1) is the goods market equation of Germany, (2) is the goods market equation of France, (3) is the goods market equation of America, (4) is the money market equation of Europe, (5) is the money market equation of America, (6) is the production function of Germany, (7) is the production function of France, (8) is the production function of America, (9) is the wage equation of Germany, (10) is the wage equation of France, and (11) is the wage equation of America.

The exogenous variables are European money supply M_{12}, American money supply M_3, the German investment parameter b_1, the French investment parameter b_2, the American investment parameter b_3, German labour supply N_1, French labour supply N_2, American labour supply N_3, German productivity a_1, French productivity a_2, and American productivity a_3. The endogenous variables are the price of German goods P_1, the price of French goods P_2, the price of American goods P_3, German nominal wages w_1, French nominal wages w_2, American nominal wages w_3, the exchange rate e, the world interest rate r, German output Y_1, French output Y_2, and American output Y_3.

Equation (6) gives German output, equation (7) gives French output, and equation (8) gives American output. Then equations (1) until (5) give the price of German goods, the price of French goods, the price of American goods, the exchange rate, and the world interest rate. Finally equation (9) gives German nominal wages, equation (10) gives French nominal wages, and equation (11) gives American nominal wages.

Next have a look at monetary policy in Europe. An increase in European money supply causes a depreciation of the euro. This in turn raises both German and French nominal wages. Therefore the prices of German and French goods move up. On the other hand, American nominal wages and the price of American goods do not change. In a numerical example, a 1 percent increase in European money supply causes a 1 percent depreciation of the euro, a 1 percent increase in German nominal wages, a 1 percent increase in French nominal wages, a 1 percent increase in the price of German goods, and a 1 percent increase in the price of French goods. For the proof see Carlberg (2001).

Chapter 2
Given Money Growth

1. The Dynamic Model

Here the focus is on steady-state inflation in Germany, France and America, given steady-state growth. We assume that nominal wages and prices are flexible, so there is always full employment in Germany, France and America. To illustrate the problem, consider a numerical example. Let German output grow at a constant rate of 1 percent, let French output grow at a constant rate of 3 percent, let American output grow at a constant rate of 2 percent, let European money supply grow at a constant rate of 3 percent, and let American money supply grow at a constant rate of 4 percent. This gives rise to a number of questions.

At what rate does the price of German goods grow? And at what rate does the price of French goods grow? The consumer price index of Germany includes the price of German goods, the price of French goods, the price of American goods, and the price of the dollar. Then at what rate does the consumer price index of Germany grow? The consumer price index of France includes the price of French goods, the price of German goods, the price of American goods, and the price of the dollar. Then at what rate does the consumer price index of France grow?

It proves useful to reformulate the static model with flexible wages as follows:

$$P_1 Y_1 = c P_1 Y_1 + P_1 b_1 r^{-\varepsilon} + m P_2 Y_2 + 0.5 q e P_3 Y_3 - (m+q) P_1 Y_1 \tag{1}$$

$$P_2 Y_2 = c P_2 Y_2 + P_2 b_2 r^{-\varepsilon} + m P_1 Y_1 + 0.5 q e P_3 Y_3 - (m+q) P_2 Y_2 \tag{2}$$

$$P_3 Y_3 = c P_3 Y_3 + P_3 b_3 r^{-\varepsilon} + q P_1 Y_1 / e + q P_2 Y_2 / e - q P_3 Y_3 \tag{3}$$

$$M_{12} = k P_1 Y_1 r^{-\eta} + k P_2 Y_2 r^{-\eta} \tag{4}$$

$$M_3 = k P_3 Y_3 r^{-\eta} \tag{5}$$

$$Y_1 = a_1 N_1 \tag{6}$$

$$Y_2 = a_2 N_2 \tag{7}$$

$$Y_3 = a_3 N_3 \tag{8}$$

$$w_1 = a_1 P_1 / g \tag{9}$$

$$w_2 = a_2 P_2 / g \tag{10}$$

$$w_3 = a_3 P_3 / g \tag{11}$$

Equation (1) is the goods market equation of Germany, (2) is the goods market equation of France, (3) is the goods market equation of America, (4) is the money market equation of Europe, (5) is the money market equation of America, (6) is the production function of Germany, (7) is the production function of France, (8) is the production function of America, (9) is the wage equation of Germany, (10) is the wage equation of France, and (11) is the wage equation of America.

In the dynamic model, we make the following assumptions:

$$\hat{M}_{12} = \text{const} \tag{12}$$

$$\hat{M}_3 = \text{const} \tag{13}$$

$$\hat{N}_1 = \text{const} \tag{14}$$

$$\hat{N}_2 = \text{const} \tag{15}$$

$$\hat{N}_3 = \text{const} \tag{16}$$

$$\hat{a}_1 = \text{const} \tag{17}$$

$$\hat{a}_2 = \text{const} \tag{18}$$

$$\hat{a}_3 = \text{const} \tag{19}$$

$$\hat{b}_1 = \hat{Y}_1 \tag{20}$$

$$\hat{b}_2 = \hat{Y}_2 \tag{21}$$

$$\hat{b}_3 = \hat{Y}_3 \tag{22}$$

$$r = \text{const} \tag{23}$$

Equation (12) has it that European money supply grows at the constant rate $\hat{M}_{12}$. Equation (13) has it that American money supply grows at the constant rate $\hat{M}_3$. Equation (14) has it that German labour supply grows at the constant rate $\hat{N}_1$. Equation (15) has it that French labour supply grows at the constant rate $\hat{N}_2$. Equation (16) has it that American labour supply grows at the constant rate $\hat{N}_3$. Equation (17) has it that German productivity grows at the constant rate $\hat{a}_1$. Equation (18) has it that French productivity grows at the constant rate $\hat{a}_2$. Equation (19) has it that American productivity grows at the constant rate $\hat{a}_3$.

In equation (20), $\hat{b}_1$ symbolizes the rate of growth of autonomous investment in Germany, and $\hat{Y}_1$ is the rate of growth of German output. Equation (20) has it that, in the steady state, the growth of autonomous investment in Germany equals output growth in Germany. This is a natural assumption. In equation (21), $\hat{b}_2$ stands for the rate of growth of autonomous investment in France, and $\hat{Y}_2$ is the rate of growth of French output. Equation (21) has it that, in the steady state, the growth of autonomous investment in France equals output growth in France. In equation (22), $\hat{b}_3$ designates the rate of growth of autonomous investment in America, and $\hat{Y}_3$ is the rate of growth of American output. Equation (22) has it that, in the steady state, the growth of autonomous investment in America equals output growth in America. And equation (23) has it that, in the steady state, the world interest rate is constant. This is a natural assumption as well.

Now the static model will be restated in terms of growth rates. To begin with, regroup equations (1) and (2) as follows:

$$(1-c+m+q)P_1Y_1 = P_1b_1r^{-\varepsilon} + mP_2Y_2 + 0.5qeP_3Y_3 \tag{24}$$

$$(1-c+m+q)P_2Y_2 = P_2b_2r^{-\varepsilon} + mP_1Y_1 + 0.5qeP_3Y_3 \tag{25}$$

Then take the difference between equations (24) and (25):

$$(1-c+2m+q)P_1Y_1 - P_1b_1r^{-\varepsilon} = (1-c+2m+q)P_2Y_2 - P_2b_2r^{-\varepsilon} \tag{26}$$

Noting equations (20) and (23), the left-hand side of equation (26) grows at the rate $\hat{P}_1 + \hat{Y}_1$. And noting equations (21) and (23), the right-hand side of equation (26) grows at the rate $\hat{P}_2 + \hat{Y}_2$. Of course, the left-hand side and the right-hand side of equation (26) grow at the same rate. This implies:

$$\hat{P}_1 + \hat{Y}_1 = \hat{P}_2 + \hat{Y}_2 \tag{27}$$

That means, German income (as measured in euros) and French income (as measured in euros) grow at the same rate.

Further, in equation (1), all terms except $0.5qeP_3Y_3$ grow at the rate $\hat{P}_1 + \hat{Y}_1$. As a consequence, $0.5qeP_3Y_3$ grows at the rate $\hat{P}_1 + \hat{Y}_1$ too. This implies:

$$\hat{P}_1 + \hat{Y}_1 = \hat{e} + \hat{P}_3 + \hat{Y}_3 \tag{28}$$

That is to say, German income (as measured in euros) and American income (as measured in euros) grow at the same rate. As a corollary, French income (as measured in euros) and American income (as measured in euros) grow at the same rate.

Moreover, equation (4) can be transformed this way:

$$\hat{M}_{12} = \pi(\hat{P}_1 + \hat{Y}_1) + (1 - \pi)(\hat{P}_2 + \hat{Y}_2) \tag{29}$$

Here π is the share of German income P_1Y_1 in European income $P_1Y_1 + P_2Y_2$. Correspondingly, $1 - \pi$ is the share of French income in European income. Equation (29), together with equation (27), yields:

$$\hat{M}_{12} = \hat{P}_1 + \hat{Y}_1 \tag{30}$$

$$\hat{M}_{12} = \hat{P}_2 + \hat{Y}_2 \tag{31}$$

That is, European money supply (as measured in euros) and German income (as measured in euros) grow at the same rate. Similarly, European money supply (as measured in euros) and French income (as measured in euros) grow at the same rate.

On this foundation, the dynamic model can be characterized by a system of ten equations:

$$\hat{P}_1 + \hat{Y}_1 = \hat{e} + \hat{P}_3 + \hat{Y}_3 \tag{32}$$

$$\hat{M}_{12} = \hat{P}_1 + \hat{Y}_1 \tag{33}$$

$$\hat{M}_{12} = \hat{P}_2 + \hat{Y}_2 \tag{34}$$

$$\hat{M}_3 = \hat{P}_3 + \hat{Y}_3 \tag{35}$$

$$\hat{Y}_1 = \hat{a}_1 + \hat{N}_1 \tag{36}$$

$$\hat{Y}_2 = \hat{a}_2 + \hat{N}_2 \tag{37}$$

$$\hat{Y}_3 = \hat{a}_3 + \hat{N}_3 \tag{38}$$

$$\hat{w}_1 = \hat{a}_1 + \hat{P}_1 \tag{39}$$

$$\hat{w}_2 = \hat{a}_2 + \hat{P}_2 \tag{40}$$

$$\hat{w}_3 = \hat{a}_3 + \hat{P}_3 \tag{41}$$

Equation (32) is called the goods market equation, (33) is called the money market equation of Germany, (34) is called the money market equation of France, (35) is the money market equation of America, (36) is the production function of Germany, (37) is the production function of France, (38) is the production function of America, (39) is the wage equation of Germany, (40) is the wage equation of France, and (41) is the wage equation of America.

$\hat{P}_1$ is the rate of growth of the price of German goods. Put another way, $\hat{P}_1$ is the rate of producer inflation in Germany. By analogy, $\hat{P}_2$ is the rate of growth of the price of French goods. Put differently, $\hat{P}_2$ is the rate of producer inflation in France. And $\hat{P}_3$ is the rate of growth of the price of American goods. In other words, $\hat{P}_3$ is the rate of producer inflation in America. ê is the rate of growth of the nominal exchange rate. That means, ê is the rate of depreciation. According to equation (32), the rate of depreciation depends on nominal income growth in Germany $\hat{P}_1 + \hat{Y}_1$ and on nominal income growth in America $\hat{P}_3 + \hat{Y}_3$.

According to equation (33), nominal income growth in Germany is determined by money growth in Europe. According to equation (34), nominal income growth in France is also determined by money growth in Europe. According to equation (35), nominal income growth in America is determined by money growth in America. According to equation (36), output growth in Germany is determined by productivity growth in Germany and by labour growth in Germany. According to equation (37), output growth in France is determined by productivity growth in France and by labour growth in France. According to equation (38), output growth in America is determined by productivity growth in America and by labour growth in America.

In equation (39), $\hat{w}_1$ is the rate of growth of German nominal wages. According to equation (39), nominal wage growth in Germany depends on productivity growth in Germany and on producer inflation in Germany. In equation (40), $\hat{w}_2$ is the rate of growth of French nominal wages. According to equation (40), nominal wage growth in France depends on productivity growth in France and on producer inflation in France. In equation (41), $\hat{w}_3$ is the rate of growth of American nominal wages. According to equation (41), nominal wage growth in America depends on productivity growth in America and on producer inflation in America.

The exogenous variables are money growth in Europe $\hat{M}_{12}$, money growth in America $\hat{M}_3$, productivity growth in Germany $\hat{a}_1$, productivity growth in France $\hat{a}_2$, productivity growth in America $\hat{a}_3$, labour growth in Germany $\hat{N}_1$, labour growth in France $\hat{N}_2$, and labour growth in America $\hat{N}_3$. The endogenous variables are producer inflation in Germany $\hat{P}_1$, producer inflation in France $\hat{P}_2$, producer inflation in America $\hat{P}_3$, nominal depreciation $\hat{e}$, output growth in Germany $\hat{Y}_1$, output growth in France $\hat{Y}_2$, output growth in America $\hat{Y}_3$, nominal wage growth in Germany $\hat{w}_1$, nominal wage growth in France $\hat{w}_2$, and nominal wage growth in America $\hat{w}_3$.

Equation (36) gives output growth in Germany, equation (37) gives output growth in France, and equation (38) gives output growth in America. Then equation (33) gives producer inflation in Germany, equation (34) gives producer inflation in France, and equation (35) gives producer inflation in America. Then equation (32) gives the rate of depreciation. Finally equation (39) gives nominal wage growth in Germany, equation (40) gives nominal wage growth in France, and equation (41) gives nominal wage growth in America.

2. Inflation and Depreciation

2.1. Producer Inflation

Producer inflation in Germany refers to the price of German goods, as measured in euros. Producer inflation in France refers to the price of French goods, as measured in euros. The model can be reduced to a system of two equations:

$$\hat{M}_{12} = \hat{P}_1 + \hat{Y}_1 \tag{1}$$

$$\hat{M}_{12} = \hat{P}_2 + \hat{Y}_2 \tag{2}$$

Equation (1) is the money market equation of Germany, and equation (2) is the money market equation of France. Here the exogenous variables are money growth in Europe, output growth in Germany, and output growth in France. The endogenous variables are producer inflation in Germany and producer inflation in France.

Obviously the solution is:

$$\hat{P}_1 = \hat{M}_{12} - \hat{Y}_1 \tag{3}$$

$$\hat{P}_2 = \hat{M}_{12} - \hat{Y}_2 \tag{4}$$

As a result, according to equation (3), the price of German goods grows at a constant rate. Producer inflation in Germany depends on money growth in Europe and on output growth in Germany. However, it does not depend on output growth in France. According to equation (4), the price of French goods also grows at a constant rate. Producer inflation in France is determined by money growth in Europe and by output growth in France. An increase in European money growth raises both producer inflation in Germany and producer inflation in France. An increase in German output growth lowers producer inflation in Germany but has no effect on producer inflation in France.

Conversely, an increase in French output growth lowers producer inflation in France but has no effect on producer inflation in Germany.

In the country where output growth in high, producer inflation will be low. And in the country where output growth is low, producer inflation will be high. To illustrate this, consider a numerical example. Let output growth in Germany be 1 percent, let output growth in France be 3 percent, and let money growth in Europe be 3 percent. Then, as a result, producer inflation in Germany is 2 percent, and producer inflation in France is 0 percent.

2.2. Nominal Depreciation

The model can be condensed to a system of three equations:

$$\hat{P}_1 + \hat{Y}_1 = \hat{e} + \hat{P}_3 + \hat{Y}_3 \tag{1}$$

$$\hat{M}_{12} = \hat{P}_1 + \hat{Y}_1 \tag{2}$$

$$\hat{M}_3 = \hat{P}_3 + \hat{Y}_3 \tag{3}$$

Equation (1) is the goods market equation, (2) is the money market equation of Germany, and (3) is the money market equation of America. The exogenous variables are money growth in Europe, money growth in America, output growth in Germany, and output growth in America. The endogenous variables are nominal depreciation, producer inflation in Germany, and producer inflation in America.

Equations (1), (2) and (3) yield:

$$\hat{e} = \hat{M}_{12} - \hat{M}_3 \tag{4}$$

As a result, the nominal exchange rate grows (or declines) at a constant rate. The rate of depreciation depends on money growth in Europe and on money growth in America. However, it does not depend on output growth in Germany, on output growth in France, or on output growth in America. In the region where money growth is high, the currency will depreciate. And in the region where money growth is low, the currency will appreciate.

To be more specific, if money growth in Europe exceeds money growth in America, then the euro will depreciate and the dollar will appreciate. The other way round, if money growth in Europe falls short of money growth in America, then the euro will appreciate and the dollar will depreciate. For instance, let money growth in Europe be 3 percent, and let money growth in America be 4 percent. Then, as a result, the euro appreciates at a rate of 1 percent. That is to say, the dollar depreciates at a rate of 1 percent.

To sum up, the rate of depreciation is determined by money growth in Europe and by money growth in America. In short, the rate of depreciation is driven by the money growth differential. But be careful. The rate of depreciation does not depend on producer inflation in Germany, on producer inflation in France, or on producer inflation in America.

2.3. Real Depreciation

1) The relative price of French goods. Here the real exchange rate is defined as the price of French goods, as measured in German goods:

$$R_{21} = P_2 / P_1 \tag{1}$$

An increase in the relative price of French goods raises the competitiveness of German goods. Equation (1) can be expressed in terms of growth rates as $\hat{R}_{21} = \hat{P}_2 - \hat{P}_1$. Here $\hat{R}_{21}$ denotes the rate of growth of the real exchange rate. Put differently, $\hat{R}_{21}$ is the rate of real depreciation. The model can be compressed to a system of two equations:

$$\hat{P}_1 + \hat{Y}_1 = \hat{P}_2 + \hat{Y}_2 \tag{2}$$

$$\hat{R}_{21} = \hat{P}_2 - \hat{P}_1 \tag{3}$$

Equation (2) is the goods market equation, and equation (3) defines the real exchange rate. The exogenous variables are output growth in Germany and output growth in France. The endogenous variable is real depreciation.

The model can be solved as follows:

$$\hat{R}_{21} = \hat{Y}_1 - \hat{Y}_2 \tag{4}$$

As a result, the real exchange rate grows at a constant rate. Put another way, the relative price of French goods grows at a constant rate. That means, the competitiveness of German goods grows at a constant rate. According to equation (4), the growth of the relative price of French goods is determined by output growth in Germany and by output growth in France.

If output growth in France is high, the relative price of French goods will decline. And if output growth in France is low, the relative price of French goods will increase. If output growth in Germany is high, the relative price of French goods will increase. And if output growth in Germany is low, the relative price of French goods will decline. To see this more clearly, have a look at a numerical example. Let output growth in Germany be 1 percent, and let output growth in France be 3 percent. Then, as a result, the relative price of French goods declines at a rate of 2 percent. That is to say, the relative price of German goods grows at a rate of 2 percent.

As regards competitiveness, the general findings can be restated as follows. If output growth in Germany is high, the competitiveness of German goods will increase. However, if output growth in Germany is low, the competitiveness of German goods will decline.

We turn now to purchasing power. An increase in the relative price of French goods (as measured in German goods) reduces the purchasing power of German goods (as measured in French goods). As regards purchasing power, the general findings can be expressed as follows. If output growth in Germany is high, the purchasing power of German goods will decline. And if output growth in Germany is low, the purchasing power of German goods will increase. This is closely related to purchasing power parity. By definition, it means that purchasing power is constant. If German output and French output grow at the same rate, then the purchasing power of German goods will be constant. In other words, purchasing power parity will hold. If German output and French output grow at different rates, then the purchasing power of German goods will not be constant. In other words, purchasing power parity will not hold.

2) The relative price of American goods. Here the real exchange rate is defined as the price of American goods, as measured in German goods:

$$R_{31} = eP_3 / P_1 \tag{5}$$

An increase in the relative price of American goods raises the competitiveness of German goods but lowers the purchasing power of German goods. Equation (5) can be rewritten in terms of growth rates as $\hat{R}_{31} = \hat{e} + \hat{P}_3 - \hat{P}_1$. Accordingly, the model can be described by a system of two equations:

$$\hat{P}_1 + \hat{Y}_1 = \hat{e} + \hat{P}_3 + \hat{Y}_3 \tag{6}$$
$$\hat{R}_{31} = \hat{e} + \hat{P}_3 - \hat{P}_1 \tag{7}$$

Equations (6) and (7) give:

$$\hat{R}_{31} = \hat{Y}_1 - \hat{Y}_3 \tag{8}$$

As a result, the growth of the relative price of American goods is determined by output growth in Germany and by output growth in America. If output growth in America is high, the relative price of American goods will decline. And if output growth in America is low, the relative price of American goods will increase. For instance, let output growth in Germany be 1 percent, and let output growth in America be 2 percent. Then the relative price of American goods declines at a rate 1 percent. That is, the relative price of German goods grows at a rate of 1 percent.

Finally compare nominal depreciation and real depreciation. Nominal depreciation is determined by money growth in Europe and by money growth in America. Real depreciation, on the other hand, is determined by output growth in Germany, by output growth in France, and by output growth in America. In short, nominal depreciation is driven by the money growth differential. And real depreciation is driven by the output growth differential.

2.4. Consumer Inflation

1) The consumer price index of Germany. German consumption includes German goods, French goods and American goods. Therefore, the consumer price index of Germany includes the price of German goods, the price of French goods, the price of American goods, and the price of the dollar. The consumer price index of Germany is defined as:

$$J_1 = P_1^\alpha P_2^\beta (eP_3)^\gamma \tag{1}$$

Here P_1 denotes the price of German goods, as measured in euros. P_2 is the price of French goods, as measured in euros. P_3 is the price of American goods, as measured in dollars. e is the price of the dollar, as measured in euros. So eP_3 is the price of American goods, as measured in euros. α is the share of German goods in German consumption, β is the share of French goods in German consumption, and γ is the share of American goods in German consumption. Then J_1 is the consumer price index of Germany, as measured in euros.

Equation (1) can be expressed in terms of growth rates:

$$\hat{J}_1 = \alpha\hat{P}_1 + \beta\hat{P}_2 + \gamma\hat{P}_3 + \gamma\hat{e} \tag{2}$$

$\hat{J}_1$ symbolizes the rate of growth of the consumer price index in Germany. Put differently, $\hat{J}_1$ is the rate of consumer inflation in Germany. According to equation (2), consumer inflation in Germany includes producer inflation in

Germany, producer inflation in France, producer inflation in America, and the appreciation of the dollar.

2) The consumer price index of France. French consumption includes French goods, German goods and American goods. Therefore, the consumer price index of France includes the price of French goods, the price of German goods, the price of American goods, and the price of the dollar. The consumer price index of France is defined as:

$$J_2 = P_2^{\alpha} P_1^{\beta} (eP_3)^{\gamma} \tag{3}$$

Here α stands for the share of French goods in French consumption, β is the share of German goods in French consumption, and γ is the share of American goods in French consumption. Then J_2 is the consumer price index to France, as measured in euros.

Equation (3) can be reformulated in terms of growth rates:

$$\hat{J}_2 = \alpha\hat{P}_2 + \beta\hat{P}_1 + \gamma\hat{P}_3 + \gamma\hat{e} \tag{4}$$

$\hat{J}_2$ designates the rate of growth of the consumer price index in France. Put another way, $\hat{J}_2$ is the rate of consumer inflation in France. According to equation (4), consumer inflation in France includes producer inflation in France, producer inflation in Germany, producer inflation in America, and the appreciation of the dollar.

3) The model. On this basis, the model can be captured by a system of six equations:

$$\hat{P}_1 + \hat{Y}_1 = \hat{e} + \hat{P}_3 + \hat{Y}_3 \tag{5}$$

$$\hat{M}_{12} = \hat{P}_1 + \hat{Y}_1 \tag{6}$$

$$\hat{M}_{12} = \hat{P}_2 + \hat{Y}_2 \tag{7}$$

$$\hat{M}_3 = \hat{P}_3 + \hat{Y}_3 \tag{8}$$

$$\hat{J}_1 = \alpha\hat{P}_1 + \beta\hat{P}_2 + \gamma\hat{P}_3 + \gamma\hat{e} \tag{9}$$

$$\hat{J}_2 = \alpha\hat{P}_2 + \beta\hat{P}_1 + \gamma\hat{P}_3 + \gamma\hat{e} \tag{10}$$

Equation (5) is the goods market equation, (6) is the money market equation of Germany, (7) is the money market equation of France, (8) is the money market equation of America, (9) is the consumer price index of Germany, and (10) is the consumer price index of France. The exogenous variables are money growth in Europe, money growth in America, output growth in Germany, output growth in France, and output growth in America. The endogenous variables are producer inflation in Germany, producer inflation in France, producer inflation in America, nominal depreciation, consumer inflation in Germany, and consumer inflation in France.

4) Consumer inflation in Germany. Equations (5), (6), (7) and (8) provide:

$$\hat{P}_1 = \hat{M}_{12} - \hat{Y}_1 \tag{11}$$

$$\hat{P}_2 = \hat{M}_{12} - \hat{Y}_2 \tag{12}$$

$$\hat{P}_3 = \hat{M}_3 - \hat{Y}_3 \tag{13}$$

$$\hat{e} = \hat{M}_{12} - \hat{M}_3 \tag{14}$$

Next substitute these equations into equation (9) to arrive at:

$$\hat{J}_1 = \hat{M}_{12} - \alpha\hat{Y}_1 - \beta\hat{Y}_2 - \gamma\hat{Y}_3 \tag{15}$$

As a result, according to equation (15), the consumer price index of Germany grows at a constant rate. Consumer inflation in Germany depends on money growth in Europe, on output growth in Germany, on output growth in France, and on output growth in America. However, it does not depend on money growth in America. An increase in European money growth raises consumer inflation in Germany. An increase in German output growth lowers consumer inflation in Germany. And what is more, an increase in French output growth lowers consumer inflation in Germany too. Similarly, an increase in American output growth lowers consumer inflation in Germany as well.

What are the causal links? An increase in European money growth raises producer inflation in Germany, producer inflation in France, and the appreciation of the dollar. On those grounds, consumer inflation in Germany goes up. An increase in German output growth lowers producer inflation in Germany and, hence, consumer inflation in Germany. An increase in French output growth lowers producer inflation in France and, hence, consumer inflation in Germany. An increase in American output growth lowers producer inflation in America and, hence, consumer inflation in Germany.

5) Consumer inflation in France. Insert equations (11), (12), (13) and (14) into equation (10) to conclude:

$$\hat{J}_2 = \hat{M}_{12} - \alpha\hat{Y}_2 - \beta\hat{Y}_1 - \gamma\hat{Y}_3 \tag{16}$$

That means, the consumer price index of France grows at a constant rate. Consumer inflation in France is determined by money growth in Europe, by output growth in France, by output growth in Germany, and by output growth in America. An increase in European money growth drives up consumer inflation in France. An increase in French output growth cuts down consumer inflation in France. An increase in German output growth also cuts down consumer inflation in France. And an increase in American output growth has the same effect.

In the country where output growth is high, consumer inflation will be low. And in the country where output growth is low, consumer inflation will be high. Further, if $\hat{Y}_1 > \hat{Y}_2$, then $\hat{J}_1 > \hat{P}_1$. Conversely, if $\hat{Y}_1 < \hat{Y}_2$, then $\hat{J}_1 < \hat{P}_1$. That is to say, in the country where output growth is high, consumer inflation will exceed producer inflation. And in the country where output growth is low, consumer inflation will fall short of producer inflation.

6) A numerical example. Let output growth in Germany be 1 percent, let output growth in France be 3 percent, let output growth in America be 2 percent, and let money growth in Europe be 3 percent. Besides, let the share of German goods in German consumption be 0.7, let the share of French goods in German consumption be 0.2, and let the share of American goods in German consumption be 0.1. By symmetry, let the share of French goods in French consumption be 0.7, let the share of German goods in French consumption be 0.2, and let the share of American goods in French consumption be 0.1.

Then, as a result, consumer inflation in Germany is 1.5 percent, and consumer inflation in France is 0.5 percent. Compare this with producer inflation. Producer inflation in Germany is 2 percent, and producer inflation in France is 0 percent. So consumer inflation differs remarkably from producer inflation. Table 12 gives an overview of the conclusions drawn in Section 2.

Table 12
Inflation and Depreciation
Given Output Growth and Money Growth

Output Growth in Germany	1
Output Growth in France	3
Output Growth in America	2
Money Growth in Europe	3
Money Growth in America	3
Producer Inflation in Germany	2
Producer Inflation in France	0
Consumer Inflation in Germany	1.5
Consumer Inflation in France	0.5
Appreciation of the Euro	0
Depreciation of the Dollar	0
Decline of German Competitiveness Relative to France	2
Decline of German Competitiveness Relative to America	1
Growth of French Competitiveness Relative to Germany	2
Growth of French Competitiveness Relative to America	1

3. Wage Growth

3.1. Productivity Growth

1) The model. This section deals with the growth of nominal wages, producer real wages and consumer real wages, given productivity growth. The relevant model can be encapsulated in a system of ten equations:

$$\hat{P}_1 + \hat{Y}_1 = \hat{e} + \hat{P}_3 + \hat{Y}_3 \tag{1}$$

$$\hat{M}_{12} = \hat{P}_1 + \hat{Y}_1 \tag{2}$$

$$\hat{M}_{12} = \hat{P}_2 + \hat{Y}_2 \tag{3}$$

$$\hat{M}_3 = \hat{P}_3 + \hat{Y}_3 \tag{4}$$

$$\hat{Y}_1 = \hat{a}_1 \tag{5}$$

$$\hat{Y}_2 = \hat{a}_2 \tag{6}$$

$$\hat{Y}_3 = \hat{a}_3 \tag{7}$$

$$\hat{w}_1 = \hat{a}_1 + \hat{P}_1 \tag{8}$$

$$\hat{w}_2 = \hat{a}_2 + \hat{P}_2 \tag{9}$$

$$\hat{w}_3 = \hat{a}_3 + \hat{P}_3 \tag{10}$$

Equation (1) is the goods market equation, (2) is the money market equation of Germany, (3) is the money market equation of France, (4) is the money market equation of America, (5) is the production function of Germany, (6) is the production function of France, (7) is the production function of America, (8) is the wage equation of Germany, (9) is the wage equation of France, and (10) is the wage equation of America.

The exogenous variables are money growth in Europe $\hat{M}_{12}$, money growth in America $\hat{M}_3$, productivity growth in Germany $\hat{a}_1$, productivity growth in France $\hat{a}_2$, and productivity growth in America $\hat{a}_3$. The endogenous variables are producer inflation in Germany $\hat{P}_1$, producer inflation in France $\hat{P}_2$, producer inflation in America $\hat{P}_3$, nominal depreciation $\hat{e}$, output growth in Germany $\hat{Y}_1$, output growth in France $\hat{Y}_2$, output growth in America $\hat{Y}_3$, nominal wage growth in Germany $\hat{w}_1$, nominal wage growth in France $\hat{w}_2$, and nominal wage growth in America $\hat{w}_3$.

2) The growth of nominal wages. Equations (2) and (5) imply $\hat{P}_1 = \hat{M}_{12} - \hat{a}_1$. This together with equation (8) yields:

$$\hat{w}_1 = \hat{M}_{12} \tag{11}$$

As a result, according to equation (11), nominal wages in Germany grow at a constant rate. Nominal wage growth in Germany depends on money growth in Europe. However, it does not depend on productivity growth in Germany. By analogy we have:

$$\hat{w}_2 = \hat{M}_{12} \tag{12}$$

That means, nominal wage growth in France is determined by money growth in Europe. For instance, let productivity growth in Germany be 1 percent, let productivity growth in France be 3 percent, and let money growth in Europe be 3 percent. Then nominal wage growth in Germany is 3 percent, and nominal wage growth in France is equally 3 percent. It is worth pointing out that nominal wages in Germany and France grow at the same rate, although Germany and France differ in productivity growth.

3) The growth of producer real wages. Producer real wages in Germany are defined as nominal wages in Germany divided by the price of German goods w_1 / P_1. Correspondingly, producer real wages in France are defined as nominal wages in France divided by the price of French goods w_2 / P_2. Producer real wages in Germany measure the real cost of labour in Germany. And producer real wages in France measure the real cost of labour in France. Producer real wages can be expressed in terms of growth rates. $\hat{w}_1 - \hat{P}_1$ is the rate of growth of producer real wages in Germany. And $\hat{w}_2 - \hat{P}_2$ is the rate of growth of producer real wages in France. Now equations (8) and (9) provide:

$$\hat{w}_1 - \hat{P}_1 = \hat{a}_1 \tag{13}$$

$$\hat{w}_2 - \hat{P}_2 = \hat{a}_2 \tag{14}$$

As a result, according to equation (13), producer real wages in Germany grow at a constant rate. The growth of producer real wages in Germany is determined by productivity growth in Germany. And according to equation (14), the growth of producer real wages in France is driven by productivity growth in France. In the country where productivity growth is high, the growth of producer real wages will be high. And in the country where productivity growth is low, the growth of producer real wages will be low. For instance, let productivity growth in Germany be 1 percent, and let productivity growth in France be 3 percent. Then the growth of producer real wages in Germany is 1 percent, and the growth of producer real wages in France is 3 percent.

4) The growth of consumer real wages. Consumer real wages in Germany are defined as nominal wages in Germany divided by the consumer price index of Germany w_1 / J_1. Similarly, consumer real wages in France are defined as nominal wages in France divided by the consumer price index of France w_2 / J_2. German nominal wages are spent on German goods, on French goods, and on American goods. So consumer real wages in Germany measure the purchasing power of German nominal wages. French nominal wages are spent on French goods, on German goods, and on American goods. So consumer real wages in France measure the purchasing power of French nominal wages. Consumer real wages can be expressed in terms of growth rates. $\hat{w}_1 - \hat{J}_1$ is the rate of growth of consumer real wages in Germany. And $\hat{w}_2 - \hat{J}_2$ is the rate of growth of consumer real wages in France.

Consumer inflation in Germany is given by:

$$\hat{J}_1 = \hat{M}_{12} - \alpha\hat{Y}_1 - \beta\hat{Y}_2 - \gamma\hat{Y}_3 \tag{15}$$

For the proof see Section 2.4. above. Next substitute equations (5), (6) and (7) into equation (15) to get $\hat{J}_1 = \hat{M}_{12} - \alpha\hat{a}_1 - \beta\hat{a}_2 - \gamma\hat{a}_3$. Then take account of equation (11) and rearrange:

$$\hat{w}_1 - \hat{J}_1 = \alpha\hat{a}_1 + \beta\hat{a}_2 + \gamma\hat{a}_3 \tag{16}$$

As a result, according to equation (16), consumer real wages in Germany grow at a constant rate. The growth of consumer real wages in Germany depends on productivity growth in Germany, on productivity growth in France, and on productivity growth in America. But it does not depend on money growth in Europe or on money growth in America. An increase in German productivity growth raises the growth of consumer real wages in Germany. And what is more, an increase in French productivity growth also raises the growth of consumer real wages in Germany. Likewise, an increase in American productivity growth raises the growth of consumer real wages in Germany.

Along the same lines it can be shown that:

$$\hat{w}_2 - \hat{J}_2 = \alpha\hat{a}_2 + \beta\hat{a}_1 + \gamma\hat{a}_3 \tag{17}$$

That is to say, the growth of consumer real wages in France is determined by productivity growth in France, by productivity growth in Germany, and by productivity growth in America. In the country where productivity growth is high, the growth of consumer real wages will be high. And in the country where productivity growth is low, the growth of consumer real wages will be low.

To see this more clearly, have a look at a numerical example. Let productivity growth in Germany be 1 percent, let productivity growth in France be 3 percent, and let productivity growth in America be 2 percent. Besides, let the share of French goods in German consumption be 0.2, and let the share of American goods in German consumption be 0.1. Symmetrically, let share of German goods in French consumption by 0.2, and let the share of American goods in French consumption be 0.1.

Then, as a result, the growth of consumer real wages in Germany is 1.5 percent, and the growth of consumer real wages in France is 2.5 percent. Compare this with the growth of producer real wages. The growth of producer real wages in Germany is 1 percent, and the growth of producer real wages in France is 3 percent. Thus the growth of consumer real wages differs substantially from the growth of producer real wages. Table 13 presents a synopsis.

Table 13
Wage Growth
Given Productivity Growth and Money Growth

Productivity Growth in Germany	1
Productivity Growth in France	3
Productivity Growth in America	2
Money Growth in Europe	3
Growth of Nominal Wages in Germany	3
Growth of Nominal Wages in France	3
Growth of Producer Real Wages in Germany	1
Growth of Producer Real Wages in France	3
Growth of Consumer Real Wages in Germany	1.5
Growth of Consumer Real Wages in France	2.5

3.2. Labour Growth

1) The model. This section is devoted to the growth of nominal wages, producer real wages and consumer real wages, given labour growth. The model can be enshrined in a system of ten equations:

$$\hat{P}_1 + \hat{Y}_1 = \hat{e} + \hat{P}_3 + \hat{Y}_3 \tag{1}$$

$$\hat{M}_{12} = \hat{P}_1 + \hat{Y}_1 \tag{2}$$

$$\hat{M}_{12} = \hat{P}_2 + \hat{Y}_2 \tag{3}$$

$$\hat{M}_3 = \hat{P}_3 + \hat{Y}_3 \tag{4}$$

$$\hat{Y}_1 = \hat{N}_1 \tag{5}$$

$$\hat{Y}_2 = \hat{N}_2 \tag{6}$$

$$\hat{Y}_3 = \hat{N}_3 \tag{7}$$

$$\hat{w}_1 = \hat{P}_1 \tag{8}$$

$$\hat{w}_2 = \hat{P}_2 \tag{9}$$

$$\hat{w}_3 = \hat{P}_3 \tag{10}$$

Equation (1) is the goods market equation, (2) is the money market equation of Germany, (3) is the money market equation of France, (4) is the money market equation of America, (5) is the production function of Germany, (6) is the production function of France, (7) is the production function of America, (8) is the wage equation of Germany, (9) is the wage equation of France, and (10) is the wage equation of America.

The exogenous variables are money growth in Europe $\hat{M}_{12}$, money growth in America $\hat{M}_3$, labour growth in Germany $\hat{N}_1$, labour growth in France $\hat{N}_2$, and labour growth in America $\hat{N}_3$. The endogenous variables are producer inflation in Germany $\hat{P}_1$, producer inflation in France $\hat{P}_2$, producer inflation in America $\hat{P}_3$, nominal depreciation $\hat{e}$, output growth in Germany $\hat{Y}_1$, output growth in France $\hat{Y}_2$, output growth in America $\hat{Y}_3$, nominal wage growth in Germany $\hat{w}_1$, nominal wage growth in France $\hat{w}_2$, and nominal wage growth in America $\hat{w}_3$.

2) The growth of nominal wages. Equations (2) and (5) provide $\hat{P}_1 = \hat{M}_{12} - \hat{N}_1$. This together with equation (8) yields:

$$\hat{w}_1 = \hat{M}_{12} - \hat{N}_1 \tag{11}$$

As a result, according to equation (11), nominal wages in Germany grow at a constant rate. Nominal wage growth in Germany is determined by money growth in Europe and by labour growth in Germany. An increase in European money growth raises nominal wage growth in Germany. On the other hand, an increase in German labour growth lowers nominal wage growth in Germany.

By analogy we have:

$$\hat{w}_2 = \hat{M}_{12} - \hat{N}_2 \tag{12}$$

That means, nominal wage growth in France is determined by money growth in Europe and by labour growth in France. In the country where labour growth is high, nominal wage growth will be low. And in the country where labour growth is low, nominal wage growth will be high.

To illustrate this, consider some numerical examples. Let us start with numerical example number one. Let labour growth in Germany be 1 percent, let labour growth in France be 3 percent, and let money growth in Europe be 3 percent. Then nominal wage growth in Germany is 2 percent, and nominal wage growth in France is 0 percent. We proceed now to numerical example number two. Let labour growth in Germany be −1 percent, let labour growth in France be 1 percent, and let money growth in Europe be 1 percent. Then nominal wage growth in Germany is 2 percent, and nominal wage growth in France is 0 percent.

3) The growth of producer real wages. From equations (8) and (9), it follows immediately that:

$$\hat{w}_1 - \hat{P}_1 = 0 \tag{13}$$

$$\hat{w}_2 - \hat{P}_2 = 0 \tag{14}$$

According to equation (13), producer real wages in Germany are constant. And according to equation (14), producer real wages in France are constant as well. This holds although there is labour growth. And this holds although the countries differ in labour growth.

4) The growth of consumer real wages. Consumer inflation in Germany is given by:

$$\hat{J}_1 = \hat{M}_{12} - \alpha\hat{Y}_1 - \beta\hat{Y}_2 - \gamma\hat{Y}_3 \tag{15}$$

For the proof see Section 2.4. above. Next insert equations (5), (6) and (7) into equation (15) to get $\hat{J}_1 = \hat{M}_{12} - \alpha\hat{N}_1 - \beta\hat{N}_2 - \gamma\hat{N}_3$. Then take account of equation (11) and solve for:

$$\hat{w}_1 - \hat{J}_1 = \beta\hat{N}_2 + \gamma\hat{N}_3 - (\beta + \gamma)\hat{N}_1 \tag{16}$$

As a result, according to equation (16), consumer real wages in Germany grow at a constant rate. The growth of consumer real wages in Germany depends on labour growth in Germany, on labour growth in France, and on labour growth in America. However, it does not depend on money growth in Europe or on money growth in America. An increase in German labour growth cuts down the growth of consumer real wages in Germany. Conversely, an increase in French labour growth drives up the growth of consumer real wages in Germany. And an increase in American labour growth has the same effect.

What is the relationship between cause and effect? First consider an increase in German labour growth. Initially let German labour growth, French labour growth and American labour growth be the same. Therefore German output growth, French output growth and American output growth are the same. The relative price of French goods is constant, as is the relative price of American goods. So consumer real wages in Germany are constant too. In this situation, German labour growth speeds up. Therefore German output growth speeds up. The relative price of French goods starts to grow, as does the relative price of American goods. So consumer real wages in Germany start to decline.

Second consider an increase in French labour growth. Initially let German labour growth, French labour growth and American labour growth be the same. Therefore German output growth, French output growth and American output growth are the same. The relative price of French goods is constant, as is the relative price of American goods. So consumer real wages in Germany are constant too. In this situation, French labour growth speeds up. Therefore French output growth speeds up. The relative price of French goods starts to decline. And the relative price of American goods stays constant. So consumer real wages in Germany start to grow.

In the same way it can be derived that:

$$\hat{w}_2 - \hat{J}_2 = \beta\hat{N}_1 + \gamma\hat{N}_3 - (\beta + \gamma)\hat{N}_2 \tag{17}$$

That is to say, the growth of consumer real wages in France is determined by labour growth in France, by labour growth in Germany, and by labour growth in America. In the country where labour growth is high, consumer real wages will decline. And in the country where labour growth is low, consumer real wages will increase.

To see this more clearly, have a look at some numerical examples. Let us begin with numerical example number one. Let labour growth in Germany be 1 percent, let labour growth in France be 3 percent, and let labour growth in America be 2 percent. Further, let the share of French goods in German consumption be 0.2, and let the share of American goods in German consumption be 0.1. Symmetrically, let the share of German goods in French consumption be 0.2, and let the share of American goods in French consumption be 0.1.

Then, as a result, the growth of consumer real wages in Germany is 0.5 percent, and the growth of consumer real wages in France is − 0.5 percent. Compare this with the growth of producer real wages. The growth of producer real wages in Germany is zero, as is the growth of producer real wages in France. Hence the growth of consumer real wages differs substantially from the growth of producer real wages.

We turn now to numerical example number two. Let labour growth in Germany be − 1 percent, let labour growth in France be 1 percent, and let labour growth in America be equally 1 percent. Then the growth of consumer real wages in Germany is 0.6 percent, and the growth of consumer real wages in France is − 0.4 percent. Table 14 gives an overview. In addition, Table 15 compares labour growth with productivity growth. As can be learned from these tables, wage growth is a process of many speeds.

Table 14

Wage Growth

Given Labour Growth and Money Growth

Labour Growth in Germany	1	− 1
Labour Growth in France	3	1
Labour Growth in America	2	1
Money Growth in Europe	3	1
Growth of Nominal Wages in Germany	2	2
Growth of Nominal Wages in France	0	0
Growth of Producer Real Wages in Germany	0	0
Growth of Producer Real Wages in France	0	0
Growth of Consumer Real Wages in Germany	0.5	0.6
Growth of Consumer Real Wages in France	− 0.5	− 0.4

Table 15

Comparing Productivity Growth and Labour Growth

Given Money Growth

Productivity Growth in Germany	1	0
Productivity Growth in France	3	0
Productivity Growth in America	2	0
Labour Growth in Germany	0	1
Labour Growth in France	0	3
Labour Growth in America	0	2
Money Growth in Europe	3	3
Growth of Nominal Wages in Germany	3	2
Growth of Nominal Wages in France	3	0
Growth of Producer Real Wages in Germany	1	0
Growth of Producer Real Wages in France	3	0
Growth of Consumer Real Wages in Germany	1.5	0.5
Growth of Consumer Real Wages in France	2.5	− 0.5

4. Nominal and Real Interest Rates

1) The model. The model can be captured by a system of nine equations:

$$\hat{P}_1 + \hat{Y}_1 = \hat{e} + \hat{P}_3 + \hat{Y}_3 \tag{1}$$

$$\hat{M}_{12} = \hat{P}_1 + \hat{Y}_1 \tag{2}$$

$$\hat{M}_{12} = \hat{P}_2 + \hat{Y}_2 \tag{3}$$

$$\hat{M}_3 = \hat{P}_3 + \hat{Y}_3 \tag{4}$$

$$i_1 = i_2 \tag{5}$$

$$i_1 = i_3 + \hat{e} \tag{6}$$

$$r_1 = i_1 - \hat{P}_1 \tag{7}$$

$$r_2 = i_2 - \hat{P}_2 \tag{8}$$

$$r_3 = i_3 - \hat{P}_3 \tag{9}$$

Equation (1) is the goods market equation, (2) is the money market equation of Germany, (3) is the money market equation of France, and (4) is the money market equation of America. Equation (5) is the interest parity between Germany and France. i_1 denotes the nominal interest rate in Germany, and i_2 is the nominal interest rate in France. The interest parity between Germany and France is the outcome of interest arbitrage. Equation (6) is the open interest parity between Germany and America. i_3 symbolizes the nominal interest rate in America, and $\hat{e}$ is the rate of depreciation. The open interest parity between Germany and America is the outcome of interest arbitrage.

Equation (7) is the Fisher equation of Germany. r_1 stands for the real interest rate in Germany. It is defined as the nominal interest rate in Germany minus producer inflation in Germany. Equation (8) is the Fisher equation of France. r_2 designates the real interest rate in France. It is defined as the nominal interest rate in France minus producer inflation in France. Equation (9) is the Fisher equation of America. r_3 is the real interest rate in America. It is defined as the nominal interest rate is America minus producer inflation in America.

The exogenous variables are money growth in Europe, money growth in America, output growth in Germany, output growth in France, and output growth in America. The endogenous variables are the nominal interest rate in Germany, the nominal interest rate in France, the nominal interest rate in America, the real interest rate in Germany, the real interest rate in France, the real interest rate in America, producer inflation in Germany, producer inflation in France, producer inflation in America, and nominal depreciation.

2) Nominal interest rates. According to equation (5), the nominal interest rate in Germany always equals the nominal interest rate in France. Put another way, the nominal interest differential between Germany and France is always zero. Equations (1), (2) and (4) give $\hat{e} = \hat{M}_{12} - \hat{M}_3$. This together with equations (5) and (6) yields:

$$i_1 - i_3 = i_2 - i_3 = \hat{M}_{12} - \hat{M}_3 \tag{10}$$

As a result, the nominal interest differential between Europe and America is determined by the money growth differential between Europe and America. In the region where money growth is high, the nominal interest rate will be high. And in the region where money growth is low, the nominal interest rate will be low.

To illustrate this, consider some numerical examples. Let us start with numerical example number one. Let money growth in Europe be 3 percent, and let money growth in America be 4 percent. Then the nominal interest rate in America exceeds the nominal interest rate in Europe by 1 percentage point. We proceed now to numerical example number two. Let output growth in Germany be 1 percent, let output growth in France be 3 percent, and let money growth in Europe be 3 percent. Then the nominal interest rate in Germany equals the nominal interest rate in France. Compare this with producer inflation. Producer inflation in Germany is 2 percent, and producer inflation in France is 0 percent. As a finding, the nominal interest differential is zero, although the inflation differential is positive.

3) Real interest rates. From equations (2), (3), (7) and (8) it can be derived that:

$$r_1 = i_1 - \hat{M}_{12} + \hat{Y}_1 \tag{11}$$

$$r_2 = i_2 - \hat{M}_{12} + \hat{Y}_2 \tag{12}$$

Next subtract equation (12) from equation (11), noting equation (5):

$$r_1 - r_2 = \hat{Y}_1 - \hat{Y}_2 \tag{13}$$

As a consequence, the real interest differential between Germany and France is determined by the output growth differential between Germany and France. In the country where output growth is high, the real interest rate will be high. And in the country where output growth is low, the real interest rate will be low. It is worth pointing out here that the real interest differential cannot be exploited.

By analogy we have:

$$r_1 - r_3 = \hat{Y}_1 - \hat{Y}_3 \tag{14}$$

$$r_2 - r_3 = \hat{Y}_2 - \hat{Y}_3 \tag{15}$$

According to equation (14), the real interest differential between Germany and America is determined by the output growth differential between Germany and America. According to equation (15), the real interest differential between France and America is determined by the output growth differential between France and America.

For instance, let output growth in Germany be 1 percent, let output growth in France be 3 percent, and let output growth in America be 2 percent. Then the real interest rate in France exceeds the real interest rate in Germany by 2 percentage points. The real interest rate in America exceeds the real interest rate in Germany by 1 percentage point. And the real interest rate in France exceeds the real interest rate in America by 1 percentage point.

Finally compare the nominal interest differential and the real interest differential. The nominal interest differential is determined by the money growth differential. And the real interest differential is determined by the output growth differential.

4) An important special case. Assume for the moment that the real interest rate in Germany equals output growth in Germany $r_1 = \hat{Y}_1$. And assume for the moment that the real interest rate in France equals output growth in France $r_2 = \hat{Y}_2$. Then, as a result, the nominal interest rate in Europe equals money growth in Europe:

$$i_1 = i_2 = \hat{M}_{12} \tag{16}$$

To see this more clearly, have a look at a numerical example. Let output growth in Germany be 1 percent, let output growth in France be 3 percent, and let money growth in Europe be 3 percent. Accordingly, let the real interest rate in Germany be 1 percent, and let the real interest rate in France be 3 percent. Then producer inflation in Germany is 2 percent, and producer inflation in France is 0 percent. So the nominal interest rate in Germany is $1 + 2 = 3$ percent, and the nominal interest rate in France is $3 + 0 = 3$ percent.

Now assume instead that the real interest rate in Germany exceeds output growth in Germany by 1 percentage point. And assume instead that the real interest rate in France exceeds output growth in France by equally 1 percentage point. Then, as a result, the nominal interest rate in Europe exceeds money growth in Europe by 1 percentage point.

For instance, let output growth in Germany be 1 percent, let output growth in France be 3 percent, and let money growth in Europe be 3 percent. Accordingly, let the real interest rate in Germany be $1 + 1 = 2$ percent, and let the real interest rate in France be $3 + 1 = 4$ percent. Then producer inflation in Germany is 2 percent, and producer inflation in France is 0 percent. Thus the nominal interest rate in Germany is $2 + 2 = 4$ percent, and the nominal interest rate in France is $4 + 0 = 4$ percent. Table 16 presents a synopsis.

Table 16
Nominal and Real Interest Rates
Given Output Growth and Money Growth

Output Growth in Germany	1	1
Output Growth in France	3	3
Money Growth in Europe	3	3
Real Interest Rate in Germany	1	2
Real Interest Rate in France	3	4
Producer Inflation in Germany	2	2
Producer Inflation in France	0	0
Nominal Interest Rate in Germany	3	4
Nominal Interest Rate in France	3	4

Chapter 3
Target Inflation and Required Money Growth

1. The Dynamic Model

The objective of the European central bank is to maintain price stability in Europe. Strictly speaking, the objective of the European central bank is to keep consumer inflation in Europe at target level. Let $\hat{J}_{12}$ denote the target rate of consumer inflation in Europe. The objective of the American central bank is to maintain price stability in America. Strictly speaking, the objective of the American central bank is to keep consumer inflation in America at target level. Let $\hat{J}_3$ denote the target rate of consumer inflation in America.

To illustrate the problem, consider a numerical example. Let target inflation in Europe be 1 percent, let output growth in Germany be 1 percent, let output growth in France be 3 percent, and let output growth in America be 2 percent. Then, what rate of money growth is required in Europe? Moreover, what is consumer inflation in Germany, and what is consumer inflation in France?

The consumer price index of Europe includes the consumer price index of Germany and the consumer price index of France. The consumer price index of Europe is defined as follows:

$$J_{12} = J_1^{\mu} J_2^{1-\mu} \tag{1}$$

Here J_1 symbolizes the consumer price index of Germany, as measured in euros. J_2 is the consumer price index of France, as measured in euros. μ is the share of German income $P_1 Y_1$ in European income $P_1 Y_1 + P_2 Y_2$, and $1 - \mu$ is the share of French income in European income. Then J_{12} is the consumer price index of Europe, as measured in euros. Of course, the consumer price index of Europe includes the price of German goods, the price of French goods, the price of American goods, and the price of the dollar.

Consumer inflation in Europe includes consumer inflation in Germany and consumer inflation in France. Consumer inflation in Europe is defined as:

$$\hat{J}_{12} = \mu\hat{J}_1 + (1-\mu)\hat{J}_2 \qquad (2)$$

$\hat{J}_1$ stands for consumer inflation in Germany, and $\hat{J}_2$ is consumer inflation in France. μ is the share of German income in European income, and $1-\mu$ is the share of French income in European income. Of course, consumer inflation in Europe includes producer inflation in Germany, producer inflation in France, producer inflation in America, and the appreciation of the dollar. Henceforth we assume that German income equals French income $P_1Y_1 = P_2Y_2$. That is to say, Germany and France are the same size. This implies $\mu = 0.5$ and $\hat{J}_{12} = 0.5\hat{J}_1 + 0.5\hat{J}_2$. The assumption we have just made will be relaxed below, see Chapter 4.

The model can be characterized by a system of eight equations:

$$\hat{P}_1 + \hat{Y}_1 = \hat{e} + \hat{P}_3 + \hat{Y}_3 \qquad (3)$$

$$\hat{M}_{12} = \hat{P}_1 + \hat{Y}_1 \qquad (4)$$

$$\hat{M}_{12} = \hat{P}_2 + \hat{Y}_2 \qquad (5)$$

$$\hat{M}_3 = \hat{P}_3 + \hat{Y}_3 \qquad (6)$$

$$\hat{J}_1 = \alpha\hat{P}_1 + \beta\hat{P}_2 + \gamma\hat{P}_3 + \gamma\hat{e} \qquad (7)$$

$$\hat{J}_2 = \alpha\hat{P}_2 + \beta\hat{P}_1 + \gamma\hat{P}_3 + \gamma\hat{e} \qquad (8)$$

$$\hat{J}_{12} = 0.5\hat{J}_1 + 0.5\hat{J}_2 \qquad (9)$$

$$\hat{J}_3 = (1-\gamma)\hat{P}_3 + 0.5\gamma\hat{P}_1 + 0.5\gamma\hat{P}_2 - \gamma\hat{e} \qquad (10)$$

Equation (3) is the goods market equation, (4) is the money market equation of Germany, (5) is the money market equation of France, (6) is the money market equation of America, (7) defines consumer inflation in Germany, (8) defines consumer inflation in France, (9) defines consumer inflation in Europe, and (10) defines consumer inflation in America. The exogenous variables are target inflation in Europe $\hat{J}_{12}$, target inflation in America $\hat{J}_3$, output growth in Germany $\hat{Y}_1$, output growth in France $\hat{Y}_2$, and output growth in America $\hat{Y}_3$. The endogenous variables are money growth in Europe $\hat{M}_{12}$, money growth in

America $\hat{M}_3$, nominal depreciation $\hat{e}$, producer inflation in Germany $\hat{P}_1$, producer inflation in France $\hat{P}_2$, producer inflation in America $\hat{P}_3$, consumer inflation in Germany $\hat{J}_1$, and consumer inflation in France $\hat{J}_2$.

2. Required Money Growth

Substitute equations (7) and (8) into equation (9):

$$\hat{J}_{12} = 0.5(\alpha + \beta)(\hat{P}_1 + \hat{P}_2) + \gamma(\hat{P}_3 + \hat{e}) \tag{11}$$

Now eliminate $\hat{P}_3 + \hat{e}$ by means of equation (3):

$$\hat{J}_{12} = 0.5(\alpha + \beta)(\hat{P}_1 + \hat{P}_2) + \gamma(\hat{P}_1 + \hat{Y}_1 - \hat{Y}_3) \tag{12}$$

Then get rid of $\hat{P}_1$ and $\hat{P}_2$ by making use of equations (4) and (5), respectively, and solve for:

$$\hat{M}_{12} = \hat{J}_{12} + 0.5(\alpha + \beta)(\hat{Y}_1 + \hat{Y}_2) + \gamma\hat{Y}_3 \tag{13}$$

As a result, this is the required rate of money growth in Europe. Obviously, required money growth in Europe depends on target inflation in Europe, on output growth in Germany, on output growth in France, and on output growth in America. However, it does not depend on target inflation in America. An increase in European target inflation calls for an increase in European money growth. An increase in German output growth calls for an increase in European money growth. Likewise, an increase in French output growth calls for an increase in European money growth. And what is more, an increase in American output growth calls for an increase in European money growth too.

What is the chain of cause and effect? An increase in European money growth raises consumer inflation in Germany and France, as was demonstrated above. An increase in German output growth lowers consumer inflation in both Germany and France. In order to prevent this, the European central bank has to raise its money growth. Similarly, an increase in French output growth lowers consumer inflation in both France and Germany. To prevent this, the European central bank has to raise its money growth. An increase in American output growth lowers consumer inflation in Germany and France. To counteract this, the European central bank has to raise its money growth.

To see this more clearly, have a look at some numerical examples. Let us begin with numerical example number one. Let target inflation in Europe be 1 percent, let output growth in Germany be 1 percent, let output growth in France be 3 percent, and let output growth in America be 2 percent. Besides, let the share of French goods in German consumption be 0.2, and let the share of American goods in German consumption be 0.1. Symmetrically, let the share of German goods in French consumption be 0.2, and let the share of American goods in French consumption be 0.1. Then, as a result, required money growth in Europe is 3 percent. Producer inflation in Germany is 2 percent, and producer inflation in France is 0 percent. Consumer inflation in Germany is 1.5 percent, consumer inflation in France is 0.5 percent, and consumer inflation in Europe is 1 percent. That means, consumer inflation in Europe is at target level. But, in a sense, consumer inflation in Germany is not at target level. And the same applies to consumer inflation in France.

We turn now to numerical example number two. Let target inflation in Europe be 1 percent, let output growth in Germany be 1 percent, let output growth in France be 3 percent, and let output growth in America be 3 percent (this being the only difference). In this case, required money growth in Europe is 3.1 percent. Table 17 gives an overview.

Table 17
Required Money Growth
Given Target Inflation and Output Growth

Target Inflation in Europe	1	1
Output Growth in Germany	1	1
Output Growth in France	3	3
Output Growth in America	2	3
Required Money Growth in Europe	3	3.1
Producer Inflation in Germany	2	2.1
Producer Inflation in France	0	0.1
Consumer Inflation in Germany	1.5	1.5
Consumer Inflation in France	0.5	0.5
Consumer Inflation in Europe	1	1

3. Wage Growth

This section deals with the growth of nominal wages, given productivity growth and labour growth. For the growth of producer real wages or consumer real wages see Chapter 2 above.

1) Productivity growth. The model can be represented by a system of three equations:

$$\hat{w}_1 = \hat{M}_{12} \tag{14}$$

$$\hat{w}_2 = \hat{M}_{12} \tag{15}$$

$$\hat{M}_{12} = \hat{J}_{12} + 0.5(\alpha + \beta)(\hat{a}_1 + \hat{a}_2) + \gamma \hat{a}_3 \tag{16}$$

Equations (14) and (15) come from Section 3.1 in Chapter 2. And equation (16) comes from Section 2 in Chapter 3. The exogenous variables are target inflation in Europe $\hat{J}_{12}$, productivity growth in Germany $\hat{a}_1$, productivity growth in France $\hat{a}_2$, and productivity growth in America $\hat{a}_3$. The endogenous variables are money growth in Europe $\hat{M}_{12}$, nominal wage growth in Germany $\hat{w}_1$, and nominal wage growth in France $\hat{w}_2$.

Comparing equations (14) and (15) gives at once:

$$\hat{w}_1 = \hat{w}_2 \tag{17}$$

As a first result, nominal wages in Germany and France grow at the same rate. This holds although Germany and France are allowed to differ in productivity growth.

Moreover, substituting equation (16) into equation (14) yields:

$$\hat{w}_1 = \hat{J}_{12} + 0.5(\alpha + \beta)(\hat{a}_1 + \hat{a}_2) + \gamma \hat{a}_3 \tag{18}$$

As a second result, nominal wage growth in Germany depends on target inflation in Europe, on productivity growth in Germany, on productivity growth in France, and on productivity growth in America. However, it does not depend on target inflation in America. An increase in European target inflation raises nominal wage growth in Germany. An increase in German productivity growth raises nominal wage growth in Germany. An increase in French productivity growth raises nominal wage growth in Germany. And an increase in American productivity growth has the same effect.

To illustrate this, consider a numerical example. Let target inflation in Europe be 1 percent, let productivity growth in Germany be 1 percent, let productivity growth in France be 3 percent, and let productivity growth in America be 2 percent. Further, let the share of French goods in German consumption be 0.2, and let the share of American goods in German consumption be 0.1. Symmetrically, let the share of German goods in French consumption be 0.2, and let the share of American goods in French consumption be 0.1.

Then, as a result, nominal wage growth in Germany is 3 percent. And nominal wage growth in France is equally 3 percent. An increase in European target inflation of 1 percentage point raises nominal wage growth in Germany by 1 percentage point. An increase in German productivity growth of 1 percentage point raises nominal wage growth in Germany by 0.45 percentage points. An increase in French productivity growth of 1 percentage point raises nominal wage growth in Germany by 0.45 percentage points. And an increase in American productivity growth of 1 percentage point raises nominal wage growth in Germany by 0.1 percentage points.

To sum up, nominal wage growth in Germany is determined by target inflation in Europe, by productivity growth in Germany, by productivity growth in France, and by productivity growth in America. This differs widely from the conclusions drawn under given money growth. There nominal wage growth in Germany was determined by money growth in Europe.

2) Labour growth. The model can be described by a system of three equations:

$$\hat{w}_1 = \hat{M}_{12} - \hat{N}_1 \tag{19}$$

$$\hat{w}_2 = \hat{M}_{12} - \hat{N}_2 \tag{20}$$

$$\hat{M}_{12} = \hat{J}_{12} + 0.5(\alpha + \beta)(\hat{N}_1 + \hat{N}_2) + \gamma\hat{N}_3 \tag{21}$$

Equations (19) and (20) come from Section 3.2 in Chapter 2. And equation (21) comes from Section 2 in Chapter 3. The exogenous variables are target inflation in Europe $\hat{J}_{12}$, labour growth in Germany $\hat{N}_1$, labour growth in France $\hat{N}_2$, and labour growth in America $\hat{N}_3$. The endogenous variables are money growth in Europe $\hat{M}_{12}$, nominal wage growth in Germany $\hat{w}_1$, and nominal wage growth in France $\hat{w}_2$.

This problem can be solved as follows:

$$\hat{w}_1 = \hat{J}_{12} - 0.5(1+\gamma)\hat{N}_1 + 0.5(\alpha+\beta)\hat{N}_2 + \gamma\hat{N}_3 \tag{22}$$

$$\hat{w}_2 = \hat{J}_{12} - 0.5(1+\gamma)\hat{N}_2 + 0.5(\alpha+\beta)\hat{N}_1 + \gamma\hat{N}_3 \tag{23}$$

As a finding, according to equation (22), nominal wage growth in Germany depends on target inflation in Europe, on labour growth in Germany, on labour growth in France, and on labour growth in America. But it does not depend on target inflation in America. An increase in European target inflation drives up nominal wage growth in Germany. An increase in German labour growth cuts down nominal wage growth in Germany. An increase in French labour growth drives up nominal wage growth in Germany. And an increase in American labour growth has the same effect. Similarly, according to equation (23), nominal wage growth in France is determined by target inflation in Europe, by labour growth in France, by labour growth in Germany, and by labour growth in America.

To see this more clearly, have a look at some numerical examples. Let us start with numerical example number one. Let target inflation in Europe be 1 percent, let labour growth in Germany be 1 percent, let labour growth in France be 3 percent, and let labour growth in America be 2 percent. Besides, let the share of French goods in German consumption be 0.2, let the share of American goods in German consumption be 0.1, and so on. Then, as a result, nominal wage growth in Germany is 2 percent. And nominal wage growth in France is 0 percent. In the country where labour growth is high, nominal wage growth will be low. And in the country where labour growth is low, nominal wage growth will be high.

An increase in European target inflation of 1 percentage point drives up nominal wage growth in Germany by 1 percentage point. An increase in German labour growth of 1 percentage point cuts down nominal wage growth in Germany by 0.55 percentage points. An increase in French labour growth of 1 percentage point drives up nominal wage growth in Germany by 0.45 percentage points. And an increase in American labour growth of 1 percentage point drives up nominal wage growth in Germany by 0.1 percentage points.

Let us proceed to numerical example number two. Let target inflation in Europe be 1 percent, let labour growth in Germany be −1 percent, let labour growth in France be 1 percent, and let labour growth in America be 0 percent. Then nominal wage growth in Germany is 2 percent, and nominal wage growth in France is 0 percent. Table 18 presents a synopsis.

To sum up, nominal wage growth in Germany is determined by target inflation in Europe, by labour growth in Germany, by labour growth in France, and by labour growth in America. This differs remarkably from the conclusions reached under given money growth. There nominal wage growth in Germany was determined by money growth in Europe and by labour growth in Germany.

Table 18
Wage Growth
Given Target Inflation, Productivity Growth, and Labour Growth

Target Inflation in Europe	1	1
Productivity Growth in Germany	1	0
Productivity Growth in France	3	0
Productivity Growth in America	2	0
Labour Growth in Germany	0	1
Labour Growth in France	0	3
Labour Growth in America	0	2
Growth of Nominal Wages in Germany	3	2
Growth of Nominal Wages in France	3	0
Growth of Producer Real Wages in Germany	1	0
Growth of Producer Real Wages in France	3	0
Growth of Consumer Real Wages in Germany	1.5	0.5
Growth of Consumer Real Wages in France	2.5	− 0.5

Chapter 4
The Union Countries Differ in Size

1) The static model. Assume that Germany is large and France is small. In terms of the model this means that the marginal import rate of Germany relative to France in small, and that the marginal import rate of France relative to Germany is large $m_1 < m_2$. Now $P_1 Y_1$ denotes German income as measured in euros, $P_2 Y_2$ is French income as measured in euros, $m_1 P_1 Y_1$ is German imports from France, and $m_2 P_2 Y_2$ is French imports from Germany.

Further, assume for the moment that the current account between Germany and France is balanced $m_1 P_1 Y_1 = m_2 P_2 Y_2$. This yields immediately:

$$\frac{P_1 Y_1}{P_2 Y_2} = \frac{m_2}{m_1} \tag{1}$$

To illustrate this, consider a numerical example. Let the marginal import rate of Germany relative to France be $m_1 = 0.1$, and let the marginal import rate of France relative to Germany be $m_2 = 0.2$. In this case we have $P_1 Y_1 = 2 P_2 Y_2$. That is to say, German income is twice as much as French income.

2) The dynamic model. Here the focus is on steady-state inflation in Germany, France and America, given steady-state growth. We assume that nominal wages and prices are flexible, hence there is always full employment in Germany, France and America. Along the same lines as in Chapter 2, the model can be represented by a system of four equations:

$$\hat{P}_1 + \hat{Y}_1 = \hat{e} + \hat{P}_3 + \hat{Y}_3 \tag{2}$$
$$\hat{M}_{12} = \hat{P}_1 + \hat{Y}_1 \tag{3}$$
$$\hat{M}_{12} = \hat{P}_2 + \hat{Y}_2 \tag{4}$$
$$\hat{M}_3 = \hat{P}_3 + \hat{Y}_3 \tag{5}$$

Equation (2) is the goods market equation, (3) is the money market equation of Germany, (4) is the money market equation of France, and (5) is the money market equation of America. The exogenous variables are money growth in Europe $\hat{M}_{12}$, money growth in America $\hat{M}_3$, output growth in Germany $\hat{Y}_1$, output growth in France $\hat{Y}_2$, and output growth in America $\hat{Y}_3$. The endogenous variables are producer inflation in Germany $\hat{P}_1$, producer inflation in France $\hat{P}_2$, producer inflation in America $\hat{P}_3$, and nominal depreciation $\hat{e}$.

3) Producer inflation and nominal depreciation. The solution to this problem is:

$$\hat{P}_1 = \hat{M}_{12} - \hat{Y}_1 \tag{6}$$

$$\hat{P}_2 = \hat{M}_{12} - \hat{Y}_2 \tag{7}$$

$$\hat{P}_3 = \hat{M}_3 - \hat{Y}_3 \tag{8}$$

$$\hat{e} = \hat{M}_{12} - \hat{M}_3 \tag{9}$$

According to equation (6), producer inflation in Germany is determined by money growth in Europe and by output growth in Germany. According to equation (9), the rate of depreciation is driven by money growth in Europe and by money growth in America.

For instance, let output growth in Germany be 1 percent, let output growth in France be 3 percent, let output growth in America be 2 percent, let money growth in Europe be 3 percent, and let money growth in America be 4 percent. Then producer inflation in Germany is 2 percent, producer inflation in France is 0 percent, producer inflation in America is 2 percent, the appreciation of the euro is 1 percent, and the depreciation of the dollar is 1 percent. All of this supports the conclusions drawn in Chapter 2 above. Put another way, the relative size of union countries does not matter here.

4) Consumer inflation. Consumer inflation in Germany is defined as:

$$\hat{J}_1 = \alpha_1 \hat{P}_1 + \beta_1 \hat{P}_2 + \gamma_1 \hat{P}_3 + \gamma_1 \hat{e} \tag{10}$$

α_1 symbolizes the share of German goods in German consumption, β_1 is the share of French goods in German consumption, and γ_1 is the share of American goods in German consumption, with $\alpha_1 + \beta_1 + \gamma_1 = 1$. Consumer inflation in France is defined as:

$$\hat{J}_2 = \alpha_2 \hat{P}_2 + \beta_2 \hat{P}_1 + \gamma_2 \hat{P}_3 + \gamma_2 \hat{e} \tag{11}$$

α_2 is the share of French goods in French consumption, β_2 is the share of German goods in French consumption, and γ_2 is the share of American goods in French consumption, with $\alpha_2 + \beta_2 + \gamma_2 = 1$. We still assume that Germany is large and France is small. In terms of the model this means that the share of French goods in German consumption is less than the share of German goods in French consumption $\beta_1 < \beta_2$ (and $\alpha_1 > \alpha_2$).

Now substitute equations (6), (7), (8) and (9) into equation (10) to check:

$$\hat{J}_1 = \hat{M}_{12} - \alpha_1 \hat{Y}_1 - \beta_1 \hat{Y}_2 - \gamma_1 \hat{Y}_3 \tag{12}$$

Obviously, consumer inflation in Germany is determined by money growth in Europe, by output growth in Germany, by output growth in France, and by output growth in America. By analogy, consumer inflation in France is:

$$\hat{J}_2 = \hat{M}_{12} - \alpha_2 \hat{Y}_2 - \beta_2 \hat{Y}_1 - \gamma_2 \hat{Y}_3 \tag{13}$$

To see this more clearly, have a look at a numerical example. Let output growth in Germany be 1 percent, let output growth in France be 3 percent, let output growth in America be 2 percent, and let money growth in Europe be 3 percent. Moreover, let the share of German goods in German consumption be 0.8, let the share of French goods in German consumption be 0.1, and let the share of American goods in German consumption be 0.1. Asymmetrically, let the share of French goods in French consumption be 0.7, let the share of German goods in French consumption be 0.2, and let the share of American goods in French consumption be 0.1. Then, as a result, consumer inflation in Germany is 1.7 percent, and consumer inflation in France is 0.5 percent. This differs from the conclusions drawn in Chapter 2 above. In other words, the relative size of union countries does matter here.

5) Target inflation and required money growth. Let $\hat{J}_{12}$ designate the target rate of consumer inflation in Europe. Consumer inflation in Europe is defined as:

$$\hat{J}_{12} = \mu\hat{J}_1 + (1-\mu)\hat{J}_2 \tag{14}$$

μ is the share of German income $P_1 Y_1$ in European income $P_1 Y_1 + P_2 Y_2$, and $1-\mu$ is the share of French income in European income. Henceforth let the share of German income be $\mu = 2/3$. The model can be described by a system of three equations:

$$\hat{J}_1 = \hat{M}_{12} - \alpha_1\hat{Y}_1 - \beta_1\hat{Y}_2 - \gamma_1\hat{Y}_3 \tag{15}$$

$$\hat{J}_2 = \hat{M}_{12} - \alpha_2\hat{Y}_2 - \beta_2\hat{Y}_1 - \gamma_2\hat{Y}_3 \tag{16}$$

$$\hat{J}_{12} = \frac{2}{3}\hat{J}_1 + \frac{1}{3}\hat{J}_2 \tag{17}$$

Equation (15) gives consumer inflation in Germany, (16) gives consumer inflation in France, and (17) defines consumer inflation in Europe. The exogenous variables are target inflation in Europe $\hat{J}_{12}$, output growth in Germany, output growth in France, and output growth in America. The endogenous variables are money growth in Europe, consumer inflation in Germany, and consumer inflation in France. Next eliminate $\hat{J}_1$ and $\hat{J}_2$ in equation (17), assume $\gamma = \gamma_1 = \gamma_2$, and solve for:

$$\hat{M}_{12} = \hat{J}_{12} + \frac{2\alpha_1 + \beta_2}{3}\hat{Y}_1 + \frac{\alpha_2 + 2\beta_1}{3}\hat{Y}_2 + \gamma\hat{Y}_3 \tag{18}$$

Evidently, required money growth in Europe is determined by target inflation in Europe, by output growth in Germany, by output growth in France, and by output growth in America.

To illustrate this, consider a numerical example. Let target inflation in Europe be 1 percent, let output growth in Germany be 1 percent, let output growth in France be 3 percent, and let output growth in America be 2 percent. Besides, let the share of German goods in German consumption be 0.8, and let the share of French goods in German consumption be 0.1. Asymmetrically, let the share of French goods in French consumption be 0.7, and let the share of German goods in French consumption be 0.2. Then, as a result, required money growth in Europe is 2.7 percent. Consumer inflation in Germany is 1.4 percent, consumer inflation in France is 0.2 percent, and consumer inflation in Europe is 1 percent. This differs from the conclusions drawn in Chapter 3 above. That means, the relative size of union countries does matter here.

Part Four

A One-Good Model
of the
World Economy

Chapter 1
The World of Two Monetary Regions

1. The Static Model

The world consists of two monetary regions, say Europe and America. The exchange rate between Europe and America is flexible. So far, in Parts Two and Three, we assumed that European goods and American goods were imperfect substitutes for each other. Now, in Part Four, we assume that there is a single good in the world economy. This good is produced in both Europe and America. Apart from this we take the same approach as before. Wages are flexible. European labour demand equals European labour supply. And American labour demand equals American labour supply. As a consequence, there is full employment in Europe and America. N_1 denotes European labour supply, and N_2 is American labour supply. European and American labour supply are given exogenously ($N_1 = \text{const}$, $N_2 = \text{const}$).

The static model can be characterized by a system of seven equations:

$$M_1 V_1 = P_1 Y_1 \tag{1}$$

$$M_2 V_2 = P_2 Y_2 \tag{2}$$

$$P_1 = e P_2 \tag{3}$$

$$Y_1 = a_1 N_1 \tag{4}$$

$$Y_2 = a_2 N_2 \tag{5}$$

$$w_1 = a_1 P_1 / g \tag{6}$$

$$w_2 = a_2 P_2 / g \tag{7}$$

Equation (1) is the quantity equation of Europe. M_1 symbolizes European money supply, as measured in euros. V_1 is the velocity of circulation in Europe. P_1 is the price of European goods, as measured in euros. And Y_1 is European output. It is assumed that, in the steady state, European velocity is constant.

Equation (2) is the quantity equation of America. M_2 is American money supply, as measured in dollars. V_2 is the velocity of circulation in America. P_2 is the price of American goods, as measured in dollars. And Y_2 is American output. It is assumed that, in the steady state, American velocity is constant.

Equation (3) is the law of one price. e is the exchange rate between the dollar and the euro. More exactly, e is the price of the dollar, as measured in euros. Then eP_2 is the price of American goods, as measured in euros. The message of equation (3) is that the price of European goods (as measured in euros) equals the price of American goods (as measured in euros). This is the outcome of arbitrage, given that European goods and American goods are perfect substitutes for each other. In fact, European goods and American goods are identical.

Equation (4) is the production function of Europe. It states that European output Y_1 depends on European labour supply N_1 and on European labour productivity a_1. Equation (5) is the production function of America. It states that American output Y_2 depends on American labour supply N_2 and on American labour productivity a_2. Equation (6) is the wage equation of Europe. w_1 stands for European nominal wages, and g is the markup factor. It is assumed that, in the steady state, the markup factor is constant. Equation (7) is the wage equation of America. w_2 designates American nominal wages.

The exogenous variables are European money supply M_1, American money supply M_2, European labour supply N_1, American labour supply N_2, European productivity a_1, and American productivity a_2. The endogenous variables are the price of European goods P_1, the price of American goods P_2, European nominal wages w_1, American nominal wages w_2, the exchange rate e, European output Y_1, and American output Y_2.

2. The Dynamic Model

Here the focus is on steady-state inflation in Europe and America, given steady-state growth. We assume that nominal wages and prices are flexible, so there is always full employment in Europe and America. To illustrate the problem, consider a numerical example. Let European output grow at a constant rate of 2 percent, let American output grow at a constant rate of 3 percent, let European money supply grow at a constant rate of 3 percent, and let American money supply grow at a constant rate of 5 percent. Then, at what rate does the price of European goods grow? At what rate does the price of American goods grow? At what rate does the price of the euro change? And at what rate does the price of the dollar change?

In the dynamic model, we make the following assumptions:

$$\hat{M}_1 = \text{const} \tag{1}$$

$$\hat{M}_2 = \text{const} \tag{2}$$

$$\hat{N}_1 = \text{const} \tag{3}$$

$$\hat{N}_2 = \text{const} \tag{4}$$

$$\hat{a}_1 = \text{const} \tag{5}$$

$$\hat{a}_2 = \text{const} \tag{6}$$

Equation (1) has it that European money supply grows at the constant rate $\hat{M}_1$. Equation (2) has it that American money supply grows at the constant rate $\hat{M}_2$. Equation (3) has it that European labour supply grows at the constant rate $\hat{N}_1$. Equation (4) has it that American labour supply grows at the constant rate $\hat{N}_2$. Equation (5) has it that European productivity grows at the constant rate $\hat{a}_1$. And equation (6) has it that American productivity grows at the constant rate $\hat{a}_2$.

On this foundation, the dynamic model can be characterized by a system of seven equations:

$$\hat{M}_1 = \hat{P}_1 + \hat{Y}_1 \tag{7}$$

$$\hat{M}_2 = \hat{P}_2 + \hat{Y}_2 \tag{8}$$

$$\hat{P}_1 = \hat{e} + \hat{P}_2 \tag{9}$$

$$\hat{Y}_1 = \hat{a}_1 + \hat{N}_1 \tag{10}$$

$$\hat{Y}_2 = \hat{a}_2 + \hat{N}_2 \tag{11}$$

$$\hat{w}_1 = \hat{a}_1 + \hat{P}_1 \tag{12}$$

$$\hat{w}_2 = \hat{a}_2 + \hat{P}_2 \tag{13}$$

Equation (7) is the money market equation of Europe, (8) is the money market equation of America, (9) is the law of one price, (10) is the production function of Europe, (11) is the production function of America, (12) is the wage equation of Europe, and (13) is the wage equation of America. The exogenous variables are money growth in Europe $\hat{M}_1$, money growth in America $\hat{M}_2$, labour growth in Europe $\hat{N}_1$, labour growth in America $\hat{N}_2$, productivity growth in Europe $\hat{a}_1$, and productivity growth in America $\hat{a}_2$. The endogenous variables are inflation in Europe $\hat{P}_1$, inflation in America $\hat{P}_2$, nominal depreciation $\hat{e}$, output growth in Europe $\hat{Y}_1$, output growth in America $\hat{Y}_2$, nominal wage growth in Europe $\hat{w}_1$, and nominal wage growth in America $\hat{w}_2$.

3. Inflation and Depreciation

The model can be reduced to a system of three equations:

$$\hat{M}_1 = \hat{P}_1 + \hat{Y}_1 \tag{1}$$

$$\hat{M}_2 = \hat{P}_2 + \hat{Y}_2 \tag{2}$$

$$\hat{P}_1 = \hat{e} + \hat{P}_2 \tag{3}$$

Here the exogenous variables are money growth in Europe, money growth in America, output growth in Europe, and output growth in America. The endogenous variables are inflation in Europe, inflation in America, and nominal depreciation. Obviously the solution is:

$$\hat{P}_1 = \hat{M}_1 - \hat{Y}_1 \tag{4}$$

$$\hat{P}_2 = \hat{M}_2 - \hat{Y}_2 \tag{5}$$

$$\hat{e} = \hat{P}_1 - \hat{P}_2 \tag{6}$$

$$\hat{e} = (\hat{M}_1 - \hat{M}_2) - (\hat{Y}_1 - \hat{Y}_2) \tag{7}$$

As a result, according to equation (4), inflation in Europe depends on money growth in Europe and on output growth in Europe. However, it does not depend on money growth in America or on output growth in America. According to equation (5), inflation in America is determined by money growth in America and by output growth in America. According to equation (6), the rate of depreciation is determined by inflation in Europe and by inflation in America. In the region where inflation is high, the currency will depreciate. And in the region where inflation is low, the currency will appreciate. To be more specific, if inflation in Europe is high, the euro will depreciate. And if inflation in Europe is low, the euro will appreciate. Correspondingly, if inflation in America is high, the dollar will depreciate. And if inflation in America is low, the dollar will appreciate.

According to equation (7), the rate of depreciation is determined by money growth in Europe, by money growth in America, by output growth in Europe, and by output growth in America. In the region where money growth is high, other things being equal, the currency will depreciate. And in the region where money growth is low, the currency will appreciate. In the region where output growth is high, other things being equal, the currency will appreciate. And in the region where output growth in low, the currency will depreciate.

To illustrate this, consider a numerical example. Let output growth in Europe be 2 percent, let output growth in America be 3 percent, let money growth in Europe be 3 percent, and let money growth in America be 5 percent. Then, as a result, inflation in Europe is 1 percent, inflation in America is 2 percent, the appreciation of the euro is 1 percent, and the depreciation of the dollar is 1 percent.

This is in sharp contrast to the conclusions drawn from the two-good model, see Part Two above. There, consumer inflation in Europe was determined by money growth in Europe, by output growth in Europe, and by output growth in America. Here, there is no difference between producer inflation and consumer inflation. There, the rate of depreciation was determined by money growth in Europe and by money growth in America. However, the rate of depreciation was not determined by output growth in Europe or by output growth in America. Likewise, the rate of depreciation was not determined by inflation in Europe or by inflation in America.

The last point refers to real depreciation. The real exchange rate is defined as the price of American goods, as measured in European goods $R = eP_2 / P_1$. Owing to the law of one price $P_1 = eP_2$, we get:

$$R = 1 \tag{8}$$

That is to say, the real exchange rate is constant. More precisely, there is no such thing as a real exchange rate.

4. Wage Growth

The solution to the full model presented in Section 1 is:

$$\hat{w}_1 = \hat{M}_1 - \hat{N}_1 \tag{1}$$
$$\hat{w}_2 = \hat{M}_2 - \hat{N}_2 \tag{2}$$
$$\hat{w}_1 - \hat{P}_1 = \hat{a}_1 \tag{3}$$
$$\hat{w}_2 - \hat{P}_2 = \hat{a}_2 \tag{4}$$

According to equation (1), nominal wage growth in Europe depends on money growth in Europe and on labour growth in Europe. However, it does not depend on productivity growth in Europe. According to equation (2), nominal wage growth in America is determined by money growth in America and by labour growth in America. According to equation (3), real wage growth in Europe depends on productivity growth in Europe. But it does not depend on labour growth in Europe. And according to equation (4), real wage growth in America is determined by productivity growth in America.

This is in remarkable contrast to the results obtained in the two-good model. There, the growth of consumer real wages in Europe was driven by productivity growth in Europe, by labour growth in Europe, by productivity growth in America, and by labour growth in America. Here, there is no difference between the growth of producer real wages and the growth of consumer real wages.

5. Nominal and Real Interest Rates

1) The model. The model can be captured by a system of six equations:

$$\hat{M}_1 = \hat{P}_1 + \hat{Y}_1 \tag{1}$$

$$\hat{M}_2 = \hat{P}_2 + \hat{Y}_2 \tag{2}$$

$$\hat{P}_1 = \hat{e} + \hat{P}_2 \tag{3}$$

$$i_1 = i_2 + \hat{e} \tag{4}$$

$$r_1 = i_1 - \hat{P}_1 \tag{5}$$

$$r_2 = i_2 - \hat{P}_2 \tag{6}$$

Equation (4) is the open interest parity. i_1 denotes the nominal interest rate in Europe, i_2 is the nominal interest rate in America, and $\hat{e}$ is the rate of depreciation. Equation (5) is the Fisher equation of Europe. r_1 symbolizes the real interest rate in Europe. The real interest rate in Europe is defined as the nominal interest rate in Europe minus inflation in Europe. Correspondingly, equation (6) is the Fisher equation of America. r_2 stands for the real interest rate in America. The exogenous variables are money growth in Europe, money growth in America, output growth in Europe, and output growth in America. The endogenous variables are the nominal interest rate in Europe, the nominal interest rate in America, the real interest rate in Europe, the real interest rate in America, inflation in Europe, inflation in America, and nominal depreciation.

2) Nominal interest rates. To begin with, the comparison of equations (3) and (4) yields:

$$i_1 - i_2 = \hat{P}_1 - \hat{P}_2 \tag{7}$$

As a result, the nominal interest differential is determined by the inflation differential. In the region where inflation is high, the nominal interest rate will be high. And in the region where inflation is low, the nominal interest rate will be low. This differs widely from the conclusions drawn in the two-good model.

Further, from equations (1), (2) and (3) it follows that $\hat{e} = (\hat{M}_1 - \hat{M}_2) - (\hat{Y}_1 - \hat{Y}_2)$. This together with equation (4) provides:

$$i_1 - i_2 = (\hat{M}_1 - \hat{M}_2) - (\hat{Y}_1 - \hat{Y}_2) \tag{8}$$

As a result, the nominal interest differential is determined by the money growth differential and by the output growth differential. In the region where money growth is high, other things being equal, the nominal interest rate will be high. And in the region where money growth is low, the nominal interest rate will be low. In the region where output growth is high, other things being equal, the nominal interest rate will be low. And in the region where output growth is low, the nominal interest rate will be high.

To see this more clearly, have a look at a numerical example. Let output growth in Europe be 2 percent, let output growth in America be 3 percent, let money growth in Europe be 3 percent, and let money growth in America be 5 percent. That means, inflation in Europe is 1 percent, and inflation in America is 2 percent. So the nominal interest rate in America exceeds the nominal interest rate in Europe by 1 percentage point.

This is in sharp contrast to the conclusions reached in the two-good model. There the nominal interest differential was determined by the money growth differential. However, it was not determined by the output growth differential. And it was not determined by the inflation differential either.

3) Real interest rates. Take the difference between equations (5) and (6) to find out $r_1 - r_2 = (i_1 - i_2) - (\hat{P}_1 - \hat{P}_2)$. From this together with equation (7) it can be derived that:

$$r_1 = r_2 \tag{9}$$

As a consequence, the real interest rate in Europe equals the real interest rate in America. This is in clear contrast to the results obtained in the two-good model. There the real interest differential was determined by the output growth differential.

6. Target Inflation and Required Money Growth

1) The model. The objective of the European central bank is to maintain price stability in Europe. Strictly speaking, the objective of the European central bank is to keep inflation in Europe at target level. Note that here there is no difference between producer inflation and consumer inflation. Let $\hat{P}_1$ designate the target rate of inflation in Europe. The objective of the American central bank is to maintain price stability in America. Strictly speaking, the objective of the American central bank is to keep inflation in America at target level. Let $\hat{P}_2$ designate the target rate of inflation in America.

To illustrate the problem, consider a numerical example. Let target inflation in Europe be 1 percent, let target inflation in America be 2 percent, let output growth in Europe be 2 percent, and let output growth in America be 3 percent. Then, what rate of money growth is required in Europe? And what rate of money growth is required in America? Moreover, what is the rate of depreciation?

The model can be characterized by a system of three equations:

$$\hat{M}_1 = \hat{P}_1 + \hat{Y}_1 \tag{1}$$

$$\hat{M}_2 = \hat{P}_2 + \hat{Y}_2 \tag{2}$$

$$\hat{P}_1 = \hat{e} + \hat{P}_2 \tag{3}$$

The exogenous variables are target inflation in Europe $\hat{P}_1$, target inflation in America $\hat{P}_2$, output growth in Europe $\hat{Y}_1$, and output growth in America $\hat{Y}_2$. The endogenous variables are money growth in Europe $\hat{M}_1$, money growth in America $\hat{M}_2$, and nominal depreciation $\hat{e}$.

2) Required money growth. As a result, according to equation (1), required money growth in Europe depends on target inflation in Europe and on output growth in Europe. However, it does not depend on target inflation in America or on output growth in America. According to equation (2), required money growth in America is determined by target inflation in America and by output growth in America. To see this more clearly, have a look at a numerical example. Let target inflation in Europe be 1 percent, let target inflation in America be 2 percent, let output growth in Europe be 2 percent, and let output growth in America be 3 percent. Then, as a result, required money growth in Europe is 3 percent. And required money growth in America is 5 percent.

This is in remarkable contrast to the conclusions drawn in the two-good model. There required money growth in Europe was determined by target inflation in Europe, by output growth in Europe, and by output growth in America.

3) Nominal depreciation. Equation (3) gives immediately:

$$\hat{e} = \hat{P}_1 - \hat{P}_2 \tag{4}$$

As a result, the rate of depreciation depends on target inflation in Europe and on target inflation in America. In the region where target inflation is high, the currency will depreciate. And in the region where target inflation is low, the currency will appreciate.

To be more explicit, if target inflation in Europe is high, the euro will depreciate. And if target inflation in Europe is low, the euro will appreciate. Correspondingly, if target inflation in America is high, the dollar will depreciate. And if target inflation in America is low, the dollar will appreciate. For instance, let target inflation in Europe be 1 percent, and let target inflation in America be 2 percent. Then the appreciation of the euro is 1 percent. In other words, the depreciation of the dollar is 1 percent.

This is in sharp contrast to the conclusions drawn from the two-good model. There the rate of depreciation was determined by target inflation in Europe, by target inflation in America, by output growth in Europe, and by output growth in America.

4) Nominal wage growth. The model can be condensed to a system of two equations:

$$\hat{w}_1 = \hat{P}_1 + \hat{a}_1 \tag{5}$$
$$\hat{w}_2 = \hat{P}_2 + \hat{a}_2 \tag{6}$$

As a result, according to equation (5), nominal wage growth in Europe is determined by target inflation in Europe and by productivity growth in Europe. According to equation (6), nominal wage growth in America is determined by target inflation in America and by productivity growth in America.

To illustrate this, consider a numerical example. Let target inflation in Europe be 1 percent, let target inflation in America be 2 percent, let productivity growth in Europe be 2 percent, and let productivity growth in America be 3 percent. Then nominal wage growth in Europe is 3 percent, and nominal wage growth in America is 5 percent.

To a certain extent, this differs from the results obtained in the two-good model. There, nominal wage growth in Europe was determined by target inflation in Europe, by productivity growth in Europe, and by productivity growth in America.

5) Nominal interest rates. The model can be compressed to a system of two equations:

$$\hat{P}_1 = \hat{e} + \hat{P}_2 \tag{7}$$
$$i_1 = i_2 + \hat{e} \tag{8}$$

This yields:

$$i_1 - i_2 = \hat{P}_1 - \hat{P}_2 \tag{9}$$

As a result, the nominal interest differential is determined by the target inflation differential. In the region where target inflation is high, the nominal interest rate will be high. And in the region where target inflation is low, the nominal interest rate will be low.

For instance, let target inflation in Europe be 1 percent, and let target inflation in America be 2 percent. Then the nominal interest rate in America exceeds the nominal interest rate in Europe by 1 percentage point. Again, this differs from the conclusions reached in the two-good model.

Chapter 2
The Monetary Union of Two Countries

1. The Static Model

The world consists of two monetary regions, say Europe and America. The exchange rate between Europe and America is flexible. Europe in turn consists of two countries, say Germany and France. Germany and France form a monetary union. There is only one good in the world economy. This good is produced in Germany, France and America. Wages are flexible. German labour demand equals German labour supply. French labour demand equals French labour supply. And American labour demand equals American labour supply. As a consequence, there is always full employment in Germany, France and America. N_1 denotes German labour supply, N_2 is French labour supply, and N_3 is American labour supply. German, French and American labour supply are given exogenously ($N_1 = \text{const}$, $N_2 = \text{const}$, $N_3 = \text{const}$).

The static model can be characterized by a system of six equations:

$$M_{12}V_{12} = P_1Y_1 + P_2Y_2 \tag{1}$$

$$P_1 = P_2 \tag{2}$$

$$Y_1 = a_1N_1 \tag{3}$$

$$Y_2 = a_2N_2 \tag{4}$$

$$w_1 = a_1P_1 / g \tag{5}$$

$$w_2 = a_2P_2 / g \tag{6}$$

Equation (1) is the quantity equation of Europe. M_{12} symbolizes European money supply, as measured in euros. V_{12} is the velocity of circulation in Europe. P_1 is the price of German goods, as measured in euros. P_2 is the price of French goods, as measured in euros. Y_1 is German output, and Y_2 is French output. It is assumed that, in the steady state, European velocity is constant. Equation (2) is the law of one price. The message of equation (2) is that the price of German goods (as measured in euros) is equal to the price of French goods (as measured in euros). This is the outcome of arbitrage, given that German goods and French goods are perfect substitutes for each other. In fact, German goods and French goods are identical.

Equation (3) is the production function of Germany. It states that German output Y_1 depends on German labour supply N_1 and on German labour productivity a_1. Equation (4) is the production function of France. It states that French output Y_2 depends on French labour supply N_2 and on French labour productivity a_2. Equation (5) is the wage equation of Germany. w_1 stands for German nominal wages, and g is the markup factor. It is assumed that, in the steady state, the markup factor is constant. Equation (6) is the wage equation of France. w_2 designates French nominal wages.

The exogenous variables are European money supply M_{12}, German labour supply N_1, French labour supply N_2, German productivity a_1, and French productivity a_2. The endogenous variables are the price of German goods P_1, the price of French goods P_2, German nominal wages w_1, French nominal wages w_2, German output Y_1, and French output Y_2.

2. The Dynamic Model

Here the focus is on steady-state inflation in Germany, France and America, given steady-state growth. We assume that nominal wages and prices are flexible, so there is always full employment in Germany, France and America. To illustrate the problem, consider a numerical example. Let German output grow at a constant rate of 1 percent, let French output grow at a constant rate of 3 percent, and let European money supply grow at a constant rate of 3 percent. Then, at what rate does the price of German goods grow? And at what rate does the price of French goods grow?

In the dynamic model, we make the following assumptions:

$$\hat{M}_{12} = \text{const} \tag{1}$$

$$\hat{N}_1 = \text{const} \tag{2}$$

$$\hat{N}_2 = \text{const} \tag{3}$$

$$\hat{a}_1 = \text{const} \tag{4}$$

$$\hat{a}_2 = \text{const} \tag{5}$$

Equation (1) has it that European money supply grows at the constant rate $\hat{M}_{12}$. Equation (2) has it that German labour supply grows at the constant rate $\hat{N}_1$. Equation (3) has it that French labour supply grows at the constant rate $\hat{N}_2$. Equation (4) has it that German productivity grows at the constant rate $\hat{a}_1$. And equation (5) has it that French productivity grows at the constant rate $\hat{a}_2$.

Now the static model will be reformulated in terms of growth rates. Let us begin with the money market equation:

$$\hat{M}_{12} = \frac{P_1 Y_1}{P_1 Y_1 + P_2 Y_2}(\hat{P}_1 + \hat{Y}_1) + \frac{P_2 Y_2}{P_1 Y_1 + P_2 Y_2}(\hat{P}_2 + \hat{Y}_2) \tag{6}$$

Here $P_1 Y_1 / (P_1 Y_1 + P_2 Y_2)$ is the share of German income in European income. And $P_2 Y_2 / (P_1 Y_1 + P_2 Y_2)$ is the share of French income in European income. Next take account of the law of one price:

$$\hat{M}_{12} = \frac{Y_1}{Y_1 + Y_2}(\hat{P}_1 + \hat{Y}_1) + \frac{Y_2}{Y_1 + Y_2}(\hat{P}_2 + \hat{Y}_2) \tag{7}$$

Here $Y_1 / (Y_1 + Y_2)$ is the share of German output in European output And $Y_2 / (Y_1 + Y_2)$ is the share of French output in European output.

On this foundation, the dynamic model can be characterized by a system of six equations:

$$\hat{M}_{12} = \frac{Y_1}{Y_1 + Y_2}(\hat{P}_1 + \hat{Y}_1) + \frac{Y_2}{Y_1 + Y_2}(\hat{P}_2 + \hat{Y}_2) \tag{8}$$

$$\hat{P}_1 = \hat{P}_2 \tag{9}$$

$$\hat{Y}_1 = \hat{a}_1 + \hat{N}_1 \tag{10}$$

$$\hat{Y}_2 = \hat{a}_2 + \hat{N}_2 \tag{11}$$

$$\hat{w}_1 = \hat{a}_1 + \hat{P}_1 \tag{12}$$

$$\hat{w}_2 = \hat{a}_2 + \hat{P}_2 \tag{13}$$

Equation (8) is the money market equation of Europe. (9) is the law of one price. (10) is the production function of Germany. (11) is the production function of France. (12) is the wage equation of Germany. And (13) is the wage equation of France. The exogenous variables are money growth in Europe $\hat{M}_{12}$, labour growth in Germany $\hat{N}_1$, labour growth in France $\hat{N}_2$, productivity growth in Germany $\hat{a}_1$, and productivity growth in France $\hat{a}_2$. The endogenous variables are inflation in Germany $\hat{P}_1$, inflation in France $\hat{P}_2$, output growth in Germany $\hat{Y}_1$, output growth in France $\hat{Y}_2$, nominal wage growth in Germany $\hat{w}_1$, and nominal wage growth in France $\hat{w}_2$.

3. Given Money Growth

The model can be reduced to a system of two equations:

$$\hat{M}_{12} = \frac{Y_1}{Y_1 + Y_2}(\hat{P}_1 + \hat{Y}_1) + \frac{Y_2}{Y_1 + Y_2}(\hat{P}_2 + \hat{Y}_2) \tag{1}$$

$$\hat{P}_1 = \hat{P}_2 \tag{2}$$

Here the exogenous variables are money growth in Europe, output growth in Germany, and output growth in France. The endogenous variables are inflation in Germany and inflation in France.

As a first result, according to equation (2), inflation in Germany equals inflation in France. This differs substantially from the conclusions drawn in the three-good model, see Part Three above. Now eliminate $\hat{P}_2$ in equation (1) with the help of equation (2) and solve for:

$$\hat{P}_1 = \hat{M}_{12} - \frac{Y_1}{Y_1 + Y_2}\hat{Y}_1 - \frac{Y_2}{Y_1 + Y_2}\hat{Y}_2 \tag{3}$$

According to equation (3), inflation in Germany is determined by money growth in Europe, by output growth in Germany, and by output growth in France. An increase in European money growth raises German inflation. On the other hand, an increase in German output growth lowers German inflation. And what is more, an increase in French output growth lowers German inflation too.

It is worth pointing out that here the rate of inflation in Germany is not constant. Rather, over time, the rate of inflation in Germany goes down. The reason for this is that, over time, the rate of output growth in Europe goes up. For instance, let German output growth fall short of French output growth (that is $\hat{Y}_1 < \hat{Y}_2$). Then the rate of inflation in Germany converges to $\hat{M}_{12} - \hat{Y}_2$ from above. Figure 1 shows the time path of inflation in Germany.

To see this more clearly, have a look at a numerical example. Let output growth in Germany be 1 percent, let output growth in France be 3 percent, let the initial share of German output in European output be 0.5, and let money growth in Europe be 3 percent. Then, as a result, inflation in Germany is 1 percent. And inflation in France is equally 1 percent. Over time, the rate of inflation in Europe goes down, converging to zero percent.

This is in sharp contrast to the conclusions drawn in the three-good model. There, inflation in Germany generally differed from inflation in France. Producer inflation in Germany was determined by money growth in Europe and by output growth in Germany. Consumer inflation in Germany was determined by money growth in Europe, by output growth in Germany, by output growth in France, and by output growth in America. The rate of producer inflation was constant, as was the rate of consumer inflation.

176

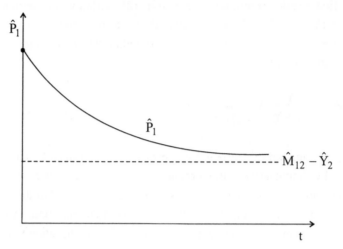

Figure 1
Inflation in Germany
(Given Money Growth and Output Growth)

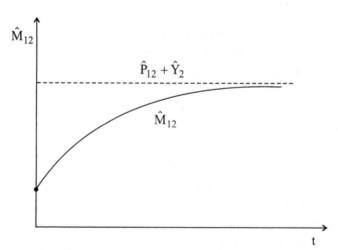

Figure 2
Required Money Growth in Europe
(Given Target Inflation and Output Growth)

4. Target Inflation and Required Money Growth

The objective of the European central bank is to maintain price stability in Europe. Strictly speaking, the objective of the European central bank is to keep inflation in Europe at target level. Let $\hat{P}_{12}$ designate the target rate of inflation in Europe. To illustrate the problem, consider a numerical example. Let target inflation in Europe be 1 percent, let output growth in Germany be 1 percent, and let output growth in France be 3 percent. Then, what rate of money growth is required in Europe?

Starting from equations (1), (2) and (3) in the previous section, the model can be condensed to a single equation:

$$\hat{M}_{12} = \hat{P}_{12} + \frac{Y_1}{Y_1 + Y_2}\hat{Y}_1 + \frac{Y_2}{Y_1 + Y_2}\hat{Y}_2 \tag{1}$$

Here the exogenous variables are target inflation in Europe $\hat{P}_{12}$, output growth in Germany $\hat{Y}_1$, and output growth in France $\hat{Y}_2$. The endogenous variable is money growth in Europe $\hat{M}_{12}$.

As a result, according to equation (1), required money growth in Europe is determined by target inflation in Europe, by output growth in Germany, and by output growth in France. For instance, let target inflation in Europe be 1 percent, let output growth in Germany be 1 percent, let output growth in France be 3 percent, and let the initial share of German output in European output be 0.5. Then required money growth in Europe is 3 percent. Over time, the required rate of money growth in Europe goes up, converging to 4 percent. Figure 2 shows the time path of required money growth in Europe.

This is in remarkable contrast to the conclusions reached in the three-good model. There, required money growth in Europe was determined by target inflation in Europe, by output growth in Germany, by output growth in France, and by output growth in America. In addition, the required rate of money growth in Europe was constant.

Part Five

Microfoundations
for a
Monetary Union

Chapter 1
The World of Two Monetary Regions

1. The Approach

The world consists of two monetary regions, say Europe and America. The exchange rate between Europe and America can be flexible or fixed. The monetary regions are completely specialized in production. Europe produces European goods, while America produces American goods. European goods and American goods are imperfect substitutes in consumption. The monetary regions are the same size and have the same behavioural functions. This assumption will be relaxed below, see Chapter 2.

European households consume both European goods and American goods. European households maximize utility subject to the budget constraint. The exogenous variables are European income, the price of European goods, the price of American goods, and the price of the dollar. The endogenous variables are the European consumption of European goods and the European consumption of American goods. Then what are the demand functions of European households?

American households consume both American goods and European goods. American households maximize utility subject to the budget constraint. The exogenous variables are American income, the price of American goods, the price of European goods, and the price of the euro. The endogenous variables are the American consumption of American goods and the American consumption of European goods. Then what are the demand functions of American households?

Next have a look at the market for European goods. European output is determined by the European consumption of European goods, by the American consumption of European goods, and by the autonomous demand for European goods. That is, European output is determined by the autonomous demand for European goods, by American income, by the price of European goods, by the price of American goods, and by the price of the euro.

Besides have a look at the market for American goods. American output is determined by the American consumption of American goods, by the European consumption of American goods, and by the autonomous demand for American goods. That is, American output is determined by the autonomous demand for American goods, by European income, by the price of American goods, by the price of European goods, and by the price of the dollar.

Further topics are:
- a first model of Europe and America
- the consumption, export and import functions of Europe
- the consumption, export and import functions of America
- a second model of Europe and America.

2. The Demand Functions of European Households

The utility function of European households is:

$$U_1 = \alpha \log C_{11} + \beta \log C_{12} + \gamma \log S_1 \tag{1}$$

Here C_{11} denotes the European consumption of European goods, as measured in European goods. C_{12} is the European consumption of American goods, as measured in American goods. S_1 is European savings, as measured in European goods. U_1 is European utility. α, β and γ are positive constants with $\alpha + \beta + \gamma = 1$.

The budget constraint of European households is:

$$P_1 Y_1 = P_1 C_{11} + e P_2 C_{12} + P_1 S_1 \tag{2}$$

Y_1 symbolizes European income, as measured in European goods. P_1 is the price of European goods, as measured in euros. P_2 is the price of American goods, as measured in dollars. e is the exchange rate between the dollar and the euro. More exactly, e is the price of the dollar, as measured in euros. Then eP_2 is the price of American goods, as measured in euros. P_1Y_1 is European income, as measured in euros. P_1C_{11} is the European consumption of European goods, as measured in euros. eP_2C_{12} is the European consumption of American goods, as measured in euros. And P_1S_1 is European savings, as measured in euros. According to the budget constraint, an increase in the price of European goods causes an increase in European income, as measured in euros. This is in sharp contrast to the assumptions made in standard microeconomic analysis.

European households maximize utility subject to the budget constraint. The exogenous variables are European income Y_1, the price of European goods P_1, the price of American goods P_2, and the price of the dollar e. The endogenous variables are the European consumption of European goods C_{11}, the European consumption of American goods C_{12}, and European savings S_1. The Lagrangian of this problem is:

$$L_1 = \alpha \log C_{11} + \beta \log C_{12} + \gamma \log S_1 + \lambda(P_1C_{11} + eP_2C_{12} + P_1S_1 - P_1Y_1) \quad (3)$$

The first-order conditions for maximizing the Lagrangian are:

$$\frac{\partial L_1}{\partial C_{11}} = \frac{\alpha}{C_{11}} + \lambda P_1 = 0 \quad (4)$$

$$\frac{\partial L_1}{\partial C_{12}} = \frac{\beta}{C_{12}} + \lambda eP_2 = 0 \quad (5)$$

$$\frac{\partial L_1}{\partial S_1} = \frac{\gamma}{S_1} + \lambda P_1 = 0 \quad (6)$$

The first-order conditions together with the budget constraint yield the shares of expenditures in income:

$$P_1C_{11} = \alpha P_1 Y_1 \quad (7)$$
$$eP_2C_{12} = \beta P_1 Y_1 \quad (8)$$
$$P_1S_1 = \gamma P_1 Y_1 \quad (9)$$

From this, the demand functions of European households can be derived immediately:

$$C_{11} = \alpha Y_1 \tag{10}$$

$$C_{12} = \beta P_1 Y_1 / e P_2 \tag{11}$$

$$S_1 = \gamma Y_1 \tag{12}$$

Equation (10) gives the European consumption of European goods. As a result, an increase in European income, as measured in European goods, causes a proportionate increase in the European consumption of European goods. However, an increase in the price of European goods has no effect on the European consumption of European goods. That means, in this case, the own price elasticity of demand is zero. This differs widely from standard microeconomic analysis. There the own price elasticity of demand is −1. The underlying reason is that here an increase in the price of European goods causes a proportionate increase in European income, as measured in euros. Moreover, an increase in the price of American goods has no effect on the European consumption of European goods. That is to say, in this case, the cross price elasticity of demand is zero. This is well in line with standard microeconomic analysis. Likewise, an appreciation of the dollar has no effect on the European consumption of European goods.

Equation (11) gives the European consumption of American goods. As a result, a 1 percent increase in European income, as measured in European goods, causes a 1 percent increase in the European consumption of American goods. A 1 percent increase in the price of European goods causes a 1 percent increase in the European consumption of American goods. That is to say, in this case, the cross price elasticity of demand is 1. This differs from standard microeconomic analysis. There the cross price elasticity of demand is zero. Again, the underlying reason is that a 1 percent increase in the price of European goods causes a 1 percent increase in European income, as measured in euros. Further, a 1 percent increase in the price of American goods causes a 1 percent decline in the European consumption of American goods. That means, in this case, the own price elasticity of demand is −1. This is in line with standard microeconomic analysis. Similarly, a 1 percent appreciation of the dollar causes a 1 percent decline in the European consumption of American goods.

Equation (12) gives European savings. As a result, an increase in European income (as measured in European goods) causes a proportionate increase in European savings (as measured in European goods). An increase in the price of European goods has no effect on European savings. An increase in the price of American goods has no effect on European savings either. And the same holds for an appreciation of the dollar.

3. The Demand Functions of American Households

The utility function of American households is:

$$U_2 = \alpha \log C_{22} + \beta \log C_{21} + \gamma \log S_2 \tag{1}$$

Here C_{22} stands for the American consumption of American goods, as measured in American goods. C_{21} is the American consumption of European goods, as measured in European goods. S_2 is American savings, as measured in American goods. And U_2 is American utility.

The budget constraint of American households is:

$$P_2 Y_2 = P_2 C_{22} + P_1 C_{21} / e + P_2 S_2 \tag{2}$$

Y_2 designates American income, as measured in American goods. $1/e$ is the price of the euro, as measured in dollars. Then P_1 / e is the price of European goods, as measured in dollars. $P_2 Y_2$ is American income, as measured in dollars. $P_2 C_{22}$ is the American consumption of American goods, as measured in dollars. $P_1 C_{21} / e$ is the American consumption of European goods, as measured in dollars. $P_2 S_2$ is American savings, as measured in dollars. According to the budget constraint, an increase in the price of American goods causes an increase in American income, as measured in dollars. This is in remarkable contrast to the assumptions made in standard microeconomic analysis.

American households maximize utility subject to the budget constraint. The exogenous variables are American income Y_2, the price of American goods P_2, the price of European goods P_1, and the price of the euro $1/e$. The endogenous variables are the American consumption of American goods C_{22}, the American consumption of European goods C_{21}, and American savings S_2. The Lagrangian of this problem is:

$$L_2 = \alpha \log C_{22} + \beta \log C_{21} + \gamma \log S_2 + \lambda(P_2 C_{22} + P_1 C_{21}/e + P_2 S_2 - P_2 Y_2)$$

(3)

The first-order conditions for maximizing the Lagrangian are:

$$\frac{\partial L_2}{\partial C_{22}} = \frac{\alpha}{C_{22}} + \lambda P_2 = 0$$

(4)

$$\frac{\partial L_2}{\partial C_{21}} = \frac{\beta}{C_{21}} + \lambda P_1/e = 0$$

(5)

$$\frac{\partial L_2}{\partial S_2} = \frac{\gamma}{S_2} + \lambda P_2 = 0$$

(6)

The first-order conditions together with the budget constraint provide the shares of expenditures in income:

$$P_2 C_{22} = \alpha P_2 Y_2$$

(7)

$$P_1 C_{21}/e = \beta P_2 Y_2$$

(8)

$$P_2 S_2 = \gamma P_2 Y_2$$

(9)

From this, the demand functions of American households can be obtained at once:

$$C_{22} = \alpha Y_2$$

(10)

$$C_{21} = \beta e P_2 Y_2 / P_1$$

(11)

$$S_2 = \gamma Y_2$$

(12)

Equation (10) gives the American consumption of American goods. As an outcome, an increase in American income, as measured in American goods, causes a proportionate increase in the American consumption of American goods. However, an increase in the price of American goods has no effect on the American consumption of American goods. The reason for this is that an increase in the price of American goods causes a proportionate increase in American income, as measured in dollars. Moreover, an increase in the price of European goods has no effect on the American consumption of American goods either. Likewise, an appreciation of the euro has no effect on the American consumption of American goods.

Equation (11) gives the American consumption of European goods. As an outcome, a 1 percent increase in American income, as measured in American goods, causes a 1 percent increase in the American consumption of European goods. A 1 percent increase in the price of American goods causes a 1 percent increase in the American consumption of European goods. This differs clearly from standard microeconomic analysis. Again, the reason for this is that a 1 percent increase in the price of American goods causes a 1 percent increase in American income, as measured in dollars. Further, a 1 percent increase in the price of European goods causes a 1 percent decline in the American consumption of European goods. Similarly, a 1 percent appreciation of the euro causes a 1 percent decline in the American consumption of European goods.

Equation (12) gives American savings. As an outcome, an increase in American income (as measured in American goods) causes a proportionate increase in American savings (as measured in American goods). An increase in the price of American goods has no effect on American savings. An increase in the price of European goods has no effect on American savings either. And the same holds for an appreciation of the euro.

4. The Market for European Goods

According to Sections 2 and 3, the demand functions for European goods are:

$$C_{11} = \alpha Y_1 \tag{1}$$

$$C_{21} = \beta e P_2 Y_2 / P_1 \tag{2}$$

$$A_1 = \text{const} \tag{3}$$

Equation (1) gives the European consumption of European goods. Equation (2) gives the American consumption of European goods. And equation (3) gives the autonomous demand for European goods, think for instance of investment or government purchases.

European output Y_1 is determined by the demand for European goods:

$$Y_1 = A_1 + C_{11} + C_{21} \tag{4}$$

Taking account of the demand functions (1) until (3), we arrive at the goods market equation of Europe:

$$Y_1 = A_1 + \alpha Y_1 + \beta e P_2 Y_2 / P_2 \tag{5}$$

As a result, European output is determined by the autonomous demand for European goods, by American income, by the price of European goods, by the price of American goods, and by the price of the euro. An increase in the autonomous demand for European goods raises European output. An increase in American income raises European output. An increase in the price of European goods lowers European output. An increase in the price of American goods raises European output. And an appreciation of the euro lowers European output.

5. The Market for American Goods

According to Sections 2 and 3, the demand functions for American goods are:

$$C_{22} = \alpha Y_2 \tag{1}$$

$$C_{12} = \beta P_1 Y_1 / e P_2 \tag{2}$$

$$A_2 = \text{const} \tag{3}$$

Equation (1) gives the American consumption of American goods. Equation (2) gives the European consumption of American goods. And equation (3) gives the autonomous demand for American goods, think for example of investment or government purchases.

American output Y_2 is determined by the demand for American goods:

$$Y_2 = A_2 + C_{22} + C_{12} \tag{4}$$

Upon substituting the demand functions (1) until (3), we reach the goods market equation of America:

$$Y_2 = A_2 + \alpha Y_2 + \beta P_1 Y_1 / e P_2 \tag{5}$$

As a result, American output is determined by the autonomous demand for American goods, by European income, by the price of American goods, by the price of European goods, and by the price of the dollar. An increase in the autonomous demand for American goods raises American output. An increase in European income raises American output. An increase in the price of American goods lowers American output. An increase in the price of European goods raises American output. And an appreciation of the dollar lowers American output.

6. A First Model of Europe and America

According to Sections 4 and 5, the model can be represented by a system of two equations:

$$Y_1 = A_1 + \alpha Y_1 + \beta e P_2 Y_2 / P_1 \tag{1}$$

$$Y_2 = A_2 + \alpha Y_2 + \beta P_1 Y_1 / e P_2 \tag{2}$$

Equation (1) is the goods market equation of Europe, as measured in European goods. And equation (2) is the goods market equation of America, as measured in American goods. Here the exogenous variables are the autonomous demand for European goods A_1, the autonomous demand for American goods A_2, the price of European goods P_1, the price of American goods P_2, and the price of the dollar e. The endogenous variables are European output Y_1 and American output Y_2.

An increase in the autonomous demand for European goods raises European output and, hence, American output. An increase in the price of European goods lowers European output but raises American output. Likewise, an appreciation of the euro lowers European output but raises American output. Besides, according to equations (1) and (2), if $P_1 A_1 = e P_2 A_2$, then $P_1 Y_1 = e P_2 Y_2$. That means, if the autonomous demand for European goods (as measured in euros) equals the autonomous demand for American goods (as measured in euros), then European income (as measured in euros) will equal American income (as measured in euros).

7. The Consumption, Export and Import Functions of Europe

European output is determined by the demand for European goods $Y_1 = A_1 + C_{11} + C_{21}$, as is well known. This equation can be rewritten as follows:

$$P_1Y_1 = P_1A_1 + (P_1C_{11} + eP_2C_{12}) + P_1C_{21} - eP_2C_{12} \tag{1}$$

Here $(P_1C_{11} + eP_2C_{12})$ is European consumption, as measured in euros. It includes both European goods and American goods. P_1C_{21} is European exports, as measured in euros. And eP_2C_{12} is European imports, as measured in euros.

Moreover, it proves useful to measure European consumption, European exports and European imports in terms of European goods. $C_{11} + eP_2C_{12} / P_1$ is European consumption, as measured in European goods. Of course, European consumption still consists of European goods and American goods. Let C_1 denote European consumption, as measured in European goods:

$$C_1 = C_{11} + eP_2C_{12} / P_1 \tag{2}$$

C_{21} is European exports, as measured in European goods. Of course, European exports consist of European goods. Let X_1 denote European exports, as measured in European goods:

$$X_1 = C_{21} \tag{3}$$

And eP_2C_{12} / P_1 is European imports, as measured in European goods. Of course, European imports consist of American goods. Let Q_1 denote European imports, as measured in European goods:

$$Q_1 = eP_2C_{12} / P_1 \tag{4}$$

Now insert equations (2), (3) and (4) in equation (1) to verify:

$$Y_1 = A_1 + C_1 + X_1 - Q_1 \tag{5}$$

That is to say, the market for European goods is in equilibrium if European output equals the autonomous demand for European goods plus European consumption plus European exports minus European imports.

According to Sections 2 and 3, the relevant demand functions are:

$$C_{11} = \alpha Y_1 \tag{6}$$
$$C_{12} = \beta P_1 Y_1 / e P_2 \tag{7}$$
$$C_{21} = \beta e P_2 Y_2 / P_1 \tag{8}$$

Next put those demand functions into equations (2), (3) and(4):

$$C_1 = (\alpha + \beta) Y_1 \tag{9}$$
$$X_1 = \beta e P_2 Y_2 / P_1 \tag{10}$$
$$Q_1 = \beta Y_1 \tag{11}$$

As a result, equation (9) is the consumption function of Europe, (10) is the export function of Europe, and (11) is the import function of Europe.

Equation (9) gives European consumption, as measured in European goods. As a finding, European consumption (as measured in European goods) is proportional to European income (as measured in European goods). However, European consumption (as measured in European goods) does not depend on the price of European goods, on the price of American goods, or on the price of the dollar. An increase in the price of European goods has no effect on European consumption (as measured in European goods). An increase in the price of American goods has no effect on European consumption (as measured in European goods). And an appreciation of the dollar has no effect on European consumption (as measured in European goods).

Equation (10) gives European exports, as measured in European goods. As a finding, European exports are an increasing function of American income. A 1 percent increase in American income, as measured in American goods, causes a 1 percent increase in European exports. A 1 percent increase in the price of American goods causes a 1 percent increase in European exports. The reason for this effect is that a 1 percent increase in the price of American goods causes a 1 percent increase in American income, as measured in dollars. A 1 percent increase in the price of European goods causes a 1 percent decline in European exports. And a 1 percent appreciation of the euro causes a 1 percent decline in European exports.

Equation (11) gives European imports, as measured in European goods. As a finding, European imports (as measured in European goods) are proportional to European income (as measured in European goods). However, European imports (as measured in European goods) do not depend on the price of American goods, on the price of the dollar, or on the price of European goods. An increase in the price of American goods has no effect on European imports (as measured in European goods). An appreciation of the dollar has no effect on European imports (as measured in European goods). And an increase in the price of European goods has no effect on European imports (as measured in European goods).

Finally the consumption, export and import functions of Europe can be restated as follows:

$$C_1 = cY_1 \tag{12}$$

$$X_1 = qeP_2 Y_2 / P_1 \tag{13}$$

$$Q_1 = qY_1 \tag{14}$$

Here $c = \alpha + \beta$ is the marginal consumption rate, and $q = \beta$ is the marginal import rate. Equation (12) is the consumption function of Europe, (13) is the export function of Europe, and (14) is the import function of Europe. European output is determined by the demand for European goods $Y_1 = A_1 + C_1 + X_1 - Q_1$. Taking account of the consumption, export and import functions of Europe, we arrive at the goods market equation of Europe:

$$Y_1 = A_1 + cY_1 + qeP_2 Y_2 / P_1 - qY_1 \tag{15}$$

8. The Consumption, Export and Import Functions of America

American output is determined by the demand for American goods $Y_2 = A_2 + C_{22} + C_{12}$, as is well known. This equation can be rewritten as follows:

$$P_2 Y_2 = P_2 A_2 + (P_2 C_{22} + P_1 C_{21} / e) + P_2 C_{12} - P_1 C_{21} / e \tag{1}$$

Here $(P_2 C_{22} + P_1 C_{21} / e)$ is American consumption, as measured in dollars. It includes both American goods and European goods. $P_2 C_{12}$ is American exports, as measured in dollars. And $P_1 C_{21} / e$ is American imports, as measured in dollars.

Further, it proves useful to measure American consumption, American exports and American imports in terms of American goods. $C_{22} + P_1 C_{21} / e P_2$ is American consumption, as measured in American goods. Of course, American consumption still consists of American goods and European goods. Let C_2 denote American consumption, as measured in American goods:

$$C_2 = C_{22} + P_1 C_{21} / e P_2 \tag{2}$$

C_{12} is American exports, as measured in American goods. Of course, American exports consist of American goods. Let X_2 denote American exports, as measured in American goods:

$$X_2 = C_{12} \tag{3}$$

And $P_1 C_{21} / e P_2$ is American imports, as measured in American goods. Of course, American imports consist of European goods. Let Q_2 denote American imports, as measured in American goods:

$$Q_2 = P_1 C_{21} / e P_2 \tag{4}$$

Now insert equations (2), (3) and (4) in equation (1) to check:

$$Y_2 = A_2 + C_2 + X_2 - Q_2 \tag{5}$$

That means, the market for American goods is in equilibrium if American output equals the autonomous demand for American goods plus American consumption plus American exports minus American imports.

According to Sections 2 and 3, the relevant demand functions are:

$$C_{22} = \alpha Y_2 \tag{6}$$

$$C_{21} = \beta e P_2 Y_2 / P_1 \tag{7}$$

$$C_{12} = \beta P_1 Y_1 / e P_2 \tag{8}$$

Next put those demand functions into equations (2), (3) and (4):

$$C_2 = (\alpha + \beta) Y_2 \tag{9}$$

$$X_2 = \beta P_1 Y_1 / e P_2 \tag{10}$$

$$Q_2 = \beta Y_2 \tag{11}$$

As a result, equation (9) is the consumption function of America, (10) is the export function of America, and (11) is the import function of America.

Equation (9) gives American consumption, as measured in American goods. As a finding, American consumption (as measured in American goods) is proportional to American income (as measured in American goods). However, American consumption (as measured in American goods) does not depend on the price of American goods, on the price of European goods, or on the price of the euro. An increase in the price of American goods has no effect on American consumption (as measured in American goods). An increase in the price of European goods has no effect on American consumption (as measured in American goods). And an appreciation of the euro has no effect on American consumption (as measured in American goods).

Equation (10) gives American exports, as measured in American goods. As a finding, American exports are an increasing function of European income. A 1 percent increase in European income, as measured in European goods, causes a 1 percent increase in American exports. A 1 percent increase in the price of European goods causes a 1 percent increase in American exports. The reason for this effect is that a 1 percent increase in the price of European goods causes a 1 percent increase in European income, as measured in euros. A 1 percent increase in the price of American goods causes a 1 percent decline in American exports. And a 1 percent appreciation of the dollar causes a 1 percent decline in American exports.

Equation (11) gives American imports, as measured in American goods. As a finding, American imports (as measured in American goods) are proportional to American income (as measured in American goods). However, American imports (as measured in American goods) do not depend on the price of European goods, on the price of the euro, or on the price of American goods. An increase in the price of European goods has no effect on American imports (as measured in American goods). An appreciation of the euro has no effect on American imports (as measured in American goods). And an increase in the price of American goods has no effect on American imports (as measured in American goods).

Finally the consumption, export and import functions of America can be restated as follows:

$$C_2 = cY_2 \tag{12}$$

$$X_2 = qP_1 Y_1 / eP_2 \tag{13}$$

$$Q_2 = qY_2 \tag{14}$$

Here $c = \alpha + \beta$ is the marginal consumption rate, and $q = \beta$ is the marginal import rate. Equation (12) is the consumption function of America, (13) is the export function of America, and (14) is the import function of America. American output is determined by the demand for American goods $Y_2 = A_2 + C_2 + X_2 - Q_2$. Upon substituting the consumption, export and import functions of America, we reach the goods market equation of America:

$$Y_2 = A_2 + cY_2 + qP_1Y_1 / eP_2 - qY_2 \qquad (15)$$

9. A Second Model of Europe and America

According to Sections 7 and 8, the model can be characterized by a system of two equations:

$$Y_1 = A_1 + cY_1 + qeP_2Y_2 / P_1 - qY_1 \qquad (1)$$

$$Y_2 = A_2 + cY_2 + qP_1Y_1 / eP_2 - qY_2 \qquad (2)$$

Equation (1) is the goods market equation of Europe, as measured in European goods. And equation (2) is the goods market equation of America, as measured in American goods. Here the exogenous variables are the autonomous demand for European goods A_1, the autonomous demand for American goods A_2, the price of European goods P_1, the price of American goods P_2, and the price of the dollar e. The endogenous variables are European output Y_1 and American output Y_2.

An increase in the autonomous demand for American goods raises American output and, hence, European output. An increase in the price of American goods lowers American output but raises European output. Likewise, an appreciation of the dollar lowers American output but raises European output. Essentially, this model forms the basis for the model developed in Part Two. It goes without saying that the second model of Europe and America is equivalent to the first model of Europe and America, see Section 6 above.

By the way, European exports (as measured in dollars) are identical to American imports (as measured in dollars) $qP_2Y_2 = qP_2Y_2$. On the other hand, European exports (as measured in dollars) generally differ from European imports (as measured in dollars) $qP_2Y_2 \neq qP_1Y_1 / e$.

Chapter 2
The Monetary Regions Differ in Size

1. The Model

The world consists of two monetary regions, say Europe and America. The monetary regions are completely specialized in production. Europe produces European goods, while America produces American goods. European goods and American goods are imperfect substitutes in consumption. So far, in Chapter 1, we assumed that Europe and America were the same size. Now, in Chapter 2, we assume that Europe is small and America is large.

As a point of reference, consider a simple model where the monetary regions are the same size:

$$Y_1 = A_1 + cY_1 + qeP_2Y_2 / P_1 - qY_1 \tag{1}$$

$$Y_2 = A_2 + cY_2 + qP_1Y_1 / eP_2 - qY_2 \tag{2}$$

Equation (1) is the goods market equation of Europe, as measured in European goods. And equation (2) is the goods market equation of America, as measured in American goods. The exogenous variables are the autonomous demand for European goods A_1, the autonomous demand for American goods A_2, the price of European goods P_1, the price of American goods P_2, and the price of the dollar e. The endogenous variables are European output Y_1 and American output Y_2.

Next consider a simple model where the monetary regions differ in size:

$$Y_1 = A_1 + cY_1 + q_2eP_2Y_2 / P_1 - q_1Y_1 \tag{3}$$

$$Y_2 = A_2 + cY_2 + q_1P_1Y_1 / eP_2 - q_2Y_2 \tag{4}$$

Here q_1 is the marginal import rate of Europe, and q_2 is the marginal import rate of America. We assume that Europe is small and America is large. In terms of the model this means that the marginal import rate of Europe is large, and the marginal import rate of America is small $q_1 > q_2$. Equation (1) is the goods market equation of Europe, and equation (2) is the goods market equation of America. The exogenous variables are A_1, A_2, P_1, P_2 and e. The endogenous variables are Y_1 and Y_2.

2. The Exact Solution

To simplify notation, let be $P_1 = eP_2$. Then the model can be written as follows:

$$Y_1 = A_1 + cY_1 + q_2Y_2 - q_1Y_1 \tag{1}$$

$$Y_2 = A_2 + cY_2 + q_1Y_1 - q_2Y_2 \tag{2}$$

First take an increase in the autonomous demand for European goods. Then what will be the effect on European output, and what on American output? As a result, the relevant multipliers are:

$$\frac{dY_1}{dA_1} = \frac{1-c+q_2}{(1-c)(1-c+q_1+q_2)} \tag{3}$$

$$\frac{dY_2}{dA_1} = \frac{q_1}{(1-c)(1-c+q_1+q_2)} \tag{4}$$

Second take an increase in the autonomous demand for American goods. Then how will American output respond, and how European output? The respective multipliers are:

$$\frac{dY_2}{dA_2} = \frac{1-c+q_1}{(1-c)(1-c+q_1+q_2)} \tag{5}$$

$$\frac{dY_1}{dA_2} = \frac{q_2}{(1-c)(1-c+q_1+q_2)} \tag{6}$$

To illustrate this, consider some numerical examples. Let us begin with numerical example number one. Assume for the time being that Europe and America are the same size. Let the marginal consumption rate be $c = 0.72$, let the marginal import rate of Europe be $q_1 = 0.08$, and let the marginal import rate of America be equally $q_2 = 0.08$. Then, as a result, an increase in the autonomous demand for European goods of 100 causes an increase in European output of 292, and increase in American output of 65, and an increase in world output of 357. That is to say, the domestic effect in Europe is 292, and the spillover effect in America is 65. Similarly, an increase in the autonomous demand for American goods of 100 causes an increase in American output of 292, an increase in European output of 65, and an increase in world output of 357. That means, the domestic effect in America is 292, and the spillover effect in Europe is 65.

We come now to numerical example number two. Assume that Europe is small and America is large. Let the marginal consumption rate be $c = 0.72$, let the marginal import rate of Europe be $q_1 = 0.16$, and let the marginal import rate of America be $q_2 = 0.04$. Then, as a result, an increase in the autonomous demand for European goods of 100 causes an increase in European output of 238, an increase in American output of 119, and an increase in world output of 357. In this case, the domestic effect in Europe is 238, and the spillover effect in America is 119. The other way round, an increase in the autonomous demand for American goods of 100 causes an increase in American output of 327, an increase in European output of 30, and an increase in world output of 357. In this case, the domestic effect in America is 327, and the spillover effect in Europe is 30.

The general point here is as follows. In the small region, the domestic effect will be small. And in the large region, the domestic effect will be large. Further, in the small region, the (incoming) spillover effect will be small. And in the large region, the (incoming) spillover effect will be large.

We proceed now to numerical example number three. Assume that Europe is very small and America is very large. Let the marginal consumption rate be $c = 0.72$, let the marginal import rate of Europe be $q_1 = 0.40$, and let the marginal import rate of America be $q_2 = 0$. Then, as a result, an increase in the autonomous demand for European goods of 100 causes an increase in European output of 147, an increase in American output of 210, and an increase in world output of 357. In this case, the spillover effect is larger than the domestic effect. Conversely, an increase in the autonomous demand for American goods of 100 causes an increase in American output of 357, an increase in European output of 0, and an increase in world output of 357. In this case, the domestic effect reaches a maximum, while the spillover effect reaches a minimum.

3. An Approximate Solution
for the Small Monetary Region

An increase in the autonomous demand for European goods has three effects: The primary effect in Europe, the spillover from Europe to America, and the repercussion from America to Europe. For the approximate solution we assume that the repercussion effect is zero. This gives rise to the question how large the associated error is.

To answer this question, consider a simple model:

$$Y_1 = A_1 + cY_1 + q_2 Y_2 - q_1 Y_1 \tag{1}$$

$$Y_2 = A_2 + cY_2 + q_1 Y_1 - q_2 Y_2 \tag{2}$$

Equation (1) is the goods market equation of Europe, and equation (2) is the goods market equation of America. The exogenous variables are the autonomous demand for European goods A_1 and the autonomous demand for American goods A_2. The endogenous variables are European output Y_1 and American output Y_2.

Now consider an increase in the autonomous demand for European goods. Then what will be overall effect on European output? First take the total differential of equation (1) $dY_1 = dA_1 + cdY_1 + q_2dY_2 - q_1dY_1$. Then solve for:

$$\frac{dY_1}{dA_1} = \frac{1}{1-c+q_1} + \frac{q_2}{1-c+q_1}\frac{dY_2}{dA_1} \tag{3}$$

Here

$$\frac{q_2}{1-c+q_1}\frac{dY_2}{dA_1} \tag{4}$$

is the repercussion effect in Europe. Next assume that the repercussion effect in Europe is zero. Then what will be the domestic effect in Europe? Obviously, the approximate solution is:

$$\frac{dY_1}{dA_1} = \frac{1}{1-c+q_1} \tag{5}$$

For instance, let the marginal consumption rate be $c = 0.72$, and let the marginal import rate of Europe be $q_1 = 0.16$. Then an increase in the autonomous demand for European goods of 100 causes an increase in European output of 227. Compare this with the exact solution given in the previous section. There, in numerical example number two, an increase in the autonomous demand for European goods of 100 caused an increase in European output of 238. So an increase in European output of 227 is a reasonably good approximation.

As a consequence, the model of a small open economy can be reduced to a single equation:

$$Y_1 = A_1 + cY_1 + q_2eP_2Y_2 / P_1 - q_1Y_1 \tag{6}$$

Equation (6) is the goods market equation of the small open economy. Here the exogenous variables are the autonomous demand for European goods A_1, American income Y_2, the price of European goods P_1, the price of American goods P_2, and the price of the dollar e. The endogenous variable is European output Y_1.

As a result, according to equation (6), an increase in the autonomous demand for European goods raises European output. An increase in American income raises European output. An increase in the price of European goods lowers European output. An increase in the price of American goods raises European output. And an appreciation of the euro lowers European output.

In addition define $h_1 = q_2 Y_2$ where h_1 is the exchange rate sensitivity of European exports. Then the model can be restated as follows:

$$Y_1 = A_1 + cY_1 + h_1 eP_2 / P_1 - q_1 Y_1 \tag{7}$$

Chapter 3
The Large Monetary Union of Two Countries

1. The Approach

The world still consists of two monetary regions, say Europe and America. The exchange rate between Europe and America can be flexible or fixed. Europe in turn consists of two countries, say Germany and France. Germany and France form a monetary union. The three spatial units are completely specialized in production. Germany produces German goods, France produces French goods, and America produces American goods. These goods are imperfect substitutes in consumption. Europe and America are the same size and have the same behavioural functions. Similarly, Germany and France are the same size and have the same behavioural functions. These assumptions will be relaxed below, see Chapter 4.

German households consume German goods, French goods and American goods. German households maximize utility subject to the budget constraint. The exogenous variables are German income, the price of German goods, the price of French goods, the price of American goods, and the price of the dollar. The endogenous variables are the German consumption of German goods, the German consumption of French goods, and the German consumption of American goods. Then what are the demand functions of German households?

French households consume French goods, German goods and American goods. French households maximize utility subject to the budget constraint. The exogenous variables are French income, the price of French goods, the price of German goods, the price of American goods, and the price of the dollar. The endogenous variables are the French consumption of French goods, the French consumption of German goods, and the French consumption of American goods. Then what are the demand functions of French households?

American households consume American goods, German goods and French goods. American households maximize utility subject to the budget constraint.

The exogenous variables are American income, the price of American goods, the price of German goods, the price of French goods, and the price of the euro. The endogenous variables are the American consumption of American goods, the American consumption of German goods, and the American consumption of French goods. Then what are the demand functions of American households?

The market for German goods. German output is determined by the German consumption of German goods, by the French consumption of German goods, by the American consumption of German goods, and by the autonomous demand for German goods. That is, German output is determined by the autonomous demand for German goods, by French income, by American income, by the price of German goods, by the price of French goods, by the price of American goods, and by the price of the euro.

The market for French goods. French output is driven by the French consumption of French goods, by the German consumption of French goods, by the American consumption of French goods, and by the autonomous demand for French goods. That is, French output is driven by the autonomous demand for French goods, by German income, by American income, by the price of French goods, by the price of German goods, by the price of American goods, and by the price of the euro.

The market for American goods. American output is determined by the American consumption of American goods, by the German consumption of American goods, by the French consumption of American goods, and by the autonomous demand for American goods. That is, American output is determined by the autonomous demand for American goods, by German income, by French income, by the price of American goods, by the price of German goods, by the price of French goods, and by the price of the dollar.

Further topics are:
- a first model of Germany, France and America
- the consumption, export and import functions of Germany
- the consumption, export and import functions of France
- the consumption, export and import functions of America
- a second model of Germany, France and America.

2. The Demand Functions of German Households

The utility function of German households is:

$$U_1 = \alpha \log C_{11} + \beta \log C_{12} + \gamma \log C_{13} + \delta \log S_1 \tag{1}$$

Here C_{11} denotes the German consumption of German goods, as measured in German goods. C_{12} is the German consumption of French goods, as measured in French goods. C_{13} is the German consumption of American goods, as measured in American goods. S_1 is German savings, as measured in German goods. U_1 is German utility. α, β, γ and δ are positive constants with $\alpha + \beta + \gamma + \delta = 1$.

The budget constraint of German households is:

$$P_1Y_1 = P_1C_{11} + P_2C_{12} + eP_3C_{13} + P_1S_1 \tag{2}$$

Y_1 symbolizes German income, as measured in German goods. P_1 is the price of German goods, as measured in euros. P_2 is the price of French goods, as measured in euros. P_3 is the price of American goods, as measured in dollars. e is the exchange rate between the dollar and the euro. More exactly, e is the price of the dollar, as measured in euros. Then eP_3 is the price of American goods, as measured in euros. P_1Y_1 is German income, as measured in euros. P_1C_{11} is the German consumption of German goods, as measured in euros. P_2C_{12} is the German consumption of French goods, as measured in euros. eP_3C_{13} is the German consumption of American goods, as measured in euros. And P_1S_1 is German savings, as measured in euros. According to the budget constraint, an increase in the price of German goods causes an increase in German income, as measured in euros. This is in sharp contrast to the assumptions made in standard microeconomic analysis.

German households maximize utility subject to the budget constraint. The exogenous variables are German income Y_1, the price of German goods P_1, the price of French goods P_2, the price of American goods P_3, and the price of the dollar e. The endogenous variables are the German consumption of German goods C_{11}, the German consumption of French goods C_{12}, the German consumption of American goods C_{13}, and German savings S_1. The first-order conditions together with the budget constraint yield the shares of expenditures in income:

$$P_1C_{11} = \alpha P_1 Y_1 \tag{3}$$

$$P_2C_{12} = \beta P_1 Y_1 \tag{4}$$

$$eP_3C_{13} = \gamma P_1 Y_1 \tag{5}$$

$$P_1S_1 = \delta P_1 Y_1 \tag{6}$$

From this, the demand functions of German households can be derived immediately:

$$C_{11} = \alpha Y_1 \tag{7}$$

$$C_{12} = \beta P_1 Y_1 / P_2 \tag{8}$$

$$C_{13} = \gamma P_1 Y_1 / eP_3 \tag{9}$$

$$S_1 = \delta Y_1 \tag{10}$$

Equation (7) gives the German consumption of German goods. As a result, an increase in German income, as measured in German goods, causes a proportionate increase in the German consumption of German goods. However, an increase in the price of German goods has no effect on the German consumption of German goods. That means, in this case, the own price elasticity of demand is zero. This differs widely from standard microeconomic analysis. There the own price elasticity of demand is -1. The underlying reason is that here an increase in the price of German goods causes a proportionate increase in German income, as measured in euros. Moreover, an increase in the price of French goods has no effect on the German consumption of German goods. That is to say, in this case, the cross price elasticity of demand is zero. This is well in line with standard microeconomic analysis. Likewise, an increase in the price of American goods has no effect on the German consumption of German goods. And an appreciation of the dollar has no effect on the German consumption of German goods either.

Equation (8) gives the German consumption of French goods. As a result, a 1 percent increase in German income, as measured in German goods, causes a 1 percent increase in the German consumption of French goods. A 1 percent increase in the price of German goods causes a 1 percent increase in the German consumption of French goods. That means, in this case, the cross price elasticity of demand is 1. This differs from standard microeconomic analysis. There the cross price elasticity of demand is zero. Again, the underlying reason is that a 1 percent increase in the price of German goods causes a 1 percent increase in German income, as measured in euros. Further, a 1 percent increase in the price of French goods causes a 1 percent decline in the German consumption of French goods. That is to say, in this case, the own price elasticity of demand is −1. This is in line with standard microeconomic analysis. In addition, an increase in the price of American goods has no effect on the German consumption of French goods. That is, in this case, the cross price elasticity of demand is zero. This is in line with standard microeconomic analysis. Similarly, an appreciation of the dollar has no effect on the German consumption of French goods.

Equation (9) gives the German consumption of American goods. As a result, a 1 percent increase in German income, as measured in German goods, causes a 1 percent increase in the German consumption of American goods. A 1 percent increase in the price of German goods causes a 1 percent increase in the German consumption of American goods. An increase in the price of French goods has no effect on the German consumption of American goods. A 1 percent increase in the price of American goods causes a 1 percent decline in the German consumption of American goods. And a 1 percent appreciation of the dollar causes a 1 percent decline in the German consumption of American goods.

Equation (10) gives German savings. As a result, an increase in German income (as measured in German goods) causes a proportionate increase in German savings (as measured in German goods). An increase in the price of German goods has no effect on German savings. An increase in the price of French goods has no effect on German savings. An increase in the price of American goods has no effect on German savings. And the same holds for an appreciation of the dollar.

3. The Demand Functions of French Households

The utility function of French households is:

$$U_2 = \alpha \log C_{22} + \beta \log C_{21} + \gamma \log C_{23} + \delta \log S_2 \tag{1}$$

Here C_{22} stands for the French consumption of French goods, as measured in French goods. C_{21} is the French consumption of German goods, as measured in German goods. C_{23} is the French consumption of American goods, as measured in American goods. S_2 is French savings, as measured in French goods. And U_2 is French utility.

The budget constraint of French households is:

$$P_2 Y_2 = P_2 C_{22} + P_1 C_{21} + e P_3 C_{23} + P_2 S_2 \tag{2}$$

Y_2 designates French income, as measured in French goods. $P_2 Y_2$ is French income, as measured in euros. $P_2 C_{22}$ is the French consumption of French goods, as measured in euros. $P_1 C_{21}$ is the French consumption of German goods, as measured in euros. $e P_3 C_{23}$ is the French consumption of American goods, as measured in euros. And $P_2 S_2$ is French savings, as measured in euros.

French households maximize utility subject to the budget constraint. The exogenous variables are French income Y_2, the price of French goods P_2, the price of German goods P_1, the price of American goods P_3, and the price of the dollar e. The endogenous variables are the French consumption of French goods C_{22}, the French consumption of German goods C_{21}, the French consumption of American goods C_{23}, and French savings S_2. The first-order conditions together with the budget constraint yield the shares of expenditures in income:

$$P_2 C_{22} = \alpha P_2 Y_2 \tag{3}$$

$$P_1 C_{21} = \beta P_2 Y_2 \tag{4}$$

$$e P_3 C_{23} = \gamma P_2 Y_2 \tag{5}$$

$$P_2 S_2 = \delta P_2 Y_2 \tag{6}$$

From this, the demand functions of French households can be obtained immediately:

$$C_{22} = \alpha Y_2 \tag{7}$$

$$C_{21} = \beta P_2 Y_2 / P_1 \tag{8}$$

$$C_{23} = \gamma P_2 Y_2 / e P_3 \tag{9}$$

$$S_2 = \delta Y_2 \tag{10}$$

Equation (7) gives the French consumption of French goods. As an outcome, it is proportional to French income. However, it does not depend on the price of French goods. Equation (8) gives the French consumption of German goods. As an outcome, it is proportional to French income and to the price of French goods. It is inversely proportional to the price of German goods. Equation (9) gives the French consumption of American goods. As an outcome, it is proportional to French income and to the price of French goods. It is inversely proportional to the price of American goods and to the price of the dollar. Equation (10) gives French savings. As an outcome, they are proportional to French income.

4. The Demand Functions of American Households

The utility function of American households is:

$$U_3 = (\alpha + \beta) \log C_{33} + 0.5\gamma \log C_{31} + 0.5\gamma \log C_{32} + \delta \log S_3 \tag{1}$$

Here C_{33} denotes the American consumption of American goods, as measured in American goods. C_{31} is the American consumption of German goods, as measured in German goods. C_{32} is the American consumption of French goods, as measured in French goods. S_3 is American savings, as measured in American goods. And U_3 is American utility.

The budget constraint of American households is:

$$P_3Y_3 = P_3C_{33} + P_1C_{31} / e + P_2C_{32} / e + P_3S_3 \qquad (2)$$

Y_3 symbolizes American income, as measured in American goods. P_3Y_3 is American income, as measured in dollars. P_3C_{33} is the American consumption of American goods, as measured in dollars. P_1C_{31} / e is the American consumption of German goods, as measured in dollars. P_2C_{32} / e is the American consumption of French goods, as measured in dollars. And P_3S_3 is American savings, as measured in dollars.

American households maximize utility subject to the budget constraint. The exogenous variables are American income Y_3, the price of American goods P_3, the price of German goods P_1, the price of French goods P_2, and the price of the euro $1/e$. The endogenous variables are the American consumption of American goods C_{33}, the American consumption of German goods C_{31}, the American consumption of French goods C_{32}, and American savings S_3. The first-order conditions together with the budget constraint yield the shares of expenditures in income:

$$P_3C_{33} = (\alpha + \beta)P_3Y_3 \qquad (3)$$

$$P_1C_{31} / e = 0.5\gamma P_3Y_3 \qquad (4)$$

$$P_2C_{32} / e = 0.5\gamma P_3Y_3 \qquad (5)$$

$$P_3S_3 = \delta P_3Y_3 \qquad (6)$$

From this, the demand functions of American households can be derived immediately:

$$C_{33} = (\alpha + \beta)Y_3 \qquad (7)$$

$$C_{31} = 0.5\gamma eP_3Y_3 / P_1 \qquad (8)$$

$$C_{32} = 0.5\gamma eP_3Y_3 / P_2 \qquad (9)$$

$$S_3 = \delta Y_3 \tag{10}$$

Equation (7) gives the American consumption of American goods. As a finding, it is proportional to American income. Equation (8) gives the American consumption of German goods. As a finding, it is proportional to American income and to the price of American goods. It is inversely proportional to the price of German goods and to the price of the euro. Equation (9) gives the American consumption of French goods. As a finding, it is proportional to American income and to the price of American goods. It is inversely proportional to the price of French goods and to the price of the euro. Equation (10) gives American savings. As a finding, they are proportional to American income.

5. The Market for German Goods

According to Sections 2, 3 and 4, the demand functions for German goods are:

$$C_{11} = \alpha Y_1 \tag{1}$$

$$C_{21} = \beta P_2 Y_2 / P_1 \tag{2}$$

$$C_{31} = 0.5\gamma e P_3 Y_3 / P_1 \tag{3}$$

$$A_1 = \text{const} \tag{4}$$

Equation (1) gives the German consumption of German goods. Equation (2) gives the French consumption of German goods. Equation (3) gives the American consumption of German goods. And equation (4) gives the autonomous demand for German goods, think for instance of investment or government purchases.

German output Y_1 is determined by the demand for German goods:

$$Y_1 = A_1 + C_{11} + C_{21} + C_{31} \tag{5}$$

Taking account of the demand functions (1) until (4), we arrive at the goods market equation of Germany:

$$Y_1 = A_1 + \alpha Y_1 + \beta P_2 Y_2 / P_1 + 0.5 \gamma e P_3 Y_3 / P_1 \tag{6}$$

As a result, German output is determined by the autonomous demand for German goods, by French income, by American income, by the price of German goods, by the price of French goods, by the price of American goods, and by the price of the euro. An increase in the autonomous demand for German goods raises German output. An increase in French income raises German output. An increase in American income raises German output. An increase in the price of German goods lowers German output. An increase in the price of French goods raises German output. An increase in the price of American goods raises German output. And an appreciation of the euro lowers German output.

6. The Market for French Goods

According to Sections 2, 3 and 4, the demand functions for French goods are:

$$C_{22} = \alpha Y_2 \tag{1}$$

$$C_{12} = \beta P_1 Y_1 / P_2 \tag{2}$$

$$C_{32} = 0.5 \gamma e P_3 Y_3 / P_2 \tag{3}$$

$$A_2 = \text{const} \tag{4}$$

Equation (1) gives the French consumption of French goods. Equation (2) gives the German consumption of French goods. Equation (3) gives the American consumption of French goods. And equation (4) gives the autonomous demand for French goods, think for example of investment or government purchases.

French output Y_2 is determined by the demand for French goods:

$$Y_2 = A_2 + C_{22} + C_{12} + C_{32} \tag{5}$$

Upon substituting the demand functions (1) until (4), we reach the goods market equation of France:

$$Y_2 = A_2 + \alpha Y_2 + \beta P_1 Y_1 / P_2 + 0.5 \gamma e P_3 Y_3 / P_2 \tag{6}$$

As a result, French output is determined by the autonomous demand for French goods, by German income, by American income, by the price of French goods, by the price of German goods, by the price of American goods, and by the price of the euro. An increase in the autonomous demand for French goods raises French output. An increase in German income raises French output. An increase in American income raises French output. An increase in the price of French goods lowers French output. An increase in the price of German goods raises French output. An increase in the price of American goods raises French output. And an appreciation of the euro lowers French output.

7. The Market for American Goods

According to Sections 2, 3 and 4, the demand functions for American goods are:

$$C_{33} = (\alpha + \beta) Y_3 \tag{1}$$

$$C_{13} = \gamma P_1 Y_1 / e P_3 \tag{2}$$

$$C_{23} = \gamma P_2 Y_2 / e P_3 \tag{3}$$

$$A_3 = \text{const} \tag{4}$$

Equation (1) gives the American consumption of American goods. Equation (2) gives the German consumption of American goods. Equation (3) gives the French consumption of American goods. And equation (4) gives the autonomous demand for American goods.

American output Y_3 is determined by the demand for American goods:

$$Y_3 = A_3 + C_{33} + C_{13} + C_{23} \tag{5}$$

Taking account of the demand functions (1) until (4), we arrive at the goods market equation of America:

$$Y_3 = A_3 + (\alpha + \beta)Y_3 + \gamma P_1 Y_1 / eP_3 + \gamma P_2 Y_2 / eP_3 \tag{6}$$

As a result, American output is determined by the autonomous demand for American goods, by German income, by French income, by the price of American goods, by the price of German goods, by the price of French goods, and by the price of the dollar. An increase in the autonomous demand for American goods raises American output. An increase in German income raises American output. An increase in French income raises American output. An increase in the price of American goods lowers American output. An increase in the price of German goods raises American output. An increase in the price of French goods raises American output. And an appreciation of the dollar lowers American output.

8. A First Model of Germany, France and America

According to Sections 5, 6 and 7, the model can be represented by a system of three equations:

$$Y_1 = A_1 + \alpha Y_1 + \beta P_2 Y_2 / P_1 + 0.5\gamma e P_3 Y_3 / P_1 \tag{1}$$

$$Y_2 = A_2 + \alpha Y_2 + \beta P_1 Y_1 / P_2 + 0.5\gamma e P_3 Y_3 / P_2 \tag{2}$$

$$Y_3 = A_3 + (\alpha + \beta)Y_3 + \gamma P_1 Y_1 / e P_3 + \gamma P_2 Y_2 / e P_3 \tag{3}$$

Equation (1) is the goods market equation of Germany, as measured in German goods. (2) is the goods market equation of France, as measured in French goods. And (3) is the goods market equation of America, as measured in American goods. Here the exogenous variables are the autonomous demand for German goods A_1, the autonomous demand for French goods A_2, the autonomous demand for American goods A_3, the price of German goods P_1, the price of French goods P_2, the price of American goods P_3, and the price of the dollar e. The endogenous variables are German output Y_1, French output Y_2, and American output Y_3.

An increase in the autonomous demand for German goods raises German output and, hence, French output as well as American output. An increase in the price of German goods lowers German output but raises French output and American output. An appreciation of the euro lowers German output and French output but raises American output. Besides, according to equations (1) and (2), if $P_1 A_1 = P_2 A_2$, then $P_1 Y_1 = P_2 Y_2$. That means, if the autonomous demand for German goods (as measured in euros) equals the autonomous demand for French goods (as measured in euros), then German income (as measured in euros) will equal French income (as measured in euros).

9. The Consumption, Export and Import Functions of Germany

German output is determined by the demand for German goods $Y_1 = A_1 + C_{11} + C_{21} + C_{31}$, as is well known. This equation can be rewritten as follows:

$$P_1Y_1 = P_1A_1 + (P_1C_{11} + P_2C_{12} + eP_3C_{13}) + P_1C_{21} + P_1C_{31} - P_2C_{12} - eP_3C_{13} \quad (1)$$

Here $(P_1C_{11} + P_2C_{12} + eP_3C_{13})$ is German consumption, as measured in euros. It includes German goods, French goods and American goods. P_1C_{21} is German exports to France, as measured in euros. P_1C_{31} is German exports to America, as measured in euros. P_2C_{12} is German imports from France, as measured in euros. And eP_3C_{13} is German imports from America, as measured in euros.

Moreover, it proves useful to measure German consumption, German exports and German imports in terms of German goods. $C_{11} + P_2C_{12} / P_1 + eP_3C_{13} / P_1$ is German consumption, as measured in German goods. Of course, German consumption still consists of German goods, French goods and American goods. Let C_1 denote German consumption, as measured in German goods:

$$C_1 = C_{11} + P_2C_{12} / P_1 + eP_3C_{13} / P_1 \quad (2)$$

C_{21} is German exports to France, as measured in German goods. Of course, German exports to France consist of German goods. Let X_{12} denote German exports to France, as measured in German goods:

$$X_{12} = C_{21} \quad (3)$$

C_{31} is German exports to America, as measured in German goods. Of course, German exports to America consist of German goods. Let X_{13} denote German exports to America, as measured in German goods:

$$X_{13} = C_{31} \quad (4)$$

P_2C_{12} / P_1 is German imports from France, as measured in German goods. Of course, German imports from France consist of French goods. Let Q_{12} denote German imports from France, as measured in German goods:

$$Q_{12} = P_2C_{12} / P_1 \tag{5}$$

And eP_3C_{13} / P_1 is German imports from America, as measured in German goods. Of course, German imports from America consist of American goods. Let Q_{13} denote German imports from America, as measured in German goods:

$$Q_{13} = eP_3C_{13} / P_1 \tag{6}$$

Now insert equations (2) until (6) into equation (1) to verify:

$$Y_1 = A_1 + C_1 + X_{12} + X_{13} - Q_{12} - Q_{13} \tag{7}$$

That is to say, the market for German goods is in equilibrium if German output equals the autonomous demand for German goods plus German consumption plus German exports minus German imports.

According to Sections 2, 3 and 4, the relevant demand functions are:

$$C_{11} = \alpha Y_1 \tag{8}$$
$$C_{12} = \beta P_1 Y_1 / P_2 \tag{9}$$
$$C_{13} = \gamma P_1 Y_1 / eP_3 \tag{10}$$
$$C_{21} = \beta P_2 Y_2 / P_1 \tag{11}$$
$$C_{31} = 0.5\gamma eP_3 Y_3 / P_1 \tag{12}$$

Next put those demand functions into equations (2) until (6):

$$C_1 = (\alpha + \beta + \gamma)Y_1 \tag{13}$$
$$X_{12} = \beta P_2 Y_2 / P_1 \tag{14}$$

$$X_{13} = 0.5\gamma eP_3 Y_3 / P_1 \tag{15}$$

$$Q_{12} = \beta Y_1 \tag{16}$$

$$Q_{13} = \gamma Y_1 \tag{17}$$

As a result, equation (13) is the consumption function of Germany. Equations (14) and (15) are the export functions of Germany. Equations (16) and (17) are the import functions of Germany.

Equation (13) gives German consumption, as measured in German goods. As a finding, German consumption (as measured in German goods) is proportional to German income (as measured in German goods). However, German consumption (as measured in German goods) does not depend on the price of German goods, on the price of French goods, on the price of American goods, or on the price of the dollar. An increase in the price of German goods has no effect on German consumption (as measured in German goods). An increase in the price of French goods has no effect on German consumption (as measured in German goods). An increase in the price of American goods has no effect on German consumption (as measured in German goods). And an appreciation of the dollar has no effect on German consumption (as measured in German goods).

Equation (14) gives German exports to France, as measured in German goods. As a finding, German exports to France are an increasing function of French income. A 1 percent increase in French income, as measured in French goods, causes a 1 percent increase in German exports to France. A 1 percent increase in the price of French goods causes a 1 percent increase in German exports to France. The reason for this effect is that a 1 percent increase in the price of French goods causes a 1 percent increase in French income, as measured in euros. And a 1 percent increase in the price of German goods causes a 1 percent decline in German exports to France.

Equation (15) gives German exports to America, as measured in German goods. As a finding, German exports to America are an increasing function of American income. A 1 percent increase in American income, as measured in American goods, causes a 1 percent increase in German exports to America. A 1 percent increase in the price of American goods causes a 1 percent increase in

German exports to America. A 1 percent increase in the price of German goods causes a 1 percent decline in German exports to America. And a 1 percent appreciation of the euro causes a 1 percent decline in German exports to America.

Equation (16) gives German imports from France, as measured in German goods. As a finding, German imports from France (as measured in German goods) are proportional to German income (as measured in German goods). On the other hand, German imports from France (as measured in German goods) do not depend on the price of French goods or on the price of German goods. An increase in the price of French goods has no effect on German imports from France (as measured in German goods). And an increase in the price of German goods has no effect on German imports from France (as measured in German goods).

Equation (17) gives German imports from America, as measured in German goods. As a finding, German imports from America (as measured in German goods) are proportional to German income (as measured in German goods). But German imports from America (as measured in German goods) do not depend on the price of American goods, on the price of the dollar, or on the price of German goods. An increase in the price of American goods has no effect on German imports from America (as measured in German goods). An appreciation of the dollar has no effect on German imports from America (as measured in German goods). And an increase in the price of German goods has no effect on German imports from America (as measured in German goods).

Finally the consumption, export and import functions of Germany can be restated as follows:

$$C_1 = cY_1 \tag{18}$$

$$X_{12} = mP_2Y_2 \,/\, P_1 \tag{19}$$

$$X_{13} = 0.5qeP_3Y_3 \,/\, P_1 \tag{20}$$

$$Q_{12} = mY_1 \tag{21}$$

$$Q_{13} = qY_1 \tag{22}$$

Here $c = \alpha + \beta + \gamma$ is the marginal consumption rate of Germany. $m = \beta$ is the marginal import rate of Germany relative to France. At the same time, $m = \beta$ is the marginal import rate of France relative to Germany. $q = \gamma$ is the marginal import rate of Germany relative to America. At the same time, $q = \gamma$ is the (overall) marginal import rate of America. $0.5q$ is the marginal import rate of America relative to Germany. And $m + q$ is the (overall) marginal import of Germany.

Equation (18) is the consumption function of Germany. Equations (19) and (20) are the export functions of Germany. Equations (21) and (22) are the import functions of Germany. German output is determined by the demand for German goods $Y_1 = A_1 + C_1 + X_{12} + X_{13} - Q_{12} - Q_{13}$. Taking account of the consumption, export and import functions of Germany, we arrive at the goods market equation of Germany:

$$Y_1 = A_1 + cY_1 + mP_2 Y_2 / P_1 + 0.5qeP_3 Y_3 / P_1 - (m+q)Y_1 \tag{23}$$

10. The Consumption, Export and Import Functions of France

French output is determined by the demand for French goods $Y_2 = A_2 + C_{22} + C_{12} + C_{32}$, as is well known. This equation can be rewritten as follows:

$$P_2 Y_2 = P_2 A_2 + (P_2 C_{22} + P_1 C_{21} + eP_3 C_{23}) + P_2 C_{12} + P_2 C_{32} - P_1 C_{21} - eP_3 C_{23} \tag{1}$$

Here $(P_2 C_{22} + P_1 C_{21} + eP_3 C_{23})$ is French consumption, as measured in euros. It includes French goods, German goods and American goods. $P_2 C_{12}$ is French exports to Germany, as measured in euros. P_2C_{32} is French exports to America, as measured in euros. P_2C_{21} is French imports from Germany, as measured in euros. And eP_3C_{23} is French imports from America, as measured in euros.

Further, it proves useful to measure French consumption, French exports and French imports in terms of French goods. $C_{22} + P_1C_{21} / P_2 + eP_3C_{23} / P_2$ is French consumption, as measured in French goods. Of course, French consumption still consists of French goods, German goods and American goods. Let C_2 denote French consumption, as measured in French goods:

$$C_2 = C_{22} + P_1C_{21} / P_2 + eP_3C_{23} / P_2 \tag{2}$$

C_{12} is French exports to Germany, as measured in French goods. Of course, French exports to Germany consist of French goods. Let X_{21} denote French exports to Germany, as measured in French goods:

$$X_{21} = C_{12} \tag{3}$$

C_{32} is French exports to America, as measured in French goods. Of course, French exports to America consist of French goods. Let X_{23} denote French exports to America, as measured in French goods:

$$X_{23} = C_{32} \tag{4}$$

P_1C_{21} / P_2 is French imports from Germany, as measured in French goods. Of course, French imports from Germany consist of German goods. Let Q_{21} denote French imports from Germany, as measured in French goods:

$$Q_{21} = P_1C_{21} / P_2 \tag{5}$$

And eP_3C_{23} / P_2 is French imports from America, as measured in French goods. Of course, French imports from America consist of American goods. Let Q_{23} denote French imports from America, as measured in French goods:

$$Q_{23} = eP_3C_{23} / P_2 \tag{6}$$

Now insert equations (2) until (6) into equation (1) to check:

$$Y_2 = A_2 + C_2 + X_{21} + X_{23} - Q_{21} - Q_{23} \tag{7}$$

That means, the market for French goods is in equilibrium if French output equals the autonomous demand for French goods plus French consumption plus French exports minus French imports.

According to Sections 2, 3 and 4, the relevant demand functions are:

$$C_{22} = \alpha Y_2 \tag{8}$$

$$C_{21} = \beta P_2 Y_2 / P_1 \tag{9}$$

$$C_{23} = \gamma P_2 Y_2 / e P_3 \tag{10}$$

$$C_{12} = \beta P_1 Y_1 / P_2 \tag{11}$$

$$C_{32} = 0.5 \gamma e P_3 Y_3 / P_2 \tag{12}$$

Next put those demand functions into equations (2) until (6):

$$C_2 = (\alpha + \beta + \gamma) Y_2 \tag{13}$$

$$X_{21} = \beta P_1 Y_1 / P_2 \tag{14}$$

$$X_{23} = 0.5 \gamma e P_3 Y_3 / P_2 \tag{15}$$

$$Q_{21} = \beta Y_2 \tag{16}$$

$$Q_{23} = \gamma Y_2 \tag{17}$$

As a result, equation (13) is the consumption function of France. Equations (14) and (15) are the export functions of France. Equations (16) and (17) are the import functions of France.

Equation (13) gives French consumption, as measured in French goods. As a finding, French consumption (as measured in French goods) is proportional to French income (as measured in French goods). However, French consumption (as measured in French goods) does not depend on the price of French goods, on the price of German goods, on the price of American goods, or on the price of the dollar.

Equation (14) gives French exports to Germany, as measured in French goods. A 1 percent increase in German income, as measured in German goods, causes a 1 percent increase in French exports to Germany. A 1 percent increase in the price of German goods causes a 1 percent increase in French exports to Germany. The reason for this effect is that a 1 percent increase in the price of German goods causes a 1 percent increase in German income, as measured in euros. And a 1 percent increase in the price of French goods causes a 1 percent decline in French exports to Germany.

Equation (15) gives French exports to America, as measured in French goods. A 1 percent increase in American income, as measured in American goods, causes a 1 percent increase in French exports to America. A 1 percent increase in the price of American goods causes a 1 percent increase in French exports to America. A 1 percent increase in the price of French goods causes a 1 percent decline in French exports to America. And a 1 percent appreciation of the euro causes a 1 percent decline in French exports to America.

Equation (16) gives French imports from Germany, as measured in French goods. As a finding, French imports from Germany (as measured in French goods) are proportional to French income (as measured in French goods). On the other hand, French imports from Germany (as measured in French goods) do not depend on the price of German goods or on the price of French goods.

Equation (17) gives French imports from America, as measured in French goods. As a finding, French imports from America (as measured in French goods) are proportional to French income (as measured in French goods). But French imports from America (as measured in French goods) do not depend on the price of American goods, on the price of the dollar, or on the price of French goods.

Finally the consumption, export and import functions of France can be restated as follows:

$$C_2 = cY_2 \tag{18}$$

$$X_{21} = mP_1Y_1 / P_2 \tag{19}$$

$$X_{23} = 0.5qeP_3Y_3 / P_2 \tag{20}$$

$$Q_{21} = mY_2 \tag{21}$$

$$Q_{23} = qY_2 \tag{22}$$

Here $c = \alpha + \beta + \gamma$ is the marginal consumption rate of France. $m = \beta$ is the marginal import rate of France relative to Germany. At the same time, $m = \beta$ is the marginal import rate of Germany relative to France. $q = \gamma$ is the marginal import rate of France relative to America. At the same time, $q = \gamma$ is the (overall) marginal import rate of America. $0.5q$ is the marginal import rate of America relative to France. And $m + q$ is the (overall) marginal import rate of France.

Equation (18) is the consumption function of France. Equations (19) and (20) are the export functions of France. Equations (21) and (22) are the import functions of France. French output is determined by the demand for French goods $Y_2 = A_2 + C_2 + X_{21} + X_{23} - Q_{21} - Q_{23}$. Upon substituting the consumption, export and import functions of France, we reach the goods market equation of France:

$$Y_2 = A_2 + cY_2 + mP_1Y_1 / P_2 + 0.5qeP_3Y_3 / P_2 - (m+q)Y_2 \tag{23}$$

11. The Consumption, Export and Import Functions of America

American output is determined by the demand for American goods $Y_3 = A_3 + C_{33} + C_{13} + C_{23}$, as is well known. This equation can be rewritten as follows:

$$P_3Y_3 = P_3A_3 + (P_3C_{33} + P_1C_{31} / e + P_2C_{32} / e)$$
$$+ P_3C_{13} + P_3C_{23} - P_1C_{31} / e - P_2C_{32} / e \tag{1}$$

Here $(P_3C_{33} + P_1C_{31} / e + P_2C_{32} / e)$ is American consumption, as measured in dollars. It includes American goods, German goods and French goods. P_3C_{13} is American exports to Germany, as measured in dollars. P_3C_{23} is American exports to France, as measured in dollars. P_1C_{31} / e is American imports from Germany, as measured in dollars. And P_2C_{32} / e is American imports from France, as measured in dollars.

Moreover, it proves useful to measure American consumption, American exports and American imports in terms of American goods. $C_{33} + P_1C_{31} / eP_3 + P_2C_{32} / eP_3$ is American consumption, as measured in American goods. Of course, American consumption still consists of American goods, German goods and French goods. Let C_3 denote American consumption, as measured in American goods:

$$C_3 = C_{33} + P_1C_{31} / eP_3 + P_2C_{32} / eP_3 \tag{2}$$

C_{13} is American exports to Germany, as measured in American goods. Of course, American exports to Germany consist of American goods. Let X_{31} denote American exports to Germany, as measured in American goods:

$$X_{31} = C_{13} \tag{3}$$

C_{23} is American exports to France, as measured in American goods. Of course, American exports to France consist of American goods. Let X_{32} denote American exports to France, as measured in American goods:

$$X_{32} = C_{23} \tag{4}$$

P_1C_{31} / eP_3 is American imports from Germany, as measured in American goods. Of course, American imports from Germany consist of German goods. Let Q_{31} denote American imports from Germany, as measured in American goods:

$$Q_{31} = P_1 C_{31} / eP_3 \tag{5}$$

And $P_2 C_{32} / eP_3$ is American imports from France, as measured in American goods. Of course, American imports from France consist of French goods. Let Q_{32} denote American imports from France, as measured in American goods:

$$Q_{32} = P_2 C_{32} / eP_3 \tag{6}$$

Now insert equations (2) until (6) into equation (1) to verify:

$$Y_3 = A_3 + C_3 + X_{31} + X_{32} - Q_{31} - Q_{32} \tag{7}$$

That is to say, the market for American goods is in equilibrium if American output equals the autonomous demand for American goods plus American consumption plus American exports minus American imports.

According to Sections 2, 3 and 4, the relevant demand functions are:

$$C_{33} = (\alpha + \beta) Y_3 \tag{8}$$
$$C_{31} = 0.5 \gamma eP_3 Y_3 / P_1 \tag{9}$$
$$C_{32} = 0.5 \gamma eP_3 Y_3 / P_2 \tag{10}$$
$$C_{13} = \gamma P_1 Y_1 / eP_3 \tag{11}$$
$$C_{23} = \gamma P_2 Y_2 / eP_3 \tag{12}$$

Next put those demand functions into equations (2) until (6):

$$C_3 = (\alpha + \beta + \gamma) Y_3 \tag{13}$$
$$X_{31} = \gamma P_1 Y_1 / eP_3 \tag{14}$$
$$X_{32} = \gamma P_2 Y_2 / eP_3 \tag{15}$$
$$Q_{31} = 0.5 \gamma Y_3 \tag{16}$$
$$Q_{32} = 0.5 \gamma Y_3 \tag{17}$$

As a result, equation (13) is the consumption function of America. Equations (14) and (15) are the export functions of America. Equations (16) and (17) are the import functions of America.

Equation (13) gives American consumption, as measured in American goods. As a finding, American consumption (as measured in American goods) is proportional to American income (as measured in American goods). However, American consumption (as measured in American goods) does not depend on the price of American goods, on the price of German goods, on the price of French goods, or on the price of the euro.

Equation (14) gives American exports to Germany, as measured in American goods. A 1 percent increase in German income, as measured in German goods, causes a 1 percent increase in American exports to Germany. A 1 percent increase in the price of German goods causes a 1 percent increase in American exports to Germany. A 1 percent increase in the price of American goods causes a 1 percent decline in American exports to Germany. And a 1 percent appreciation of the dollar causes a 1 percent decline in American exports to Germany.

Equation (15) gives American exports to France, as measured in American goods. A 1 percent increase in French income, as measured in French goods, causes a 1 percent increase in American exports to France. A 1 percent increase in the price of French goods causes a 1 percent increase in American exports to France. A 1 percent increase in the price of American goods causes a 1 percent decline in American exports to France. And a 1 percent appreciation of the dollar causes a 1 percent decline in American exports to France.

Equation (16) gives American imports from Germany, as measured in American goods. As a finding, American imports from Germany (as measured in American goods) are proportional to American income (as measured in American goods). On the other hand, American imports from Germany (as measured in American goods) do not depend on the price of German goods, on the price of the euro, or on the price of American goods.

Equation (17) gives American imports from France, as measured in American goods. As a finding, American imports from France (as measured in American goods) are proportional to American income (as measured in American goods). But American imports from France (as measured in American goods) do not depend on the price of French goods, on the price of the euro, or on the price of American goods.

Finally the consumption, export and import functions of America can be restated as follows:

$$C_3 = cY_3 \tag{18}$$

$$X_{31} = qP_1Y_1 / eP_3 \tag{19}$$

$$X_{32} = qP_2Y_2 / eP_3 \tag{20}$$

$$Q_{31} = 0.5qY_3 \tag{21}$$

$$Q_{32} = 0.5qY_3 \tag{22}$$

Here $c = \alpha + \beta + \gamma$ is the marginal consumption rate of America. $q = \gamma$ is the (overall) marginal import rate of America. At the same time, $q = \gamma$ is the marginal import rate of Germany relative to America. At the same time, $q = \gamma$ is the marginal import rate of France relative to America. $0.5q$ is the marginal import rate of America relative to Germany. At the same time, $0.5q$ is the marginal import rate of America relative to France.

Equation (18) is the consumption function of America. Equations (19) and (20) are the export functions of America. Equations (21) and (22) are the import functions of America. American output is determined by the demand for American goods $Y_3 = A_3 + C_3 + X_{31} + X_{32} - Q_{31} - Q_{32}$. Taking account of the consumption, export and import functions of America, we arrive at the goods market equation of America:

$$Y_3 = A_3 + cY_3 + qP_1Y_1 / eP_3 + qP_2Y_2 / eP_3 - qY_3 \tag{23}$$

12. A Second Model of Germany, France and America

According to Sections 9, 10 and 11, the model can be characterized by a system of three equations:

$$Y_1 = A_1 + cY_1 + mP_2Y_2 / P_1 + 0.5qeP_3Y_3 / P_1 - (m+q)Y_1 \tag{1}$$

$$Y_2 = A_2 + cY_2 + mP_1Y_1 / P_2 + 0.5qeP_3Y_3 / P_2 - (m+q)Y_2 \tag{2}$$

$$Y_3 = A_3 + cY_3 + qP_1Y_1 / eP_3 + qP_2Y_2 / eP_3 - qY_3 \tag{3}$$

Equation (1) is the goods market equation of Germany, as measured in German goods. Equation (2) is the goods market equation of France, as measured in French goods. And equation (3) in the goods market equation of America, as measured in American goods. Here the exogenous variables are the autonomous demand for German goods A_1, the autonomous demand for French goods A_2, the autonomous demand for American goods A_3, the price of German goods P_1, the price of French goods P_2, the price of American goods P_3, and the price of the dollar e. The endogenous variables are German output Y_1, French output Y_2, and American output Y_3.

An increase in the autonomous demand for French goods raises French output and, hence, German output as well as American output. An increase in the price of French goods lowers French output but raises German output and American output. An appreciation of the euro lowers French output and German output but raises American output. Essentially, this model forms the basis for the model developed in Part Three. Needless to say, the second model of Germany, France and America is equivalent to the first model of Germany, France and America, see Section 8 above. By the way, German exports to France (as measured in euros) are identical to French imports from Germany (as measured in euros) $mP_2Y_2 = mP_2Y_2$. On the other hand, German exports to France (as measured in euros) generally differ from German imports from France (as measured in euros) $mP_2Y_2 \neq mP_1Y_1$.

Chapter 4
The Small Monetary Union of Two Countries

So far, in Chapter 3, we assumed that Europe and America were the same size. Now, in Chapter 4, we assume that Europe is small and America is large. The general model can be described by a system of three equations:

$$Y_1 = A_1 + cY_1 + m_2 P_2 Y_2 / P_1 + 0.5 q_3 e P_3 Y_3 / P_1 - (m_1 + q_1) Y_1 \tag{1}$$

$$Y_2 = A_2 + cY_2 + m_1 P_1 Y_1 / P_2 + 0.5 q_3 e P_3 Y_3 / P_2 - (m_2 + q_2) Y_2 \tag{2}$$

$$Y_3 = A_3 + cY_3 + q_1 P_1 Y_1 / e P_3 + q_2 P_2 Y_2 / e P_3 - q_3 Y_3 \tag{3}$$

Here m_1 is the marginal import rate of Germany relative to France, m_2 is the marginal import rate of France relative to Germany, q_1 is the marginal import rate of Germany relative to America, and q_2 is the marginal import rate of France relative to America. We assume that Germany and France are the same size. In terms of the model this means that the marginal import rate of Germany relative to France is equal to the marginal import rate of France relative to Germany $m_1 = m_2$. In addition, it means that the marginal import rate of Germany relative to America is equal to the marginal import rate of France relative to America $q_1 = q_2$.

q_3 is the (overall) marginal import rate of America. $0.5 q_3$ is the marginal import rate of America relative to Germany. At the same time, $0.5 q_3$ is the marginal import rate of America relative to France. We assume that Europe is small and America is large. In terms of the model this means that the marginal import rate of Europe is large, and the marginal import rate of America is small $q_1 = q_2 > q_3$.

Equation (1) is the goods market equation of Germany, equation (2) is the goods market equation of France, and equation (3) is the goods market equation of America. The exogenous variables are the autonomous demand for German goods A_1, the autonomous demand for French goods A_2, the autonomous demand for American goods A_3, the price of German goods P_1, the price of

French goods P_2, the price of American goods P_3, and the price of the dollar e. The endogenous variables are German output Y_1, French output Y_2, and American output Y_3.

We turn next to an approximate solution for the small monetary region. An increase in the autonomous demand for German goods has three effects:
- the primary effect in Germany
- the spillover to France and America
- the repercussion from France and America.

For the approximate solution we assume that the repercussion effect from America to Germany and France is zero. So we take the same approach as in Chapter 2. The model can be captured by a system of two equations:

$$Y_1 = A_1 + cY_1 + m_2 P_2 Y_2 / P_1 + 0.5 q_3 e P_3 Y_3 / P_1 - (m_1 + q_1)Y_1 \tag{4}$$

$$Y_2 = A_2 + cY_2 + m_1 P_1 Y_1 / P_2 + 0.5 q_3 e P_3 Y_3 / P_2 - (m_2 + q_2)Y_2 \tag{5}$$

Equation (4) is the goods market equation of Germany, and equation (5) is the goods market equation of France. Here the exogenous variables are the autonomous demand for German goods A_1, the autonomous demand for French goods A_2, American income Y_3, the price of German goods P_1, the price of French goods P_2, the price of American goods P_3, and the price of the dollar e. The endogenous variables are German output Y_1 and French output Y_2.

As a result, according to equations (4) and (5), an increase in the autonomous demand for German goods raises German output and, hence, French output. An increase in American income raises both German output and French output. An increase in the price of German goods lowers German output but raises French output. An appreciation of the euro lowers both German output and French output. And an increase in the price of American goods raises both German output and French output.

Synopsis

1. The World of Two Monetary Regions

1.1. Given Money Growth

Producer inflation in Europe is determined by
- money growth in Europe
- output growth in Europe.

Producer inflation in America is determined by
- money growth in America
- output growth in America.

Nominal depreciation is determined by
- money growth in Europe
- money growth in America.

Real depreciation is determined by
- output growth in Europe
- output growth in America.

Consumer inflation in Europe is determined by
- money growth in Europe
- output growth in Europe
- output growth in America.

Consumer inflation in America is determined in by
- money growth in America
- output growth in America
- output growth in Europe.

The nominal interest differential is determined by
- money growth in Europe
- money growth in America.

The real interest differential is determined by
- output growth in Europe
- output growth in America.

Nominal wage growth in Europe is determined by
- money growth in Europe
- labour growth in Europe.

Nominal wage growth in America is determined by
- money growth in America
- labour growth in America.

The growth of producer real wages in Europe is determined by
- productivity growth in Europe.

The growth of producer real wages in America is determined by
- productivity growth in America.

The growth of consumer real wages in Europe is determined by
- productivity growth in Europe
- productivity growth in America
- labour growth in Europe
- labour growth in America.

The growth of consumer real wages in America is determined by
- productivity growth in America
- productivity growth in Europe
- labour growth in America
- labour growth in Europe.

Table 19
The World of Two Monetary Regions
Given Output Growth and Money Growth

Output Growth in Europe	2
Output Growth in America	3
Money Growth in Europe	3
Money Growth in America	5
Productivity Growth in Europe	2
Productivity Growth in America	3
Producer Inflation in Europe	1
Producer Inflation in America	2
Nominal Appreciation of the Euro	2
Nominal Depreciation of the Dollar	2
Real Appreciation of European Goods	1
Real Depreciation of American Goods	1
Consumer Inflation in Europe	0.9
Consumer Inflation in America	2.1
Nominal Interest Differential	− 2
Real Interest Differential	− 1
Growth of Nominal Wages in Europe	3
Growth of Nominal Wages in America	5
Growth of Producer Real Wages in Europe	2
Growth of Producer Real Wages in America	3
Growth of Consumer Real Wages in Europe	2.1
Growth of Consumer Real Wages in America	2.9

1.2. Target Inflation and Required Money Growth

Required money growth in Europe is determined by
- target inflation in Europe
- output growth in Europe
- output growth in America.

Required money growth in America is determined by
- target inflation in America
- output growth in America
- output growth in Europe.

Nominal depreciation is determined by
- target inflation in Europe
- target inflation in America
- output growth in Europe
- output growth in America.

The nominal interest differential is determined by
- target inflation in Europe
- target inflation in America
- output growth in Europe
- output growth in America.

Nominal wage growth in Europe is determined by
- target inflation in Europe
- productivity growth in Europe
- productivity growth in America
- labour growth in Europe
- labour growth in America.

Table 20

The World of Two Monetary Regions

Given Target Inflation and Output Growth

Target Inflation in Europe	1
Target Inflation in America	2
Output Growth in Europe	2
Output Growth in America	3
Productivity Growth in Europe	2
Productivity Growth in America	3
Required Money Growth in Europe	3.1
Required Money Growth in America	4.9
Producer Inflation in Europe	1.1
Producer Inflation in America	1.9
Nominal Appreciation of the Euro	1.8
Nominal Depreciation of the Dollar	1.8
Real Appreciation of European Goods	1
Real Depreciation of American Goods	1
Consumer Inflation in Europe	1
Consumer Inflation in America	2
Nominal Interest Differential	− 1.8
Real Interest Differential	− 1
Growth of Nominal Wages in Europe	3.1
Growth of Nominal Wages in America	4.9
Growth of Producer Real Wages in Europe	2
Growth of Producer Real Wages in America	3
Growth of Consumer Real Wages in Europe	2.1
Growth of Consumer Real Wages in America	2.9

2. The Monetary Union of Two Countries

2.1. Given Money Growth

Producer inflation in Germany is determined by
- money growth in Europe
- output growth in Germany.

Producer inflation in France is determined by
- money growth in Europe
- output growth in France.

Nominal depreciation between Europe and America is determined by
- money growth in Europe
- money growth in America.

Real depreciation between Germany and France is determined by
- output growth in Germany
- output growth in France.

Consumer inflation in Germany is determined by
- money growth in Europe
- output growth in Germany
- output growth in France
- output growth in America.

Consumer inflation in France is determined by
- money growth in Europe
- output growth in France
- output growth in Germany
- output growth in America.

The nominal interest differential between Germany and France is zero.

The real interest differential between Germany and France is determined by
- output growth in Germany
- output growth in France.

Nominal wage growth in Germany is determined by
- money growth in Europe
- labour growth in Germany.

Nominal wage growth in France is determined by
- money growth in Europe
- labour growth in France.

The growth of producer real wages in Germany is determined by
- productivity growth in Germany.

The growth of producer real wages in France is determined by
- productivity growth in France.

The growth of consumer real wages in Germany is determined by
- productivity growth in Germany
- productivity growth in France
- productivity growth in America
- labour growth in Germany
- labour growth in France
- labour growth in America.

The growth of consumer real wages in France is determined by
- productivity growth in France
- productivity growth in Germany
- productivity growth in America
- labour growth in France
- labour growth in Germany
- labour growth in America.

Table 21

The Monetary Union of Two Countries

Given Output Growth and Money Growth

Output Growth in Germany	1
Output Growth in France	3
Output Growth in America	2
Money Growth in Europe	3
Productivity Growth in Germany	1
Productivity Growth in France	3
Productivity Growth in America	2
Producer Inflation in Germany	2
Producer Inflation in France	0
Real Appreciation of German Goods	2
Real Depreciation of French Goods	2
Consumer Inflation in Germany	1.5
Consumer Inflation in France	0.5
Nominal Interest Differential	0
Real Interest Differential	− 2
Growth of Nominal Wages in Germany	3
Growth of Nominal Wages in France	3
Growth of Producer Real Wages in Germany	1
Growth of Producer Real Wages in France	3
Growth of Consumer Real Wages in Germany	1.5
Growth of Consumer Real Wages in France	2.5

2.2. Target Inflation and Required Money Growth

Required money growth in Europe is determined by
- target inflation in Europe
- output growth in Germany
- output growth in France
- output growth in America.

The nominal interest differential between Germany and France is zero.

Nominal wage growth in Germany is determined by
- target inflation in Europe
- productivity growth in Germany
- productivity growth in France
- productivity growth in America
- labour growth in Germany
- labour growth in France
- labour growth in America.

Nominal wage growth in France is determined by
- target inflation in Europe
- productivity growth in France
- productivity growth in Germany
- productivity growth in America
- labour growth in France
- labour growth in Germany
- labour growth in America.

Table 22
The Monetary Union of Two Countries
Given Target Inflation and Output Growth

Target Inflation in Europe	1
Output Growth in Germany	1
Output Growth in France	3
Output Growth in America	2
Productivity Growth in Germany	1
Productivity Growth in France	3
Productivity Growth in America	2
Required Money Growth in Europe	3
Producer Inflation in Germany	2
Producer Inflation in France	0
Real Appreciation of German Goods	2
Real Depreciation of French Goods	2
Consumer Inflation in Germany	1.5
Consumer Inflation in France	0.5
Consumer Inflation in Europe	1
Nominal Interest Differential	0
Real Interest Differential	− 2
Growth of Nominal Wages in Germany	3
Growth of Nominal Wages in France	3
Growth of Producer Real Wages in Germany	1
Growth of Producer Real Wages in France	3
Growth of Consumer Real Wages in Germany	1.5
Growth of Consumer Real Wages in France	2.5

3. A One-Good Model of the World Economy

3.1. The World of Two Monetary Regions

1) Given Money Growth

Inflation in Europe is determined by
- money growth in Europe
- output growth in Europe.

Nominal depreciation is determined by
- money growth in Europe
- money growth in America
- output growth in Europe
- output growth in America.

Real depreciation is zero.

The nominal interest differential is determined by
- money growth in Europe
- money growth in America
- output growth in Europe
- output growth in America.

The real interest differential is zero.

Nominal wage growth in Europe is determined by
- money growth in Europe
- labour growth in Europe.

Real wage growth in Europe is determined by
- productivity growth in Europe.

Table 23
The World of Two Monetary Regions
Given Output Growth and Money Growth

Output Growth in Europe	2
Output Growth in America	3
Money Growth in Europe	3
Money Growth in America	5
Productivity Growth in Europe	2
Productivity Growth in America	3
Inflation in Europe	1
Inflation in America	2
Nominal Appreciation of the Euro	1
Nominal Depreciation of the Dollar	1
Real Appreciation of European Goods	0
Real Depreciation of American Goods	0
Nominal Interest Differential	− 1
Real Interest Differential	0
Nominal Wage Growth in Europe	3
Nominal Wage Growth in America	5
Real Wage Growth in Europe	2
Real Wage Growth in America	3

2) Target Inflation and Required Money Growth

Required money growth in Europe is determined by
- target inflation in Europe
- output growth in Europe.

Required money growth in America is determined by
- target inflation in America
- output growth in America.

Nominal depreciation is determined by
- target inflation in Europe
- target inflation in America.

The nominal interest differential is determined by
- target inflation in Europe
- target inflation in America.

Nominal wage growth in Europe is determined by
- target inflation in Europe
- productivity growth in Europe.

Nominal wage growth in America is determined by
- target inflation in America
- productivity growth in America.

Table 24
The World of Two Monetary Regions
Given Target Inflation and Output Growth

Target Inflation in Europe	1
Target Inflation in America	2
Output Growth in Europe	2
Output Growth in America	3
Productivity Growth in Europe	2
Productivity Growth in America	3
Required Money Growth in Europe	3
Required Money Growth in America	5
Nominal Appreciation of the Euro	1
Nominal Depreciation of the Dollar	1
Real Appreciation of European Goods	0
Real Depreciation of American Goods	0
Nominal Interest Differential	− 1
Real Interest Differential	0
Nominal Wage Growth in Europe	3
Nominal Wage Growth in America	5
Real Wage Growth in Europe	2
Real Wage Growth in America	3

3.2. The Monetary Union of Two Countries

1) Given Money Growth

Inflation in Germany is determined by
- money growth in Europe
- output growth in Germany
- output growth in France.

Nominal depreciation between Europe and America is determined by
- money growth in Europe
- money growth in America
- output growth in Germany
- output growth in France
- output growth in America.

Real depreciation between Germany and France is zero.

The nominal interest differential between Germany and France is zero.

The real interest differential between Germany and France is zero.

Nominal wage growth in Germany is determined by
- money growth in Europe
- productivity growth in Germany
- productivity growth in France
- labour growth in Germany
- labour growth in France.

Real wage growth in Germany is determined by
- productivity growth in Germany.

Table 25

The Monetary Union of Two Countries

Given Output Growth and Money Growth

Output Growth in Germany	1
Output Growth in France	3
Money Growth in Europe	3
Productivity Growth in Germany	1
Productivity Growth in France	3
Inflation in Germany	1
Inflation in France	1
Real Appreciation of German Goods	0
Real Depreciation of French Goods	0
Nominal Interest Differential	0
Real Interest Differential	0
Nominal Wage Growth in Germany	2
Nominal Wage Growth in France	4
Real Wage Growth in Germany	1
Real Wage Growth in France	3

2) Target Inflation and Required Money Growth

Required money growth in Europe is determined by
- target inflation in Europe
- output growth in Germany
- output growth in France.

Nominal depreciation between Europe and America is determined by
- target inflation in Europe
- target inflation in America.

The nominal interest differential between Germany and France is zero.

Nominal wage growth in Germany is determined by
- target inflation in Europe
- productivity growth in Germany.

Nominal wage growth in France is determined by
- target inflation in Europe
- productivity growth in France.

Table 26

The Monetary Union of Two Countries

Given Target Inflation and Output Growth

Target Inflation in Europe	1
Output Growth in Germany	1
Output Growth in France	3
Productivity Growth in Germany	1
Productivity Growth in France	3
Required Money Growth in Europe	3
Inflation in Germany	1
Inflation in France	1
Real Appreciation of German Goods	0
Real Depreciation of French Goods	0
Nominal Interest Differential	0
Real Interest Differential	0
Nominal Wage Growth in Germany	2
Nominal Wage Growth in France	4
Real Wage Growth in Germany	1
Real Wage Growth in France	3

Conclusion

1. The World of Two Monetary Regions

1.1. Given Money Growth

1) The model. The world consists of two monetary regions, say Europe and America. The exchange rate between Europe and America is flexible. Here the focus is on steady-state inflation in Europe and America, given steady-state growth. Nominal wages and prices are flexible, so there is full employment in Europe and America. European goods and American goods are imperfect substitutes for each other. The monetary regions are the same size and have the same behavioural functions.

2) Producer inflation. Producer inflation in Europe refers to the price of European goods, as measured in euros. Producer inflation in America refers to the price of American goods, as measured in dollars. As a result, producer inflation in Europe is determined by money growth in Europe and by output growth in Europe. Correspondingly, producer inflation in America is determined by money growth in America and by output growth in America.

In the region where money growth is high, other things being equal, producer inflation will be high. And in the region where money growth is low, producer inflation will be low. In the region where output growth is high, other things being equal, producer inflation will be low. And in the region where output growth is low, producer inflation will be high. For instance, let output growth in Europe be 2 percent, let output growth in America be 3 percent, let money growth in Europe be 3 percent, and let money growth in America be 5 percent. Then producer inflation in Europe is 1 percent, and producer inflation in America is 2 percent.

3) Nominal depreciation. As a result, the rate of depreciation is determined by money growth in Europe and by money growth in America. In the region where money growth is high, the currency will depreciate. And in the region where money growth is low, the currency will appreciate. To be more specific, if

money growth in Europe is high, the euro will depreciate. And if money growth in Europe is low, the euro will appreciate. Correspondingly, if money growth in America is high, the dollar will depreciate. And if money growth in America is low, the dollar will appreciate.

To illustrate this, consider some numerical examples. Let us begin with numerical example number one. Let money growth in Europe be 3 percent, and let money growth in America be 5 percent. Then the price of the dollar declines at a constant rate of 2 percent. In other words, the price of the euro grows at a constant rate of 2 percent.

We proceed now to numerical example number two. Let output growth in Europe be 2 percent, let output growth in America be 3 percent, let money growth in Europe be 3 percent, and let money growth in America be 4 percent. Then producer inflation in Europe is 1 percent, producer inflation in America is 1 percent, the appreciation of the euro is 1 percent, and the depreciation of the dollar is 1 percent. Here we have an appreciation of the euro, in spite of the fact that producer inflation in Europe is equal to producer inflation in America. The general point is that the rate of depreciation does not depend on producer inflation in Europe or on producer inflation in America. This is in sharp contrast to a widely held view.

4) Real depreciation. The real exchange rate is defined as the price of American goods, as measured in European goods. An increase in the relative price of American goods lowers the purchasing power of European goods. As a result, the growth of the relative price of American goods is determined by output growth in Europe and by output growth in America.

If output growth in America is high, the relative price of American goods will decline. And if output growth in America is low, the relative price of American goods will increase. If output growth in Europe is high, the relative price of American goods will increase. And if output growth in Europe is low, the relative price of American goods will decline. For instance, let output growth in Europe be 2 percent, and let output growth in America be 3 percent. Then the relative price of American goods declines at a constant rate of 1 percent. That is to say, the relative price of European goods grows at a constant rate of 1 percent.

Finally compare nominal depreciation and real depreciation. Nominal depreciation is determined by money growth in Europe and by money growth in America. Real depreciation, on the other hand, is determined by output growth in Europe and by output growth in America. In short, nominal depreciation is driven by the money growth differential. And real depreciation is driven by the output growth differential.

5) Consumer inflation. European consumption includes both European goods and American goods. Therefore, the consumer price index of Europe includes the price of European goods, the price of American goods, and the price of the dollar. Accordingly, consumer inflation in Europe includes producer inflation in Europe, producer inflation in America, and the appreciation of the dollar.

As a result, consumer inflation in Europe is determined by money growth in Europe, by output growth in Europe, and by output growth in America. An increase in European money growth raises consumer inflation in Europe. An increase in European output growth lowers consumer inflation in Europe. And what is more, an increase in American output growth lowers consumer inflation in Europe too. Similarly, consumer inflation in America is determined by money growth in America, by output growth in America, and by output growth in Europe.

To see this more clearly, have a look at a numerical example. Let output growth in Europe be 2 percent, let output growth in America be 3 percent, let money growth in Europe be 3 percent, and let money growth in America be 5 percent. Further, let the share of American goods in European consumption be 0.1, and let the share of European goods in American consumption be equally 0.1. Then consumer inflation in Europe is 0.9 percent, and consumer inflation in America is 2.1 percent. Compare this with producer inflation. Producer inflation in Europe is 1 percent, and producer inflation in America is 2 percent.

6) The growth of nominal wages, given productivity growth. As a result, nominal wage growth in Europe is determined by money growth in Europe. And nominal wage growth in America is determined by money growth in America. In the region where money growth is high, nominal wage growth will be high. And in the region where money growth is low, nominal wage growth will be low. For instance, let money growth in Europe be 3 percent, and let money growth in

America be 5 percent. Then nominal wage growth in Europe is 3 percent, and nominal wage growth in America is 5 percent.

7) The growth of producer real wages, given productivity growth. Producer real wages in Europe are defined as nominal wages in Europe divided by the price of European goods. And producer real wages in America are defined as nominal wages in America divided by the price of American goods. Producer real wages in Europe measure the real cost of labour in Europe. And producer real wages in America measure the real cost of labour in America.

As a result, the growth of producer real wages in Europe is driven by productivity growth in Europe. And the growth of producer real wages in America is driven by productivity growth in America. In the region where productivity growth is high, the growth of producer real wages will be high. And in the region where productivity growth is low, the growth of producer real wages will be low. For instance, let productivity growth in Europe be 2 percent, and let productivity growth in America be 3 percent. Then the growth of producer real wages in Europe is 2 percent, and the growth of producer real wages in America is 3 percent.

8) The growth of consumer real wages, given productivity growth. Consumer real wages in Europe are defined as nominal wages in Europe divided by the consumer price index of Europe. Consumer real wages in America are defined as nominal wages in America divided by the consumer price index of America. European nominal wages are spent on European goods and on American goods. So consumer real wages in Europe measure the purchasing power of European nominal wages. American nominal wages are spent on American goods and on European goods. So consumer real wages in America measure the purchasing power of American nominal wages.

As a result, the growth of consumer real wages in Europe is determined by productivity growth in Europe and by productivity growth in America. Correspondingly, the growth of consumer real wages in America is determined by productivity growth in America and by productivity growth in Europe. In the region where productivity growth is high, the growth of consumer real wages will be high. And in the region where productivity growth is low, the growth of consumer real wages will be low.

To illustrate this, consider a numerical example. Let productivity growth in Europe be 2 percent, and let productivity growth in America be 3 percent. In addition, let the share of American goods in European consumption be 0.1, and let the share of European goods in American consumption be equally 0.1. Then the growth of consumer real wages in Europe is 2.1 percent, and the growth of consumer real wages in America is 2.9 percent. Compare this with the growth of producer real wages. The growth of producer real wages in Europe is 2 percent, and the growth of producer real wages in America is 3 percent.

9) The growth of nominal wages, given labour growth. As a finding, nominal wage growth in Europe is determined by money growth in Europe and by labour growth in Europe. Similarly, nominal wage growth in America is determined by money growth in America and by labour growth in America. In the region where money growth is high, nominal wage growth will be high. And in the region where money growth is low, nominal wage growth will be low. In the region where labour growth is high, nominal wage growth will be low. And in the region where labour growth is low, nominal wage growth will be high.

To see this more clearly, have a look at some numerical examples. Let us start with numerical example number one. Let labour growth in Europe be 1 percent, let labour growth in America be equally 1 percent, let money growth in Europe be 2 percent, and let money growth in America be 3 percent. Then nominal wage growth in Europe is 1 percent, and nominal wage growth in America is 2 percent. We proceed now to numerical example number two. Let labour growth in Europe be 0 percent, let labour growth in America be 1 percent, let money growth in Europe be 2 percent, and let money growth in America be equally 2 percent. Then nominal wage growth in Europe is 2 percent, and nominal wage growth in America is 1 percent.

10) The growth of producer real wages, given labour growth. As a finding, producer real wages in Europe are constant. And the same applies to producer real wages in America. This holds although there is labour growth. And this holds although the regions differ in labour growth.

11) The growth of consumer real wages, given labour growth. As a finding, the growth of consumer real wages in Europe is determined by labour growth in

Europe and by labour growth in America. Likewise, the growth of consumer real wages in America is determined by labour growth in America and by labour growth in Europe. In the region where labour growth is high, consumer real wages will decline. And in the region where labour growth is low, consumer real wages will increase. For instance, let labour growth in Europe be 0 percent, and let labour growth in America be 1 percent. Further, let the share of American goods in European consumption be 0.1, and let the share of European goods in American consumption be equally 0.1. Then the growth of consumer real wages in Europe is 0.1 percent, and the growth of consumer real wages in America is − 0.1 percent.

12) Nominal interest rates. There is perfect capital mobility between Europe and America. The nominal interest rate in Europe equals the sum of the nominal interest rate in America and the rate of depreciation. As a result, the nominal interest differential is determined by the money growth differential. In the region where money growth is high, the nominal interest rate will be high. And in the region where money growth is low, the nominal interest rate will be low. To illustrate this, consider some numerical examples. Let us start with numerical example number one. Let money growth in Europe be 3 percent, and let money growth in America be 5 percent. Then the nominal interest rate in America exceeds the nominal interest rate in Europe by 2 percentage points.

We proceed now to numerical example number two. Let output growth in Europe be 2 percent, let output growth in America be 3 percent, let money growth in Europe be 3 percent, and let money growth in America be 5 percent. Then the nominal interest rate in America exceeds the nominal interest rate in Europe by 2 percentage points. Compare this with producer inflation. Producer inflation in Europe is 1 percent, and producer inflation in America is 2 percent. So producer inflation in America exceeds producer inflation in Europe by 1 percentage point. By comparison, the nominal interest differential is greater than the inflation differential. The general point is that the nominal interest differential is not determined by the inflation differential. This is in remarkable contrast to a popular view.

13) Real interest rates. The real interest rate in Europe is defined as the nominal interest rate in Europe minus producer inflation in Europe. And the real interest rate in America is defined as the nominal interest rate in America minus

producer inflation in America. As a result, the real interest differential is determined by the output growth differential. In the region where output growth is high, the real interest rate will be high. And in the region where output growth is low, the real interest rate will be low. It is worth pointing out here that the real interest differential cannot be exploited by producers. For instance, let output growth in Europe be 2 percent, and let output growth in America be 3 percent. Then the real interest rate in America exceeds the real interest rate in Europe by 1 percentage point.

Finally compare the nominal interest differential and the real interest differential. The nominal interest differential is determined by the money growth differential. And the real interest differential is determined by the output growth differential.

1.2. Target Inflation and Required Money Growth

1) Required money growth. The objective of the European central bank is to maintain price stability in Europe. Strictly speaking, the objective of the European central bank is to keep consumer inflation in Europe at target level. The objective of the American central bank is to maintain price stability in America. Strictly speaking, the objective of the American central bank is to keep consumer inflation in America at target level.

As a result, required money growth in Europe is determined by target inflation in Europe, by output growth in Europe, and by output growth in America. An increase in European target inflation calls for an increase in European money growth. An increase in European output growth calls for an increase in European money growth too. And what is more, an increase in American output growth calls for an increase in European money growth as well. By analogy, required money growth in America is determined by target inflation in America, by output growth in America, and by output growth in Europe. In the region where target inflation is high, money growth has to be high. And in the region where target inflation is low, money growth has to be low. In the region where output growth is high, money growth has to be high. And in the region where output growth is low, money growth has to be low.

To see this more clearly, have a look at a numerical example. Let the share of American goods in European consumption be 0.1, and let the share of European goods in American consumption be equally 0.1. First consider the case that output growth in Europe equals output growth in America. Let target inflation in Europe be 1 percent, let target inflation in America be 2 percent, let output growth in Europe be 2 percent, and let output growth in America be equally 2 percent. Then required money growth in Europe is 3 percent, and required money growth in America is 4 percent. Second consider the case that target inflation in Europe equals target inflation in America. Let output growth in Europe be 2 percent, let output growth in America be 3 percent, let target inflation in Europe be 1 percent, and let target inflation in America be equally 1 percent. Then required money growth in Europe is 3.1 percent, and required money growth in America is 3.9 percent.

2) Nominal depreciation. As a result, the rate of depreciation is determined by target inflation in Europe, by target inflation in America, by output growth in Europe, and by output growth in America.

First consider the case that output growth in Europe equals output growth in America. Then the rate of depreciation is determined by the target inflation differential. In the region where target inflation is high, the currency will depreciate. And in the region where target inflation is low, the currency will appreciate. To be more specific, if target inflation in Europe is high, the euro will depreciate. And if target inflation in Europe is low, the euro will appreciate. Correspondingly, if target inflation in America is high, the dollar will depreciate. And if target inflation in America is low, the dollar will appreciate. For instance, let target inflation in Europe be 1 percent, and let target inflation in America be 2 percent. Then the appreciation of the euro is 1 percent. In other words, the depreciation of the dollar is 1 percent. How can this be explained? In the region where target inflation is high, money growth has to be high. And in the region where target inflation is low, money growth has to be low.

Second consider the case that target inflation in Europe equals target inflation in America. Then the rate of depreciation is determined by the output growth differential. In the region where output growth is high, the currency will depreciate. And in the region where output growth is low, the currency will appreciate. To be more explicit, if output growth in Europe is high, the euro will depreciate. And if output growth in Europe is low, the euro will appreciate. Correspondingly, if output growth in America is high, the dollar will depreciate. And if output growth in America is low, the dollar will appreciate. For instance, let output growth in Europe be 2 percent, and let output growth in America be 3 percent. Then the appreciation of the euro is 0.8 percent. Put differently, the depreciation of the dollar is 0.8 percent. What is the intuition about this result? In the region where output growth is high, money growth has to be high. And in the region where output growth is low, money growth has to be low.

To sum up, nominal depreciation is determined by the target inflation differential and by the output growth differential. This is in sharp contrast to the conclusions drawn under given money growth. There, nominal depreciation was determined by the money growth differential.

3) Nominal interest rates. As a result, the difference between the nominal interest rate in Europe and the nominal interest rate in America is determined by target inflation in Europe, by target inflation in America, by output growth in Europe, and by output growth in America.

First have a look at the case that output growth in Europe equals output growth in America. Then the nominal interest differential is determined by the target inflation differential. In the region where target inflation is high, the nominal interest rate will be high. And in the region where target inflation is low, the nominal interest rate will be low. For instance, let target inflation in Europe be 1 percent, and let target inflation in America be 2 percent. Then the nominal interest rate in America exceeds the nominal interest rate in Europe by 1 percentage point.

Second have a look at the case that target inflation in Europe equals target inflation in America. Then the nominal interest differential is determined by the output growth differential. In the region where output growth is high, the nominal interest rate will be high. And in the region where output growth is low, the nominal interest rate will be low. For instance, let output growth in Europe be 2 percent, and let output growth in America be 3 percent. Then the nominal interest rate in America exceeds the nominal interest rate in Europe by 0.8 percentage points. At first glance, this comes as a surprise.

To sum up, the nominal interest differential is determined by the target inflation differential and by the output growth differential. This is in remarkable contrast to the conclusions reached under given money growth. There, the nominal interest differential was determined by the money growth differential.

4) The growth of nominal wages, given productivity growth. As a result, nominal wage growth in Europe is determined by target inflation in Europe, by productivity growth in Europe, and by productivity growth in America. An increase in European target inflation raises nominal wage growth in Europe. An increase in European productivity growth raises nominal wage growth in Europe. And an increase in American productivity growth raises nominal wage growth in Europe too. Nominal wage growth in America is determined by target inflation in America, by productivity growth in America, and by productivity growth in Europe. For instance, let target inflation in Europe be 1 percent, let target inflation in America be 2 percent, let productivity growth in Europe be 2 percent, and let productivity growth in America be 3 percent. Then nominal wage growth in Europe is 3.1 percent, and nominal wage growth in America is 4.9 percent.

5) The growth of nominal wages, given labour growth. As a finding, nominal wage growth in Europe is determined by target inflation in Europe, by labour growth in Europe, and by labour growth in America. An increase in European target inflation drives up nominal wage growth in Europe. An increase in European labour growth cuts down nominal wage growth in Europe. And an increase in American labour growth drives up nominal wage growth in Europe. Nominal wage growth in America is determined by target inflation in America, by labour growth in America, and by labour growth in Europe. For instance, let target inflation in Europe be 1 percent, let target inflation in America be 2 percent, let labour growth in Europe be 0 percent, and let labour growth in America be 1 percent. Then nominal wage growth in Europe is 1.1 percent, and nominal wage growth in America is 1.9 percent.

1.3. The Monetary Regions Differ in Size

Now assume that Europe is small and America is large. In terms of the model this means that the marginal import rate of Europe is large, and the marginal import rate of America is small. For instance, let the marginal import rate of Europe be 0.2, and let the marginal import rate of America be 0.1. Then American income (as measured in euros) is twice as much as European income (as measured in euros). As a result, concerning producer inflation and nominal depreciation, the relative size of regions does not matter at all. With respect to consumer inflation, the relative size of regions matters to a limited extent. And the same holds with respect to target inflation and required money growth.

2. The Monetary Union of Two Countries

2.1. Given Money Growth

1) The model. The world consists of two monetary regions, say Europe and America. The exchange rate between Europe and America is flexible. Europe in turn consists of two countries, say Germany and France. So Germany and France form a monetary union. Here the focus is on steady-state inflation in Germany, France and America, given steady-state growth. Nominal wages and prices are flexible, thus there is full employment in Germany, France and America. German goods, French goods and American goods are imperfect substitutes for each other. The monetary regions are the same size and have the same behavioural functions. The union countries are the same size and have the same behavioural functions.

2) Producer inflation. Producer inflation in Germany refers to the price of German goods, as measured in euros. Producer inflation in France refers to the price of French goods, as measured in euros. As a result, producer inflation in Germany is determined by money growth in Europe and by output growth in Germany. Correspondingly, producer inflation in France is determined by money growth in Europe and by output growth in France. In the country where output growth in high, producer inflation will be low. And in the country where output growth is low, producer inflation will be high. To illustrate this, consider a numerical example. Let output growth in Germany be 1 percent, let output growth in France be 3 percent, and let money growth in Europe be 3 percent. Then, as a result, producer inflation in Germany is 2 percent, and producer inflation in France is 0 percent.

3) Nominal depreciation. As a result, the rate of depreciation is determined by money growth in Europe and by money growth in America. In the region where money growth is high, the currency will depreciate. And in the region where money growth is low, the currency will appreciate. To be more specific, if money growth in Europe exceeds money growth in America, then the euro will depreciate and the dollar will appreciate. The other way round, if money growth in Europe falls short of money growth in America, then the euro will appreciate

and the dollar will depreciate. For instance, let money growth in Europe be 3 percent, and let money growth in America be 4 percent. Then the euro appreciates at a rate of 1 percent. That is to say, the dollar depreciates at a rate of 1 percent.

To sum up, the rate of depreciation is determined by money growth in Europe and by money growth in America. In short, the rate of depreciation is driven by the money growth differential. But be careful. The rate of depreciation does not depend on producer inflation in Germany, on producer inflation in France, or on producer inflation in America.

4) Real depreciation. Here the real exchange rate is defined as the price of French goods, as measured in German goods. An increase in the relative price of French goods lowers the purchasing power of German goods. As a result, the growth of the relative price of French goods is determined by output growth in Germany and by output growth in France. If output growth in France is high, the relative price of French goods will decline. And if output growth in France is low, the relative price of French goods will increase. If output growth in Germany is high, the relative price of French goods will increase. And if output growth in Germany is low, the relative price of French goods will decline. For instance, let output growth in Germany be 1 percent, and let output growth in France be 3 percent. Then the relative price of French goods declines at a rate of 2 percent. That is to say, the relative price of German goods grows at a rate of 2 percent.

Finally compare nominal depreciation and real depreciation. Nominal depreciation is determined by money growth in Europe and by money growth in America. Real depreciation, on the other hand, is determined by output growth in Germany, by output growth in France, and by output growth in America. In short, nominal depreciation is driven by the money growth differential. And real depreciation is driven by the output growth differential.

5) Consumer inflation. German consumption includes German goods, French goods and American goods. Therefore, the consumer price index of Germany includes the price of German goods, the price of French goods, the price of American goods, and the price of the dollar. Accordingly, consumer inflation in

Germany includes producer inflation in Germany, producer inflation in France, producer inflation in America, and the appreciation of the dollar.

As a result, consumer inflation in Germany is determined by money growth in Europe, by output growth in Germany, by output growth in France, and by output growth in America. An increase in European money growth raises consumer inflation in Germany. An increase in German output growth lowers consumer inflation in Germany. And what is more, an increase in French output growth lowers consumer inflation in Germany too. Similarly, an increase in American output growth lowers consumer inflation in Germany as well. Consumer inflation in France is determined by money growth in Europe, by output growth in France, by output growth in Germany, and by output growth in America.

To see this more clearly, have a look at a numerical example. Let output growth in Germany be 1 percent, let output growth in France be 3 percent, let output growth in America be 2 percent, and let money growth in Europe be 3 percent. Besides, let the share of French goods in German consumption be 0.2, and let the share of American goods in German consumption be 0.1. By symmetry, let the share of German goods in French consumption be 0.2, and let the share of American goods in French consumption be 0.1. Then consumer inflation in Germany is 1.5 percent, and consumer inflation in France is 0.5 percent. Compare this with producer inflation. Producer inflation in Germany is 2 percent, and producer inflation in France is 0 percent. So consumer inflation differs remarkably from producer inflation.

6) The growth of nominal wages, given productivity growth. As a result, nominal wage growth in Germany is determined by money growth in Europe. And nominal wage growth in France is determined by money growth in Europe too. For instance, let productivity growth in Germany be 1 percent, let productivity growth in France be 3 percent, and let money growth in Europe be 3 percent. Then nominal wage growth in Germany is 3 percent, and nominal wage growth in France is equally 3 percent. It is worth pointing out that nominal wages in Germany and France grow at the same rate, although Germany and France differ in productivity growth.

7) The growth of producer real wages, given productivity growth. Producer real wages in Germany are defined as nominal wages in Germany divided by the price of German goods. And producer real wages in France are defined as nominal wages in France divided by the price of French goods. Producer real wages in Germany measure the real cost of labour in Germany. And producer real wages in France measure the real cost of labour in France.

As a result, the growth of producer real wages in Germany is determined by productivity growth in Germany. And the growth of producer real wages in France is driven by productivity growth in France. In the country where productivity growth is high, the growth of producer real wages will be high. And in the country where productivity growth is low, the growth of producer real wages will be low. For instance, let productivity growth in Germany be 1 percent, and let productivity growth in France be 3 percent. Then the growth of producer real wages in Germany is 1 percent, and the growth of producer real wages in France is 3 percent.

8) The growth of consumer real wages, given productivity growth. Consumer real wages in Germany are defined as nominal wages in Germany divided by the consumer price index of Germany. Consumer real wages in France are defined as nominal wages in France divided by the consumer price index of France. German nominal wages are spent on German goods, on French goods, and on American goods. So consumer real wages in Germany measure the purchasing power of German nominal wages. French nominal wages are spent on French goods, on German goods, and on American goods. So consumer real wages in France measure the purchasing power of French nominal wages.

As a result, the growth of consumer real wages in Germany is determined by productivity growth in Germany, by productivity growth in France, and by productivity growth in America. Correspondingly, the growth of consumer real wages in France is determined by productivity growth in France, by productivity growth in Germany, and by productivity growth in America. In the country where productivity growth is high, the growth of consumer real wages will be high. And in the country where productivity growth is low, the growth of consumer real wages will be low.

To illustrate this, consider a numerical example. Let productivity growth in Germany be 1 percent, let productivity growth in France be 3 percent, and let productivity growth in America be 2 percent. Besides, let the share of French goods in German consumption be 0.2, and let the share of American goods in German consumption be 0.1. Symmetrically, let share of German goods in French consumption by 0.2, and let the share of American goods in French consumption be 0.1. Then the growth of consumer real wages in Germany is 1.5 percent, and the growth of consumer real wages in France is 2.5 percent. Compare this with the growth of producer real wages. The growth of producer real wages in Germany is 1 percent, and the growth of producer real wages in France is 3 percent. Thus the growth of consumer real wages differs substantially from the growth of producer real wages.

9) The growth of nominal wages, given labour growth. As a finding, nominal wage growth in Germany is determined by money growth in Europe and by labour growth in Germany. Similarly, nominal wage growth in France is determined by money growth in Europe and by labour growth in France. In the country where labour growth is high, nominal wage growth will be low. And in the country where labour growth is low, nominal wage growth will be high. For instance, let labour growth in Germany be −1 percent, let labour growth in France be 1 percent, and let money growth in Europe be 1 percent. Then nominal wage growth in Germany is 2 percent, and nominal wage growth in France is 0 percent.

10) The growth of producer real wages, given labour growth. As a finding, producer real wages in Germany are constant. And the same applies to producer real wages in France. This holds although there is labour growth. And this holds although the countries differ in labour growth.

11) The growth of consumer real wages, given labour growth. As a finding, the growth of consumer real wages in Germany is determined by labour growth in Germany, by labour growth in France, and by labour growth in America. Likewise, the growth of consumer real wages in France is determined by labour growth in France, by labour growth in Germany, and by labour growth in America. In the country where labour growth is high, consumer real wages will decline. And in the country where labour growth is low, consumer real wages will increase. For instance, let labour growth in Germany be − 1 percent, let

labour growth in France be 1 percent, and let labour growth in America be 0 percent. Then the growth of consumer real wages in Germany is 0.5 percent, and the growth of consumer real wages in France is − 0.5 percent.

12) Nominal interest rates. As a result, the nominal interest differential between Germany and France is zero. Further, the nominal interest differential between Europe and America is determined by the money growth differential between Europe and America. In the region where money growth is high, the nominal interest rate will be high. And in the region where money growth is low, the nominal interest rate will be low. For instance, let money growth in Europe be 3 percent, and let money growth in America be 4 percent. Then the nominal interest rate in America exceeds the nominal interest rate in Europe by 1 percentage point.

13) Real interest rates. The real interest rate in Germany is defined as the nominal interest rate in Germany minus producer inflation in Germany. And the real interest rate in France is defined as the nominal interest rate in France minus producer inflation in France. As a result, the real interest differential between Germany and France is determined by the output growth differential between Germany and France. In the country where output growth is high, the real interest rate will be high. And in the country where output growth is low, the real interest rate will be low. It is worth pointing out here that the real interest differential cannot be exploited. For instance, let output growth in Germany be 1 percent, and let output growth in France be 3 percent. Then the real interest rate in France exceeds the real interest rate in Germany by 2 percentage points.

Finally compare the nominal interest differential and the real interest differential. The nominal interest differential is determined by the money growth differential. And the real interest differential is determined by the output growth differential.

2.2. Target Inflation and Required Money Growth

1) Required money growth. The objective of the European central bank is to maintain price stability in Europe. Strictly speaking, the objective of the European central bank is to keep consumer inflation in Europe at target level. European consumption includes German goods, French goods and American goods. Therefore, the consumer price index of Europe includes the price of German goods, the price of French goods, the price of American goods, and the price of the dollar. Accordingly, consumer inflation in Europe includes producer inflation in Germany, producer inflation in France, producer inflation in America, and the appreciation of the dollar.

As a result, required money growth in Europe is determined by target inflation in Europe, by output growth in Germany, by output growth in France, and by output growth in America. An increase in European target inflation calls for an increase in European money growth. An increase in German output growth calls for an increase in European money growth. Likewise, an increase in French output growth calls for an increase in European money growth. And what is more, an increase in American output growth calls for an increase in European money growth too.

To see this more clearly, have a look at a numerical example. Let target inflation in Europe be 1 percent, let output growth in Germany be 1 percent, let output growth in France be 3 percent, and let output growth in America be 2 percent. Then required money growth in Europe is 3 percent. Producer inflation in Germany is 2 percent, and producer inflation in France is 0 percent. Consumer inflation in Germany is 1.5 percent, consumer inflation in France is 0.5 percent, and consumer inflation in Europe is 1 percent. That means, consumer inflation in Europe is at target level. But, in a sense, consumer inflation in Germany is not at target level. And the same applies to consumer inflation in France.

2) The growth of nominal wages, given productivity growth. As a result, nominal wage growth in Germany is determined by target inflation in Europe, by productivity growth in Germany, by productivity growth in France, and by productivity growth in America. An increase in European target inflation raises

nominal wage growth in Germany. An increase in German productivity growth raises nominal wage growth in Germany. An increase in French productivity growth raises nominal wage growth in Germany. And an increase in American productivity growth has the same effect. Correspondingly, nominal wage growth in France is determined by target inflation in Europe, by productivity growth in France, by productivity growth in Germany, and by productivity growth in America.

For instance, let target inflation in Europe be 1 percent, let productivity growth in Germany be 1 percent, let productivity growth in France be 3 percent, and let productivity growth in America be 2 percent. Then nominal wage growth in Germany is 3 percent, and nominal wage growth in France is equally 3 percent. It is worth pointing out that nominal wages in Germany and France grow at the same rate, although Germany and France differ in productivity growth.

3) The growth of nominal wages, given labour growth. As a finding, nominal wage growth in Germany is determined by target inflation in Europe, by labour growth in Germany, by labour growth in France, and by labour growth in America. Similarly, nominal wage growth in France is determined by target inflation in Europe, by labour growth in France, by labour growth in Germany, and by labour growth in America. In the country where labour growth is high, nominal wage growth will be low. And in the country where labour growth is low, nominal wage growth will be high. For instance, let target inflation in Europe be 1 percent, let labour growth in Germany be −1 percent, let labour growth in France 1 percent, and let labour growth in America be 0 percent. Then nominal wage growth in Germany is 2 percent, and nominal wage growth in France is 0 percent.

2.3. The Union Countries Differ in Size

Now assume that Germany is large and France is small. In terms of the model this means that the marginal import rate of Germany relative to France is small, and the marginal import rate of France relative to Germany is large. For instance, let the marginal import rate of Germany relative to France be 0.1, and let the marginal import rate of France relative to Germany be 0.2. Then German income (as measured in euros) is twice as much as French income (as measured in euros). As a result, concerning producer inflation and nominal depreciation, the relative size of union countries does not matter at all. With respect to consumer inflation, the relative size of union countries matters to a limited extent. And the same holds with respect to target inflation and required money growth.

3. A One-Good Model of the World Economy

3.1. The World of Two Monetary Regions

1) Given money growth. First consider inflation. As a result, inflation in Europe is determined by money growth in Europe and by output growth in Europe. For instance, let output growth in Europe be 2 percent, and let money growth in Europe be 3 percent. Then inflation in Europe is 1 percent. This differs substantially from the conclusions reached in the two-good model, see Section 1 above. There, consumer inflation in Europe was determined by money growth in Europe, by output growth in Europe, and by output growth in America. Here, there is no difference between producer inflation and consumer inflation.

Second consider nominal depreciation. As a result, the rate of depreciation is determined by inflation in Europe and by inflation in America. In the region where inflation is high, the currency will depreciate. And in the region where inflation is low, the currency will appreciate. To be more specific, if inflation in Europe is high, the euro will depreciate. And if inflation in Europe is low, the euro will appreciate. Correspondingly, if inflation in America is high, the dollar will depreciate. And if inflation in America is low, the dollar will appreciate.

More exactly, the rate of depreciation is determined by money growth in Europe, by money growth in America, by output growth in Europe, and by output growth in America. In the region where money growth is high, other things being equal, the currency will depreciate. And in the region where money growth is low, the currency will appreciate. In the region where output growth is high, other things being equal, the currency will appreciate. And in the region where output growth in low, the currency will depreciate.

To illustrate this, consider a numerical example. Let output growth in Europe be 2 percent, let output growth in America be 3 percent, let money growth in Europe be 3 percent, and let money growth in America be 5 percent. Then inflation in Europe is 1 percent, inflation in America is 2 percent, the appreciation of the euro is 1 percent, and the depreciation of the dollar is 1 percent.

This is in sharp contrast to the conclusions drawn from the two-good model. There, the rate of depreciation was determined by money growth in Europe and by money growth in America. However, the rate of depreciation was not determined by output growth in Europe or by output growth in America. Likewise, the rate of depreciation was not determined by inflation in Europe or by inflation in America.

Third consider nominal interest rates. As a result, the nominal interest differential is determined by the inflation differential. In the region where inflation is high, the nominal interest rate will be high. And in the region where inflation is low, the nominal interest rate will be low. More precisely, the nominal interest differential is determined by the money growth differential and by the output growth differential. In the region where money growth is high, other things being equal, the nominal interest rate will be high. And in the region where money growth is low, the nominal interest rate will be low. In the region where output growth is high, other things being equal, the nominal interest rate will be low. And in the region where output growth is low, the nominal interest rate will be high.

For instance, let output growth in Europe be 2 percent, let output growth in America be 3 percent, let money growth in Europe be 3 percent, and let money growth in America be 5 percent. Then inflation in Europe is 1 percent, and inflation in America is 2 percent. So the nominal interest rate in America exceeds the nominal interest rate in Europe by 1 percentage point. This is in clear contrast to the conclusions reached in the two-good model. There the nominal interest differential was determined by the money growth differential. However, it was not determined by the output growth differential. And it was not determined by the inflation differential either.

Fourth consider real interest rates. As a result, the real interest rate in Europe equals the real interest rate in America. This differs widely from the conclusions drawn in the two-good model. There the real interest differential was determined by the output growth differential.

2) Target inflation and required money growth. As a result, required money growth in Europe is determined by target inflation in Europe and by output growth in Europe. For instance, let target inflation in Europe be 1 percent, and let output growth in Europe be 2 percent. Then required money growth in Europe is 3 percent. This is in remarkable contrast to the conclusions reached in the two-good model. There required money growth in Europe was determined by target inflation in Europe, by output growth in Europe, and by output growth in America.

Next consider nominal depreciation, given target inflation. As a result, the rate of depreciation is determined by target inflation in Europe and by target inflation in America. In the region where target inflation is high, the currency will depreciate. And in the region where target inflation is low, the currency will appreciate. For instance, let target inflation in Europe be 1 percent, and let target inflation in America be 2 percent. Then the appreciation of the euro is 1 percent. In other words, the depreciation of the dollar is 1 percent. This is in sharp contrast to the conclusions drawn from the two-good model. There the rate of depreciation was determined by target inflation in Europe, by target inflation in America, by output growth in Europe, and by output growth in America.

3.2. The Monetary Union of Two Countries

1) Given money growth. As a result, inflation in Germany equals inflation in France. Inflation in Germany is determined by money growth in Europe, by output growth in Germany, and by output growth in France. An increase in European money growth raises German inflation. On the other hand, an increase in German output growth lowers German inflation. And what is more, an increase in French output growth lowers German inflation too.

For instance, let output growth in Germany be 1 percent, let output growth in France be 3 percent, let the initial share of German output in European output be 0.5, and let money growth in Europe be 3 percent. Then inflation in Germany is 1 percent. And inflation in France is equally 1 percent. This differs substantially from the conclusions reached in the three-good model, see Section 2 above. There, inflation in Germany generally differed from inflation in France. Producer inflation in Germany was determined by money growth in Europe and by output growth in Germany.

2) Target inflation and required money growth. As a result, required money growth in Europe is determined by target inflation in Europe, by output growth in Germany, and by output growth in France. For instance, let target inflation in Europe be 1 percent, let output growth in Germany be 1 percent, let output growth in France be 3 percent, and let the initial share of German output in European output be 0.5. Then required money growth in Europe is 3 percent. This is in remarkable contrast to the conclusions drawn in the three-good model.

4. Microfoundations for a Monetary Union

4.1. The World of Two Monetary Regions

1) The demand functions of European households. First consider the European consumption of European goods. As a result, an increase in European income, as measured in European goods, causes a proportionate increase in the European consumption of European goods. However, an increase in the price of European goods has no effect on the European consumption of European goods. The underlying reason is that here an increase in the price of European goods causes a proportionate increase in European income, as measured in euros. Moreover, an increase in the price of American goods has no effect on the European consumption of European goods. Likewise, an appreciation of the dollar has no effect on the European consumption of European goods.

Second consider the European consumption of American goods. As a result, a 1 percent increase in European income, as measured in European goods, causes a 1 percent increase in the European consumption of American goods. A 1 percent increase in the price of European goods causes a 1 percent increase in the European consumption of American goods. The underlying reason is that a 1 percent increase in the price of European goods causes a 1 percent increase in European income, as measured in euros. Further, a 1 percent increase in the price of American goods causes a 1 percent decline in the European consumption of American goods. Similarly, a 1 percent appreciation of the dollar causes a 1 percent decline in the European consumption of American goods.

2) The market for European goods. European output is determined by the demand for European goods. As a result, an increase in the autonomous demand for European goods raises European output. An increase in American income raises European output. An increase in the price of European goods lowers European output. An increase in the price of American goods raises European output. And an appreciation of the euro lowers European output.

3) A first model of Europe and America. As a result, an increase in the autonomous demand for European goods raises European output and, hence,

American output. An increase in the price of European goods lowers European output but raises American output. Likewise, an appreciation of the euro lowers European output but raises American output.

4) The consumption, export and import functions of Europe. It proves useful to measure European consumption, European exports and European imports in terms of European goods. First consider European consumption, as measured in European goods. Of course, European consumption still consists of European goods and American goods. As a finding, an increase in European income causes a proportionate increase in European consumption. However, an increase in the price of European goods has no effect on European consumption. An increase in the price of American goods has no effect on European consumption either. And the same holds for an appreciation of the dollar.

Second consider European exports, as measured in European goods. Of course, European exports consist of European goods. As a finding, a 1 percent increase in American income causes a 1 percent increase in European exports. A 1 percent increase in the price of American goods causes a 1 percent increase in European exports. A 1 percent increase in the price of European goods causes a 1 percent decline in European exports. And a 1 percent appreciation of the euro causes a 1 percent decline in European exports.

Third consider European imports, as measured in European goods. Of course, European imports consist of American goods. As a finding, an increase in European income causes a proportionate increase in European imports. However, an increase in the price of American goods has no effect on European imports. An appreciation of the dollar has no effect on European imports either. And the same holds for an increase in the price of European goods.

4.2. The Monetary Union of Two Countries

1) The demand functions of German households. First consider the German consumption of German goods. As a result, an increase in German income, as measured in German goods, causes a proportionate increase in the German consumption of German goods. However, an increase in the price of German goods has no effect on the German consumption of German goods. The underlying reason is that here an increase in the price of German goods causes a proportionate increase in German income, as measured in euros. Moreover, an increase in the price of French goods has no effect on the German consumption of German goods. Likewise, an increase in the price of American goods has no effect on the German consumption of German goods. And an appreciation of the dollar has no effect on the German consumption of German goods either.

Second consider the German consumption of French goods. As a result, a 1 percent increase in German income, as measured in German goods, causes a 1 percent increase in the German consumption of French goods. A 1 percent increase in the price of German goods causes a 1 percent increase in the German consumption of French goods. The underlying reason is that a 1 percent increase in the price of German goods causes a 1 percent increase in German income, as measured in euros. Further, a 1 percent increase in the price of French goods causes a 1 percent decline in the German consumption of French goods. In addition, an increase in the price of American goods has no effect on the German consumption of French goods. Similarly, an appreciation of the dollar has no effect on the German consumption of French goods.

Third consider the German consumption of American goods. As a result, a 1 percent increase in German income, as measured in German goods, causes a 1 percent increase in the German consumption of American goods. A 1 percent increase in the price of German goods causes a 1 percent increase in the German consumption of American goods. An increase in the price of French goods has no effect on the German consumption of American goods. A 1 percent increase in the price of American goods causes a 1 percent decline in the German consumption of American goods. And a 1 percent appreciation of the dollar causes a 1 percent decline in the German consumption of American goods.

2) The market for German goods. German output is determined by the demand for German goods. As a result, an increase in the autonomous demand for German goods raises German output. An increase in French income raises German output. An increase in American income raises German output. An increase in the price of German goods lowers German output. An increase in the price of French goods raises German output. An increase in the price of American goods raises German output. And an appreciation of the euro lowers German output.

3) A first model of Germany, France and America. As a result, an increase in the autonomous demand for German goods raises German output and, hence, French output as well as American output. An increase in the price of German goods lowers German output but raises French output and American output. An appreciation of the euro lowers German output and French output but raises American output.

4) The consumption, export and import functions of Germany. It proves useful to measure German consumption, German exports and German imports in terms of German goods. First consider German consumption, as measured in German goods. As a finding, German consumption is proportional to German income. However, German consumption does not depend on the price of German goods, on the price of French goods, on the price of American goods, or on the price of the dollar.

Second consider German exports to France, as measured in German goods. As a finding a 1 percent increase in French income, as measured in French goods, causes a 1 percent increase in German exports to France. A 1 percent increase in the price of French goods causes a 1 percent increase in German exports to France. And a 1 percent increase in the price of German goods causes a 1 percent decline in German exports to France.

Third consider German exports to America, as measured in German goods. As a finding, a 1 percent increase in American income, as measured in American goods, causes a 1 percent increase in German exports to America. A 1 percent increase in the price of American goods causes a 1 percent increase in German exports to America. A 1 percent increase in the price of German goods causes a 1 percent decline in German exports to America. And a 1 percent appreciation of the euro causes a 1 percent decline in German exports to America.

Fourth consider German imports from France, as measured in German goods. As a finding, German imports from France are proportional to German income. On the other hand, German imports from France do not depend on the price of French goods or on the price of German goods.

Fifth consider German imports from America, as measured in German goods. As a finding, German imports from America are proportional to German income. But German imports from America do not depend on the price of American goods, on the price of the dollar, or on the price of German goods.

Result

1. The World of Two Monetary Regions

1.1. Given Money Growth

1) The model. The world consists of two monetary regions, say Europe and America. The exchange rate between Europe and America is flexible. Here the focus is on steady-state inflation in Europe and America, given steady-state growth. Nominal wages and prices are flexible, so there is full employment in Europe and America. European goods and American goods are imperfect substitutes for each other. The monetary regions are the same size and have the same behavioural functions.

2) Producer inflation. Producer inflation in Europe refers to the price of European goods, as measured in euros. As a result, producer inflation in Europe is determined by money growth in Europe and by output growth in Europe. For instance, let output growth in Europe be 2 percent, let output growth in America be 3 percent, let money growth in Europe be 3 percent, and let money growth in America be 5 percent. Then producer inflation in Europe is 1 percent, and producer inflation in America is 2 percent.

3) Nominal depreciation. As a result, the rate of depreciation is determined by money growth in Europe and by money growth in America. If money growth in Europe is high, the euro will depreciate. If money growth in Europe is low, the euro will appreciate. For instance, let money growth in Europe be 3 percent, and let money growth in America be 5 percent. Then the price of the euro grows at a constant rate of 2 percent. In other words, the price of the dollar declines at a constant rate of 2 percent. But be careful. The rate of depreciation does not depend on producer inflation in Europe or on producer inflation in America.

4) Real depreciation. The real exchange rate is defined as the price of American goods, as measured in European goods. As a result, the growth of the relative price of American goods is determined by output growth in Europe and

by output growth in America. If output growth in America is high, the relative price of American goods will decline. If output growth in America is low, the relative price of American goods will increase. For instance, let output growth in Europe be 2 percent, and let output growth in America be 3 percent. Then the relative price of American goods declines at a constant rate of 1 percent.

5) Consumer inflation. European consumption includes both European goods and American goods. Therefore, the consumer price index of Europe includes the price of European goods, the price of American goods, and the price of the dollar. Accordingly, consumer inflation in Europe includes producer inflation in Europe, producer inflation in America, and the appreciation of the dollar. As a result, consumer inflation in Europe is determined by money growth in Europe, by output growth in Europe, and by output growth in America.

For instance, let output growth in Europe be 2 percent, let output growth in America be 3 percent, let money growth in Europe be 3 percent, and let money growth in America be 5 percent. Further, let the share of American goods in European consumption be 0.1, and let the share of European goods in American consumption be equally 0.1. Then consumer inflation in Europe is 0.9 percent, and consumer inflation in America is 2.1 percent.

6) Wage growth, given productivity growth. First consider nominal wages. As a result, nominal wage growth in Europe is determined by money growth in Europe. For instance, let money growth in Europe be 3 percent. Then nominal wage growth in Europe is equally 3 percent. Second consider producer real wages. Producer real wages in Europe are defined as nominal wages in Europe divided by the price of European goods. As a result, the growth of producer real wages in Europe is determined by productivity growth in Europe. For instance, let productivity growth in Europe be 2 percent. Then the growth of producer real wages in Europe is equally 2 percent.

Third consider consumer real wages. Consumer real wages in Europe are defined as nominal wages in Europe divided by the consumer price index of Europe. As a result, the growth of consumer real wages in Europe is determined by productivity growth in Europe and by productivity growth in America. For instance, let productivity growth in Europe be 2 percent, and let productivity growth in America be 3 percent. Then the growth of consumer real wages in

Europe is 2.1 percent, and the growth of consumer real wages in America is 2.9 percent.

7) Interest rates. First consider nominal interest rates. The nominal interest rate in Europe equals the sum of the nominal interest rate in America and the rate of depreciation. As a result, the nominal interest differential is determined by the money growth differential. For instance, let money growth in Europe be 3 percent, and let money growth in America be 5 percent. Then the nominal interest rate in America exceeds the nominal interest rate in Europe by 2 percentage points. Second consider real interest rates. As a result, the real interest differential is determined by the output growth differential. For instance, let output growth in Europe be 2 percent, and let output growth in America be 3 percent. Then the real interest rate in America exceeds the real interest rate in Europe by 1 percentage point.

1.2. Target Inflation and Required Money Growth

1) Required money growth. The objective of the European central bank is to maintain price stability in Europe. Strictly speaking, the objective of the European central bank is to keep consumer inflation in Europe at target level. The objective of the American central bank is to maintain price stability in America. Strictly speaking, the objective of the American central bank is to keep consumer inflation in America at target level. As a result, required money growth in Europe is determined by target inflation in Europe, by output growth in Europe, and by output growth in America.

For instance, let target inflation in Europe be 1 percent, let target inflation in America be 2 percent, let output growth in Europe be 2 percent, and let output growth in America be 3 percent. Moreover, let the share of American goods in European consumption be 0.1, and let the share of European goods in American consumption be equally 0.1. Then required money growth in Europe is 3.1 percent, and required money growth in America is 4.9 percent.

2) Nominal depreciation. First consider the case that output growth in Europe equals output growth in America. As a result, the rate of depreciation is determined by the target inflation differential. If target inflation in Europe is high, the euro will depreciate. If target inflation in Europe is low, the euro will appreciate. For instance, let target inflation in Europe be 1 percent, and let target inflation in America be 2 percent. Then the appreciation of the euro is 1 percent.

Second consider the case that target inflation in Europe equals target inflation in America. As a result, the rate of depreciation is determined by the output growth differential. If output growth in Europe is high, the euro will depreciate. If output growth in Europe is low, the euro will appreciate. For instance, let output growth in Europe be 2 percent, and let output growth in America be 3 percent. Then the appreciation of the euro is 0.8 percent.

3) Nominal interest rates. First consider the case that output growth in Europe equals output growth in America. As a result, the nominal interest differential is determined by the target inflation differential. For instance, let target inflation in Europe be 1 percent, and let target inflation in America be 2 percent. Then the nominal interest rate in America exceeds the nominal interest rate in Europe by 1 percentage point.

Second consider the case that target inflation in Europe equals target inflation in America. As a result, the nominal interest differential is determined by the output growth differential. For instance, let output growth in Europe be 2 percent, and let output growth in America be 3 percent. Then the nominal interest rate in America exceeds the nominal interest rate in Europe by 0.8 percentage points.

4) Wage growth, given productivity growth. As a result, nominal wage growth in Europe is determined by target inflation in Europe, by productivity growth in Europe, and by productivity growth in America. For instance, let target inflation in Europe be 1 percent, let target inflation in America be 2 percent, let productivity growth in Europe be 2 percent, and let productivity growth in America be 3 percent. Then nominal wage growth in Europe is 3.1 percent, and nominal wage growth in America is 4.9 percent.

2. The Monetary Union of Two Countries

2.1. Given Money Growth

1) The model. The world consists of two monetary regions, say Europe and America. The exchange rate between Europe and America is flexible. Europe in turn consists of two countries, say Germany and France. Germany and France form a monetary union. Here the focus is on steady-state inflation in Germany, France and America, given steady-state growth. Nominal wages and prices are flexible, so there is full employment in Germany, France and America. German goods, French goods and American goods are imperfect substitutes for each other. The monetary regions are the same size and have the same behavioural functions. The union countries are the same size and have the same behavioural functions.

2) Producer inflation. Producer inflation in Germany refers to the price of German goods, as measured in euros. As a result, producer inflation in Germany is determined by money growth in Europe and by output growth in Germany. For instance, let output growth in Germany be 1 percent, let output growth in France be 3 percent, and let money growth in Europe be 3 percent. Then producer inflation in Germany is 2 percent, and producer inflation in France is 0 percent.

3) Real depreciation. Here the real exchange rate is defined as the price of French goods, as measured in German goods. As a result, the growth of the relative price of French goods is determined by output growth in Germany and by output growth in France. If output growth in France is high, the relative price of French goods will decline. If output growth in France is low, the relative price of French goods will increase. For instance, let output growth in Germany be 1 percent, and let output growth in France be 3 percent. Then the relative price of French goods declines at a rate of 2 percent.

4) Consumer inflation. German consumption includes German goods, French goods and American goods. Therefore, the consumer price index of Germany includes the price of German goods, the price of French goods, the price of American goods, and the price of the dollar. Accordingly, consumer inflation in

Germany includes producer inflation in Germany, producer inflation in France, producer inflation in America, and the appreciation of the dollar. As a result, consumer inflation in Germany is determined by money growth in Europe, by output growth in Germany, by output growth in France, and by output growth in America.

For instance, let output growth in Germany be 1 percent, let output growth in France be 3 percent, let output growth in America be 2 percent, and let money growth in Europe be 3 percent. Besides, let the share of French goods in German consumption be 0.2, and let the share of American goods in German consumption be 0.1. By symmetry, let the share of German goods in French consumption be 0.2, and let the share of American goods in French consumption be 0.1. Then consumer inflation in Germany is 1.5 percent, and consumer inflation in France is 0.5 percent.

5) Wage growth, given productivity growth. First consider nominal wages. As a result, nominal wage growth in Germany is determined by money growth in Europe. For instance, let money growth in Europe be 3 percent. Then nominal wage growth in Germany is 3 percent, and nominal wage growth in France is equally 3 percent.

Second consider producer real wages. Producer real wages in Germany are defined as nominal wages in Germany divided by the price of German goods. As a result, the growth of producer real wages in Germany is determined by productivity growth in Germany. For instance, let productivity growth in Germany be 1 percent, and let productivity growth in France be 3 percent. Then the growth of producer real wages in Germany is 1 percent, and the growth of producer real wages in France is 3 percent.

Third consider consumer real wages. Consumer real wages in Germany are defined as nominal wages in Germany divided by the consumer price index of Germany. As a result, the growth of consumer real wages in Germany is determined by productivity growth in Germany, by productivity growth in France, and by productivity growth in America. For instance, let productivity growth in Germany be 1 percent, let productivity growth in France be 3 percent, and let productivity growth in America be 2 percent. Then the growth of consumer real wages in Germany is 1.5 percent, and the growth of consumer real wages in France is 2.5 percent.

6) Nominal and real interest rates. First consider nominal interest rates. As a result, the nominal interest differential between Germany and France is zero. Second consider real interest rates. As a result, the real interest differential between Germany and France is determined by the output growth differential. For instance, let output growth in Germany be 1 percent, and let output growth in France be 3 percent. Then the real interest rate in France exceeds the real interest rate in Germany by 2 percentage points.

2.2. Target Inflation and Required Money Growth

The objective of the European central bank is to keep consumer inflation in Europe at target level. Consumer inflation in Europe includes producer inflation in Germany, producer inflation in France, producer inflation in America, and the appreciation of the dollar. As a result, required money growth in Europe is determined by target inflation in Europe, by output growth in Germany, by output growth in France, and by output growth in America.

For instance, let target inflation in Europe be 1 percent, let output growth in Germany be 1 percent, let output growth in France be 3 percent, and let output growth in America be 2 percent. Then required money growth in Europe is 3 percent. Producer inflation in Germany is 2 percent, and producer inflation in France is 0 percent. Consumer inflation in Germany is 1.5 percent, consumer inflation in France is 0.5 percent, and consumer inflation in Europe is 1 percent.

Symbols

A	autonomous demand
C	consumption
I	investment
J	consumer price index
L	money demand
M	money supply, Lagrangian
N	labour
P	producer price
Q	imports
R	real exchange rate
S	savings
U	utility
V	velocity of circulation
X	exports
Y	output, income

a	labour productivity
b	parameter of investment function
c	marginal consumption rate
d	differential
e	nominal exchange rate
g	markup factor
h	exchange rate sensitivity of exports
i	nominal interest rate
k	parameter of money demand function
m	marginal import rate
q	marginal import rate
r	real interest rate
t	time
w	nominal wage rate
z	constant

α	parameter (consumer price index, utility function)
β	parameter (consumer price index, utility function)
γ	parameter (consumer price index, utility function)
δ	parameter (consumer price index, utility function)
ε	interest elasticity of investment
η	interest elasticity of money demand
λ	multiplier
π	share

$\hat{a}$	productivity growth
$\hat{e}$	nominal depreciation
$\hat{J}$	consumer inflation
$\hat{M}$	money growth
$\hat{N}$	labour growth
$\hat{P}$	producer inflation
$\hat{R}$	real depreciation
$\hat{Y}$	output growth
$\hat{w}$	nominal wage growth

A Brief Survey of the Literature

The focus of this survey is on the macroeconomics of monetary union. It is based on that given in Carlberg (2001). As a starting point take the classic papers by Fleming (1962) and Mundell (1963, 1964, 1968). They discuss monetary and fiscal policy in an open economy characterized by perfect capital mobility. The exchange rate can either be flexible or fixed. They consider both the small open economy and the world economy made up of two large countries.

The seminal papers by Levin (1983) as well as by Rose and Sauernheimer (1983) are natural extensions of the papers by Fleming and Mundell. They deal with stabilization policy in a jointly floating currency area. It turns out, however, that the joint float produces results for the individual countries within the currency area and for the area as a whole that in some cases differ sharply from those in the Fleming and Mundell papers.

The currency area is a small open economy with perfect capital mobility. For the small currency area, the world interest rate is given exogenously. Under perfect capital mobility, the interest rate of the currency area coincides with the world interest rate. Therefore the interest rate of the currency area is constant, too. The currency area consists of two countries. The exchange rate within the currency area is pegged. The exchange rate between the currency area and the rest of the world is floating. Country 1 manufactures good 1, and country 2 manufactures good 2. These goods are imperfect substitutes. The authors examine monetary and fiscal policy by one of the countries in the currency area, paying special attention to the effects on the domestic country and the partner country. Moreover they study demand switches within the currency area as well as a realignment of the exchange rate within the currency area.

The most surprising finding is that a fiscal expansion by one of the countries in the currency area produces a contraction of economic activity in the other country. This beggar-my-neighbour effect can be so strong as to cause a decline in economic activity within the area as a whole. Conversely, a monetary expansion by one of the countries in the currency area produces an expansion of economic activity in the other country as well. Levin concludes his paper with a practical observation. Since the cross effects of fiscal expansion in one currency area country may well be negative because of the joint float, it is crucial for econometric model builders concerned with linkages within a currency area to incorporate the induced exchange rate movements into their models.

Sauernheimer (1984) argues that a depreciation brings up consumer prices. To prevent a loss of purchasing power, trade unions call for higher money wages. On that account, producer prices go up as well. He sums up that the results obtained in the 1983 papers are very robust. Moutos and Scarth (1988) further investigate the supply side and the part played by real wage rigidity. Under markup pricing, there is no beggar-my-neighbour effect of fiscal policy. Under marginal cost pricing, on the other hand, the beggar-my-neighbour effect is a serious possibility. Feuerstein and Siebke (1990) also model the supply side. In addition, they introduce exchange rate expectations. The monograph by Feuerstein (1992) contains a thorough analysis of the supply side. Beyond that the author looks into wage indexation and the role of a lead currency. Over and above that, she develops a portfolio model of a small currency area.

The books by Hansen, Heinrich and Nielsen (1992) as well as by Hansen and Nielsen (1997) are devoted to the economics of the European Community. As far as the macroeconomics of monetary union is concerned, the main topics are policy coordination, exchange rate expectations, and slow prices. In the paper by Wohltmann (1993), prices are a slow variable. Both inflation expectations and exchange rate expectations are rational. He contemplates an economy with or without wage indexation. The paper by Jarchow (1993) has a world economy that consists of three large countries. Two of them share one money. Prices are flexible, and real wages are fixed. A fiscal expansion in union country 1 enhances union income. Unfortunately, it can depress the income of union country 2. It can inflate prices in each of the union countries. A depreciation of the union currency is possible.

The present book by Carlberg is volume four of a series on monetary union. Volume two (2000) explores the scope and limits of macroeconomic policy in a monetary union. The focus is on pure policies, policy mixes, and policy coordination. The leading protagonists are the union central bank, national governments, and national trade unions. Special emphasis is put on wage shocks and wage restraint. This book develops a series of basic, intermediate, and more advanced models. A striking feature is the numerical estimation of policy multipliers. A lot of diagrams serve to illustrate the subject in hand. The monetary union is an open economy with high capital mobility. The exchange rate between the monetary union and the rest of the world is flexible. The world interest rate can be exogenous or endogenous. The union countries may differ in money demand, consumption, imports, openness, or size.

Volume three (2001) explores the new economics of monetary union. It carefully discusses the effects of shocks and policies on output and prices. Shocks and policies are country-specific or common. They occur on the demand or supply side. Countries can differ in behavioural functions. Wages can be fixed, flexible, or slow. In addition, fixed wages and flexible wages can coexist. Take for instance fixed wages in Germany and flexible wages in France. Or take fixed wages in Europe and flexible wages in America. A special feature of this book is the numerical estimation of shock and policy multipliers. Further topics are inflation and disinflation. Take for instance inflation in Germany and price stability in France. Then what policy is needed for disinflation in the union? And what will be the dynamic effects on Germany and France? Further information about these books is given on the web-page:
http://www.unibw-hamburg.de/WWEB/vwl/carlberg/netcarl1.htm

Finally have a look at a list of some recent books:
- Allsopp, C., Vines, D., eds., Macroeconomic Policy after EMU, Oxford 1998
- Begg, D., von Hagen, J., Wyplosz, C., Zimmermann, K. F., eds., EMU: Prospects and Challenges for the Euro, Cambridge 1998
- Buti, M., Sapir, A., eds., Economic Policy in EMU, Oxford 1998
- Calmfors, L., et al., EMU – A Swedish Perspective, Dordrecht 1997
- Clausen, V., Asymmetric Monetary Transmission in Europe, Berlin 2000
- De Grauwe, P., The Economics of Monetary Union, Oxford 2000
- Deissenberg, C., Owen, R., Ulph, D., eds., European Economic Integration, Oxford 1998
- Eichengreen, B., European Monetary Unification, Cambridge 1997
- Eijffinger, S., De Haan, J., European Monetary and Fiscal Policy, Oxford 2000
- Favero, C., et al., One Monetary, Many Countries, London 2000
- Gros, D., Thygesen, N., European Monetary Integration, London 1998
- Hansen, J. D., ed., European Integration, Oxford 2001

- Hughes Hallet, A., Hutchison, M. M., Jensen, S. H., eds., Fiscal Aspects of European Monetary Integration, Cambridge 1999
- Issing, O., Gaspar, V., Angeloni, I., Tristani, O., Monetary Policy in the Euro Area, Cambridge 2001
- Masson, P. R., Krueger, T. H., Turtelboom, B. G., eds., EMU and the International Monetary System, Washington 1997
- Moser, T., Schips, B., eds., EMU, Financial Markets and the World Economy, Dordrecht 2001
- Mundell, R. A., Clesse, A., eds., The Euro as a Stabilizer in the International Economic System, Dordrecht 2000
- OECD, EMU: Facts, Challenges and Policies, Paris 1999
- OECD, EMU: One Year On, Paris 2000
- Rose, K., Sauernheimer, K., Theorie der Außenwirtschaft, München 1999
- Siebert, H., ed., Quo Vadis Europe?, Tübingen 1997
- Sitz, A., Währungsunion oder Wechselkursflexibilität, Frankfurt 2001
- Smets, J., Dombrecht, M., eds., How to Promote Economic Growth in the Euro Area, Cheltenham 2001
- Von Hagen, J., Waller, C. J., eds., Regional Aspects of Monetary Policy in Europe, Dordrecht 2000

References

ALLSOPP, C., DAVIES, G., McKIBBIN, W., VINES, D., Monetary and Fiscal Stabilization of Demand Shocks within Europe, in: Review of International Economics 5(4), 1997, 55 – 76

ALLSOPP, C., McKIBBIN, W., VINES, D., Fiscal Consolidation in Europe: Some Empirical Issues, in: A. Hughes Hallett, M. M. Hutchison, S.E.H. Jensen, eds., Fiscal Aspects of European Monetary Integration, Cambridge 1999

ALLSOPP, C., VINES, D., eds., Macroeconomic Policy after EMU, Oxford 1998

ALOGOSKOUFIS, G., PORTES, R., The Euro, the Dollar, and the International Monetary System, in: P. R. Masson, T. H. Krueger, B. G. Turtelboom, eds., EMU, Washington 1997

ANDERSEN, T. M., SORENSEN, J. R., Unemployment and Fiscal Policy in an Economic and Monetary Union, in: European Journal of Political Economy 11, 1995, 27 - 43

ARGY, V., International Macroeconomics, London 1994

ARTIS, M., NIXSON, F., eds., The Economics of the European Union, Oxford 2001

BAIMBRIDGE, M., WHYMAN, P., eds., Economic and Monetary Union in Europe, Cheltenham 2001

BALDWIN, R. E., On the Microeconomics of the European Monetary Union, in: European Economy, Special Edition No 1, 1991

BAYOUMI, T., Financial Integration and Real Activity, Ann Arbor 1997

BAYOUMI, T., EICHENGREEN, B., Shocking Aspects of European Monetary Integration, in: F. Torres, F. Giavazzi, eds., Adjustment and Growth in the European Monetary Union, Cambridge 1993

BEAN, C., Economic and Monetary Union in Europe, in: Journal of Economic Perspectives 6, 1992, 31 - 52

BEAN, C., Monetary Policy under EMU, in: Oxford Review of Economic Policy 14(3), 1998, 41 - 53

BEGG, D., Alternative Exchange Rate Regimes: The Role of the Exchange Rate and the Implications for Wage-Price Adjustment, in: European Economy, Special Edition No 1, 1991

BEGG, D., VON HAGEN, J., WYPLOSZ, C., ZIMMERMANN, K. F., eds., EMU: Prospects and Challenges for the Euro, Cambridge 1998

BELKE, A., Wechselkursschwankungen, Außenhandel, und Arbeitsmärkte, Heidelberg 2001

BERNANKE, B., LAUBACH, T., MISHKIN, F., POSEN, A., Inflation Targeting, Princeton 1999

BERTOLA, G., BOERI, G., NICOLETTI, G., eds., Welfare and Employment in a United Europe, Cambridge 2000

BINI SMAGHI, L., GROS, D., Open Issues in European Central Banking, London 2000

BLANCHARD, O., Macroeconomics, Upper Saddle River 2000

BLINDER, A. S., Central Banking in Theory and Practice, Cambridge 1998

BOFINGER, P., Monetary Policy, Oxford 2001

BREUSS, F., Außenwirtschaft, Wien 1998

BRYSON, J. H., Fiscal Policy Coordination and Flexibility under European Monetary Union, in: Journal of Policy Modeling 16, 1994, 541 - 557

BRYSON, J. H., Macroeconomic Stabilization Through Monetary and Fiscal Policy Coordination: Implications for European Monetary Union, in: Open Economies Review 5, 1994, 307 - 326

BUITER, W. H., The Economic Case for Monetary Union in the European Union, in: Review of International Economics 5(4), 1997, 10 - 35

BUITER, W., CORSETTI, G., ROUBINI, N., Excessive Deficits: Sense and Nonsense in the Treaty of Maastricht, in: Economic Policy 16, 1993, 57 - 100

BURDA, M., WYPLOSZ, C., Macroeconomics, Oxford 2001

BUTI, M., SAPIR, A., eds., Economic Policy in EMU, Oxford 1998

CAESAR, R., SCHARRER, H. E., eds., European Economic and Monetary Union, Baden-Baden 2001

CALMFORS, L., Macroeconomic Policy, Wage Setting, and Employment – What Difference Does the EMU Make?, in: Oxford Review of Economic Policy 14(3), 1998, 125 - 151

CALMFORS, L., et al., EMU - A Swedish Perspective, Dordrecht 1997

CALVO, G. A., DORNBUSCH, R., OBSTFELD, M., eds., Money, Capital Mobility, and Trade, Cambridge 2001

CARLBERG, M., An Economic Analysis of Monetary Union, Berlin New York 2001

CARLBERG, M., Economic Policy in a Monetary Union, Berlin New York 2000

CARLBERG, M., European Monetary Union, Heidelberg New York 1999

CARLBERG, M., International Economic Growth, Heidelberg 1997

CARLBERG, M., Intertemporal Macroeconomics: Deficits, Unemployment, and Growth, Heidelberg New York 1998

CARLBERG, M., Sustainability and Optimality of Public Debt, Heidelberg 1995

CLAASSEN, E. M., Global Monetary Economics, Oxford 1996

CLAASSEN, E. M., ed., International and European Monetary Systems, Oxford 1990

CLAUSEN, V., Asymmetric Monetary Transmission in Europe, Berlin 2000

COHEN, D., How Will the Euro Behave?, in: P. R. Masson et al, eds., EMU, Washington 1997

COMMISSION OF THE EC, The Economics of EMU, in: European Economy, Special Edition No 1, 1991

COMMISSION OF THE EC, One Market, One Money, in: European Economy 44, 1990

COMMISSION OF THE EC, Stable Money, Sound Finances, in: European Economy 53, 1993

COMMITTEE FOR THE STUDY OF ECONOMIC AND MONETARY UNION, Report on Economic and Monetary Union in the European Community, Luxembourg 1989

DANIELS, J. P., VANHOOSE, D. D., Two-Country Models of Monetary and Fiscal Policy, in: Open Economies Review 9, 1998, 263 – 282

DE GRAUWE, P., The Economics of Monetary Union, Oxford 2000

DE GRAUWE, P., Fiscal Policies in the EMS - A Strategic Analysis, in: E.M. Claassen, ed., International and European Monetary Systems, Oxford 1990

DEISSENBERG, C., OWEN, R., ULPH, D., eds., European Economic Integration, Oxford 1998

DORNBUSCH, R., FISCHER, S., STARTZ, R., Macroeconomics, New York 2001

DULLIEN, S., HORN, G. A., Auswirkungen der Europäischen Währungsunion auf die deutsche Wirtschaft, Berlin 1999

DUWENDAG, D., KETTERER, K. H., KÖSTERS, W., POHL, R., SIMMERT, D. B., Geldtheorie und Geldpolitik in Europa, Berlin 1999

ECB, Inflation Differentials in a Monetary Union, in: Monthly Bulletin, October 1999

EICHENGREEN, B., European Monetary Unification, Cambridge 1997

EIJFFINGER, S., DE HAAN, J., European Monetary and Fiscal Policy, Oxford 2000

ENGEL, G., RÜHMANN, P., Geldpolitik und Europäische Währungsunion, Göttingen 2001

EUROPEAN CENTRAL BANK, The Monetary Policy of the ECB, Frankfurt 2001

FAVERO, C., et al., One Money, Many Countries, London 2000

FELDSTEIN, M., The European Central Bank and the Euro: The First Year, in: Journal of Policy Modeling 22, 2000, 345 - 354

FEUERSTEIN, S., Studien zur Wechselkursunion, Heidelberg 1992

FEUERSTEIN, S., SIEBKE, J., Wechselkursunion und Stabilitätspolitik, in: Zeitschrift für Wirtschafts- und Sozialwissenschaften 110, 1990, 359 – 379

FISCHER, S., Roundtable on Lessons of European Monetary Integration for the International Monetary System, in: P. R. Masson et al., eds., EMU, Washington 1997

FLEMING, J. M., Domestic Financial Policies under Fixed and Floating Exchange Rates, in: IMF Staff Papers 9, 1962, 369 - 380

FRIEDMAN, B. M., HAHN, F. H., eds., Handbook of Monetary Economics, Amsterdam 1990

GALI, J., GERTLER, M., LOPEZ-SALIDO, J. D., European Inflation Dynamics, in: European Economic Review 45, 2001, 1237 – 1270

GANDOLFO, G., International Finance and Open-Economy Macroeconomics, Berlin 2001

GIOVANNINI, A., et al., The Monetary Future of Europe, London 1993

GIOVANNINI, A., MAYER, C., eds., European Financial Integration, Cambridge 1991

GROS, D., THYGESEN, N., European Monetary Integration, London 1998

HAMADA, K., The Political Economy of International Monetary Interdependence, Cambridge 1985

HANSEN, J. D., ed., European Integration, Oxford 2001

HANSEN, J. D., HEINRICH, H., NIELSEN, J. U., An Economic Analysis of the EC, London 1992

HANSEN, J. D., NIELSEN, J. U., An Economic Analysis of the EU, London 1997

HAYO, B., Empirische und theoretische Studien zur Europäischen Währungsunion, Frankfurt 1998

HORN, G. A., SCHEREMET, W., ZWIENER, R., Wages and the Euro, Heidelberg New York 1999

HUGHES HALLET, A., HUTCHISON, M. M., JENSEN, S. H., eds., Fiscal Aspects of European Monetary Integration, Cambridge 1999

ISSING, O., GASPAR, V., ANGELONI, I., TRISTANI, O., Monetary Policy in the Euro Area, Cambridge 2001

JARCHOW, H. J., Fiskalpolitik in einer Währungsunion, in: Finanzarchiv 50, 1993, 187 - 203

JARCHOW, H. J., RÜHMANN, P., Monetäre Außenwirtschaft, Göttingen 2000

KENEN, P. B., Economic and Monetary Union in Europe, Cambridge 1995

KRUGMAN, P., Lessons of Massachusetts for EMU, in: F. Giavazzi, F. Torres, eds., The Transition to Economic and Monetary Union in Europe, Cambridge 1993

KRUGMAN, P., The Return of Depression Economics, New York 1999

KRUGMAN, P. R., OBSTFELD, M., International Economics, New York 1997

LANDMANN, O., JERGER, J., Beschäftigungstheorie, Berlin 1999

LAWLER, P., Monetary Policy and Asymmetrical Fiscal Policy in a Jointly Floating Currency Area, in: Scottish Journal of Political Economy 41, 1994, 142 - 162

LEIDERMAN, L., SVENSSON, L., eds., Inflation Targeting, London 1995

LEVIN, J. H., On the Dynamic Effects of Monetary and Fiscal Policy in a Monetary Union, in: K. V. Maskus et al., eds., Quiet Pioneering, Michigan 1997

LEVIN, J. H., A Model of Stabilization Policy in a Jointly Floating Currency Area, in: J. S. Bhandari, B. H. Putnam, eds., Economic Interdependence and Flexible Exchange Rates, Cambridge 1983

MARK, N. C., International Macroeconomics and Finance, Oxford 2001

MASSON, P. R., KRUEGER, T.H., TURTELBOOM, B. G., eds., EMU and the International Monetary System, Washington 1997

MASSON, P. R., TAYLOR, M. P., Fiscal Policy within Common Currency Areas, in: Journal of Common Market Studies 31, 1993, 29 - 44

McCALLUM, B. T., International Monetary Economics, Oxford 1995

MEADE, J., WEALE, M., Monetary Union and the Assignment Problem, in: Scandinavian Journal of Economics 97, 1995, 201-222

MOSER, T., SCHIPS, B., eds., EMU, Financial Markets and the World Economy, Dordrecht 2001

MOUTOS, T., SCARTH, W., Stabilization Policy within a Currency Area, in: Scottish Journal of Political Economy 35, 1988, 387 - 397

MÜCKL, W. J., Hg., Die Europäische Währungsunion, Paderborn 2000

MUNDELL, R. A., EMU and the International Monetary System, in: A. Giovannini et al., eds., The Monetary Future of Europe, London 1993

MUNDELL, R. A., International Economics, New York 1968

MUNDELL, R. A., CLESSE, A., eds., The Euro as a Stabilizer in the International Economic System, Dordrecht 2000

OBSTFELD, M., ROGOFF, K., Foundations of International Macroeconomics, Cambridge 1996

OECD, EMU: Facts, Challenges and Policies, Paris 1999

OECD, EMU: One Year On, Paris 2000

OHR, R., THEURL, T., Hg., Kompendium Europäische Wirtschaftspolitik, München 2000

PADOAN, P. C., ed., Monetary Union, Employment and Growth, Cheltenham 2001

PADOA-SCHIOPPA, T., et al., Efficiency, Stability, and Equity, Oxford 2000

PADOA-SCHIOPPA, T., The Road to Monetary Union in Europe, Oxford 1994

PAPADOPOULOU, D. M., Makroökonomik der Wechselkursunion, Frankfurt 1993

PENTECOST, E. J., VAN POECK, A., eds., European Monetary Integration, Cheltenham 2001

PERSSON, T., TABELLINI, G., Political Economics, Cambridge 2000

PISANI- FERRY, J., et al., A French Perspective on EMU, Paris 1993

POHL, R., GALLER, H. P., Hg., Implikationen der Währungsunion für makroökonometrische Modelle, Baden-Baden 2001

ROSE, K., SAUERNHEIMER, K., Theorie der Außenwirtschaft, München 1999

ROSE, K., SAUERNHEIMER, K., Zur Theorie eines Mischwechselkurssystems, in: M. Feldsieper, R. Groß, Hg., Wirtschaftspolitik in weltoffener Wirtschaft, Berlin 1983, 15 - 28

RÜBEL, G., Grundlagen der Monetären Außenwirtschaft, München 2001

RÜBEL, G., ed., Real and Monetary Issues of International Economic Integration, Berlin 2000

SALVATORE, D., The Euro, the Dollar, and the International Monetary System, in: Journal of Policy Modeling 22, 2000, 407 - 415

SAUERNHEIMER, K., Fiscal Policy in einer Wechselkursunion, in: Finanzarchiv 42, 1984, 143 - 157

SIEBERT, H., ed., Quo Vadis Europe?, Tübingen 1997

SIEBERT, H., Weltwirtschaft, Stuttgart 1997

SITZ, A., Währungsunion oder Wechselkursflexibilität, Frankfurt 2001

SMETS, J., DOMBRECHT, M., eds., How to Promote Economic Growth in the Euro Area, Cheltenham 2001

SPAHN, H. P., From Gold to Euro, Berlin 2001

STAHN, K., Reputation und Kooperation in einer Währungsunion, Frankfurt 2000

SVENSSON, L. E. O., Monetary Policy Issues für the Eurosystem, in: Carnegie-Rochester Conference Series on Public Policy 51, 1999, 79 - 136

TAYLOR, J. B., Macroeconomic Policy in a World Economy, New York 1993

TAYLOR, J. B., WOODFORD, M., eds., Handbook of Macroeconomics, Amsterdam 1999

TORRES, F., GIAVAZZI, F., eds., Adjustment and Growth in the European Monetary Union, Cambridge 1993

VAN DER PLOEG, F., Macroeconomic Policy Coordination and Monetary Integration: A European Perspective, The Hague 1989

VON HAGEN, J., WALLER, C. J., eds., Regional Aspects of Monetary Policy in Europe, Dordrecht 2000

VON WEIZSÄCKER, C. C., Logik der Globalisierung, Göttingen 1999

WAGNER, H., Europäische Wirtschaftspolitik, Berlin 1998

WALSH, C., Monetary Theory and Policy, Cambridge 1998

WELFENS, P. J. J., European Monetary Union and Exchange Rate Dynamics, Berlin 2000

WOHLTMANN, H. W., Transmission nationaler Wirtschaftspolitiken in einer Wechselkursunion, in: Jahrbücher für Nationalökonomie und Statistik 211, 1993, 73 - 89

Index